ELECTORAL RESERVATIONS, POLITICAL REPRESENTATION AND SOCIAL CHANGE IN INDIA

Centre de Sciences Humaines (Centre for Social Sciences and Humanities): Created in New Delhi in 1989, the CSH is part of the network of research centres of the French Ministry of Foreign Affairs. The Centre's research work is primarily oriented towards the study of issues concerning the contemporary dynamics of development in India and South Asia. The activities of the Centre are focused on four main themes, namely: Economic transition and sustainable development, political dynamics, institutional set-up and social transformations, regional dynamics in South Asia and international relations and urban dynamics.

Centre de Sciences Humaines, 2, Aurangzeb Road, New Delhi 110011, India, Tel: (91) 11 2301 62 59, Fax: (91) 11 2301 84 80
E-mail: public@csh-delhi.com
Website: http://www.csh-delhi.com

Institut Français de Pondichéry (French Institute of Pondicherry): Created in 1955, the IFP is a multidisciplinary research and advanced educational institute. Major research works are focusing on Sanskrit and Tamil Languages and literatures—in close collaboration with the Ecole Française d'Extrême-Orient—ecosystems, biodiversity and sustainability, dynamics of population and socio-economic development.

Institut Français de Pondichéry, 11 Saint Louis Street, PB 33, Pondicherry 605001, Tel: (91) 413 2334 168/2334 170, Fax: (91) 413 2339 534
E-mail: ifpdir@ifpindia.org
Website: http://www.ifpindia.org

Electoral Reservations, Political Representation and Social Change in India

A Comparative Perspective

Edited by

STÉPHANIE TAWA LAMA-REWAL

MANOHAR

CENTRE DE SCIENCES HUMAINES
2005

First published 2005

ISBN 81-7304-622-0

Published by
Ajay Kumar Jain for
Manohar Publishers & Distributors
4753/23 Ansari Road, Daryaganj
New Delhi 110 002

Printed at
Lordson Publishers Pvt Ltd
Delhi 110 007

Distributed in South Asia by
FOUNDATION BOOKS
4381/4, Ansari Road
Daryaganj, New Delhi 110 002
and its branches at Mumbai, Hyderabad,
Bangalore, Chennai, Kolkata

Contents

Acknowledgements 7

Introduction
STÉPHANIE TAWA LAMA-REWAL 9

1. A Quest for Identity through Politics: The Scheduled Castes in Uttar Pradesh
SUDHA PAI 21

2. Safeguards or Segregation? Reservations for the Scheduled Castes in Bihar
PRAKASH LOUIS 53

3. Reservations and Social Change: The Case of the North-East
WALTER FERNANDES 83

4. The Policy of Reservations for Scheduled Tribes
BHUPINDER SINGH 105

5. Electoral Reservations for Scheduled Tribes: The Legitimization of Domination
VIRGINIUS XAXA 119

6. Empowered without Reservations: OBCs in Uttar Pradesh and Bihar
MEENAKSHI JAIN 137

7. Reservations for Backward Classes in Karnataka's Panchayati Raj Institutions
K.S. NARAYANA 155

8. Reservations for Women in Urban Local Bodies: A Tentative Assessment
STÉPHANIE TAWA LAMA-REWAL 189

Contributors 209

Acknowledgements

This book is to a large extent the outcome of a seminar entitled 'Reservations and the Political Representation of Scheduled Castes, Scheduled Tribes, Other Backward Classes and Women: A Comparative Assessment', held in Delhi in April 2002.

I would like to express my gratitude to Dr Frederic Grare, the then Director of the Centre de Sciences Humaines (CSH), for encouraging me when I first explained the idea of such an exercise; for providing the much needed financial and institutional support of the CSH to the seminar logistics; and for actively participating in the discussions. I also would like to expresss special thanks to Dr Girish Kumar, my colleague at the CSH, for his invaluable suggestions regarding the concept paper and potential participants.

I am very grateful to Prof. Gopal Guru, Prof. Ghanshyam Shah, Prof. Dipankar Gupta, Prof. Susheela Kaushik, Prof. Kamlesh Mohan, Prof. Gurpreet Mahajan, Dr (Mrs) Bidyut Mohanty and Dr Mary John for actively participating in the seminar and making it such a fruitful exchange of observations and ideas. Lastly, I thank all the contributors to this volume for bearing with the long and tedious process of revisions.

STÉPHANIE TAWA LAMA-REWAL

Introduction

STÉPHANIE TAWA LAMA-REWAL

Reservations are the Indian version of quotas: a legal provision that guarantees a minimum presence in various institutions to social categories considered victims of a historical prejudice. Reservations were first established at the regional level in the princely state of Mysore in 1921,[1] and in British India through the Montague–Chelmsford Reforms in 1919. They were enshrined in the Constitution of independent India, making it a pioneer in policies of affirmative action, or 'compensatory discrimination' (Galanter, 1991). They have evoked a recurring debate, but seem nevertheless unstoppable in their slow but steady extension to new categories of beneficiaries and to new institutions. If we consider independent India only, in 1950 reservations concerned two categories: the Scheduled Castes (SC) and the Scheduled Tribes (ST), and three fields: public employment, institutions of higher education and political representation—seats were reserved in the national Parliament and in state Assemblies, in proportion to the demographic weight of SCs and STs, i.e. 15 per cent and 7.5 per cent respectively.

While the question of reservations for the SCs and STs rapidly became the object of a relative consensus, their extension to a third category, that of the Other Backward Classes (OBC), evoked repeated controversies. At the Centre, two commissions were charged with the mission of identifying communities qualifying as OBCs—under the chairmanship of Kaka Kalelkar in 1953, and B.P. Mandal in 1978. In both cases the criteria used as indicators of backwardness[2] as well as the importance of the population thus considered as potentially entitled to reservations were contested. Reservations for the OBCs were finally implemented at the state level, but only in the fields of public employment and higher education.[3]

More recently, the decentralization policy approved in 1992 introduced electoral reservations for a fourth category—women. Indeed, seats are now being reserved in local assemblies for women (33 per cent), for SCs, for STs and in some states, for OBCs (in proportion to the local demographic weight of each category), at all three levels of local self-government: village, block, and district (or municipality in urban areas). Lastly, the question of the possibility of identifying 'Most Backward Classes' among the OBCs, and 'Economically Backward Classes' among the upper castes, and making them the beneficiaries of reservations resurfaces regularly either at the Centre or in the states.

The debate around reservations is thus a complex one. It is rooted in the colonial history of India, it follows different courses at the Union and at the states levels; it is fraught with electoral calculations and it has repeatedly evoked violent reactions.[4] But this debate, on the whole, has been unevenly focussed: It has concentrated (i) on OBCs—a category characterized by the permanent controversy regarding its criteria of definition, by its inherent heterogeneity in terms of economic status, and by the size of the population it designates; (ii) on the fields of public employment and higher education—where the number of positions concerned is much greater than in the political field, and the expected benefits more direct; and (iii) with principles: the concepts of social justice, backwardness, equality, equality of opportunity, merit, and their relation with one another have been discussed at length. As far as the consequences of reservations are concerned, the debate has been restricted, for the most part, to the fields of higher education and public employment until 1996, when the Women's Reservation Bill—a legislation proposing to reserve 33 per cent of seats in state Assemblies and in the Lok Sabha for women—provoked a new controversy over the relevance and consequences of the political representation of groups through electoral reservations, both for the groups concerned and for society at large.

CROSS PERSPECTIVES ON ELECTORAL RESERVATIONS

This book is born from the observation of the compartmentalization and silences of the debate on reservations, be it political or academic, and sheds new light on the subject through a confrontation of studies of the implementation of electoral reservations[5] for the four social categories (SCs, STs, OBCs and women) to which they apply today at various levels of political life. Indeed, even though the sociological characteristics and the bases for the exclusion suffered by these categories are quite distinct, all electoral reservations clearly pertain to the same policy. They stem from a common principle—reparation; they aim at a common goal—including the excluded; and they work along a largely common institutional design—reserving constituencies.

Reservations constitute a fascinating object of observation insofar as they appear to aim at reconciling the individual and equalitarian premises of democracy with the traditionally major role of communities and hierarchies in the Indian society. Through reservations, the law tackles frontally the contrast between the political system and the social structure of India—and one can wonder which of the two comes out more transformed in the process. The book consists of a series of empirical case studies focussing on the implementation of electoral reservations for different categories, at different levels of political life, in different regions and along different time-frames—that bring elements of answer to that question.[6] The very heterogeneity of the collection, which is far from exhausting the many dimensions and variations of electoral reservations as they have been practiced throughout the country, allows us to go beyond the specific problematic usually associated with each beneficiary category, that is (to put it briefly), the impact of electoral reservations on the stigmatization suffered by SCs; on the isolation characterizing tribal societies; on the 'glass-ceiling' that limits women's political representation; and on the political mobilization of OBCs.

This collective, though partial, taking-stock exercise brings out similarities and contrasts that add to our understanding of reservations as a policy: its limitations, its principal and secondary effects. More precisely, the different papers analyse the workings of reservations (or, in the case of the OBCs as analysed by Meenakshi Jain, the absence thereof) with reference to two main issues which are closely connected yet distinct: the effectiveness of reservations as a means towards political representation, and their relevance as instruments of social change.

WHAT ARE THE CONSEQUENCES OF ELECTORAL RESERVATIONS?

The first question running through all papers is: what have been the observable consequences of electoral reservations on the political and social status of the beneficiaries, and on Indian political life as a whole?

Such a question clearly involves a number of methodological difficulties, starting with the definition of the yardstick to be used in the assessment of reservations. What *should* be expected from electoral reservations? What did the Fathers of the Constitution expect from them in the first place? Elucidating the intent of the constituents is crucial, because the fact that reservations originate from the Constitution gives them *a priori* the status of a major legislative tool in the construction of the new India born from independence. Yet, the constitutional intent is fairly vague concerning categories other than SCs and STs.

More generally, what can be the legitimate consequences of reservations? The notion of legitimacy implies a reference to the values and beliefs shared by society, which means that the yardstick for measuring the success of political reservations is to be found within the concept of representative democracy that dominates in India. The question, moreover, is obscured by the frequent confusion of the three fields to which reservations apply. Indeed controversies around notions such as the emergence of a 'creamy layer' (an elite that tends to monopolize the benefits of reservations) among the beneficiary categories, or 'the well-being of institutions' (Beteille, 1998) that may be affected by the lowering of standards produced by reservations, take an entirely different meaning when it comes to the political field. Thus, the emergence of an elite of politicians among the categories concerned is not only unavoidable—Roberto Michels famously called this phenomenon 'the iron law of oligarchy' (Michels, 1915)—but may also appear desirable. Indeed these elite, by definition, have access to such essential political resources as education and money, which may result in a greater 'well-being' of the concerned assemblies—even though the choice of indicators to measure the quality of representation is in itself an object of debate.

Should reservations, being a tool of political integration, be assessed within the political sphere only? In that case the success or failure of reservations could be measured through the number and importance of executive positions occupied by elected representatives belonging to the beneficiary categories, the type of political careers open to them, and ultimately in the number of them being elected in 'general' (i.e. non-reserved) seats.[7] Yet, there is much ambivalence inherent in the notion of political integration: it can mean co-option as well as empowerment.

The articles in this volume share two basic assumptions. One, reservations are a particular means towards political representation, with inherent effects that must be identified as precisely as possible. Two, there is a relationship between political representation and social change, notwithstanding the difficulty involved in isolating the impact of the political representation of a given group, and of the means thereof, on the social status of that group. The relationship in any case is assumed to be two-way: most studies of political sociology are based on the assumption that social change gets reflected in the sociological profile of elected representatives, but one can also imagine that the sociological composition of a representative assembly may influence the society it represents—which is in fact a major argument of the supporters of 'mirror representation'.

REPRESENTATION *vs.* REPRESENTATIVENESS

Three major themes run through the eight papers, across the diversity of their respective focuses. The first theme is the tension between representation and representativeness, insofar as reservations mechanically produce the latter, sometimes at the expense of the former. This tension appears clearly through the pre-Independence history of reservations, evoked by several papers. The constitutional reform of British India, inspired by the theory of groups' interests as well as by the intention to divide and rule, introduced group representation through separate electorates with the 1909 Indian Council Act. Separate representation ensured that a given group's preference would be represented but, more importantly in the eyes of the Congress leaders, it threatened the cohesion of Indian society. The confrontation between Mahatma Gandhi and Dr Ambedkar over the Communal Award resulting from the Second Round Table Conference (1932), where several groups—including the Depressed Classes and women—had gone to negotiate their political representation, is, therefore, a major turning point in the history of group representation in India.[8] The Communal Award included a separate electorate for the Depressed Classes, which Gandhi considered as an unacceptable division of the Hindu community, and which he opposed by a fast unto death, until Ambedkar accepted the compromise known as the Poona Pact, which replaced separate electorates with reserved seats for the Depressed Classes within the Hindu electorate.

Reservations as provided for by the Constitution are a continuation of this principle and guarantee the representativeness of elected assemblies but not the representation of the interests of the beneficiary categories, which is a major limitation of 'mirror representation'. Indeed, Galanter argues that 'reservations are designed in a way which filters and muffles the representation of the interests of the Scheduled castes and tribes insofar as they diverge from the interests of other groups' (Galanter, 1991: 51). Bhupinder Singh's paper, presenting an insider's account of the process of reforms concerning STs' political representation, provides a detailed description of the many obstacles lying between mere presence and advocacy or, to use the words of Hannah Pitkin, 'standing for' and 'acting for' (Pitkin, 1972).

What is the relationship between reservations and identity politics? Sudha Pai's article, tracing the historical process that led to the emergence of a Dalit political leadership in Uttar Pradesh, offers a wealth of insights on that complicated question. She shows that the representation of Dalit interests has come not from SC representatives elected in reserved constituencies but from a Dalit party—the Bahujan Samaj Party (BSP). In fact, the very choice of words to name the former untouchables conveys the status of identity in the political representation process. The phrase 'scheduled castes' is a typically bureaucratic, deliberately neutral appellation, while the word 'dalit' evokes a whole narrative about the historical nature and variations of the oppression suffered by the former untouchables, and their struggle to come out of it.[9] Pai's paper suggests that identity needs to be constructed and activated, that is, mobilized, in order to become a political resource.

Indeed, a comparison of the four categories benefitting from electoral reservations at various levels highlights the limits of 'the politics of numbers', and the crucial importance of mobilization. The contrast between the OBCs and women is particularly interesting insofar as both categories cover about half the population. Jain's article underlines the particular process of OBCs' political empowerment in Uttar Pradesh and Bihar; she shows that the OBCs first mobilized themselves politically through the formation of political parties dedicated to the representation of their interests, and then only demanded electoral reservations—which they obtained only at the local level, in the framework of the decentralization policy, and only in nine states. On the contrary, the case of women illustrates the difficulty of building a political identity based on gender, despite the implementation of substantial reservations at the local level since 1994,[10] the demand for reservations at the state and Union levels since 1996, and the vitality of the Indian women's movement.

Yet, a larger timeframe of observation suggests that reservations do play a role in the construction of political identities. Indeed, all political categories are historically constructed, even though some may look more 'natural' than others today. SCs, STs and OBCs are originally 'socio-administrative categories' (Jaffrelot, 2003) coined in pre-independent India, which have become political categories through the reservation policy. Women by contrast appear to be quite distinct as a political category by the fact that (i) gender is largely defined by sex, i.e. a biological fact; (ii) women are scattered, so to speak, among the various communities defined by caste, class, religion or region; and (iii) they share men's lives—in short, women do not form a group. Yet the papers by Louis, Singh and Narayana show that SCs, STs and OBCs, too, have had to overcome the heterogeneity and dispersal of the population gathered under each category in their respective mobilization process. The juxtaposition of papers also underlines that the process of political construction of the identity of each category has an impact on the others: thus, Jain mentions that the OBCs' demand for reservations was inspired by their observation of the consequences of reservations for the SCs; Tawa Lama-Rewal evokes the impact of the OBC lobby on the fate of the Women's Reservation Bill; and Fernandes underlines the gender bias inherent in several affirmative action measures targeting the STs.

ELECTORAL RESERVATIONS AS SYMBOLIC POLICIES

The second theme running through the papers is the question whether reservations are a tool of the *status quo*. Many papers actually conclude that the main benefits of electoral reservations are of a symbolic nature: they provide recognition, not redistribution, to use Nancy Fraser's distinction (Fraser, 1995). This is partly due to the institutional design of reservations, which does not favour the electoral mobilization of those voters belonging to the beneficiary category. Moreover, both Prakash Louis and Walter Fernandes situate electoral reservations within the larger package of affirmative action measures targeting respectively the SCs and the STs, and come out with similar conclusions: the inconsistency of that package makes it ineffective to tackle the structural causes of inequality. Yet, Pai's paper shows that the political representation of STs through a Dalit party such as the BSP is the indirect consequence not of electoral reservations, but of reservations in public employment and institutions of higher education, which over time resulted in the emergence of urban elite among the SCs.

Virginius Xaxa's article, presenting the implementation of reservations for the STs at the local level, analyses reservations as a means to co-opt potential dissent. Indeed, all three papers focussing on STs show the historical process of the political integration of tribes as a bartering process in which reservations were granted to STs by the Indian state in exchange for its own legitimization, which was necessary in order to exploit the rich natural resources areas traditionally inhabited by tribals. In other words these authors present reservations as an alibi, or a 'mechanism for social control' (Dushkin, 1998: 226).

The proof of the relatively innocuous nature of electoral reservations as they exist today may lie in the striking contrast between, on the one hand, the consensus over reservations whenever they apply to a relatively small population (SCs and STs), or to a level where the stakes of political life are limited (local self-government), and on the other hand, the controversy evoked by reservations for categories covering a large population at the state and Union levels (women and OBCs). Indeed, K.S. Narayana's paper, presenting the implementation of reservations for OBCs at the local level in the very region where reservations were experimented for the first time—Karnataka—ends with a series of concrete suggestions to transform the working of these reservations.

RESERVATIONS AND POLITICIZATION

Yet, reservations do affect the relationship between the beneficiary categories and political life in a variety of ways. The third idea running across the papers is that reservations always generate a minimal type of political integration that could be called the politicization of the concerned categories. Politicization happens in an oblique fashion: the implementation of reservations generates some interest for politics among the concerned populations; it offers a political socialization to those individuals benefitting from their opportunity effect;[11] it generates an elite who can act as a role model; and it establishes notabilities that are more accessible to people belonging to the beneficiary categories.

Moreover, the confrontation of studies covering different time-frames suggests that time is an important factor in the degree of political integration produced by reservations. Thus, the situation of STs vis-à-vis reservations in the 1950s, as described by Singh, was in many ways similar to that of women today. Indeed, Singh recalls how political parties, commanding all political loyalty, prevented the emergence of a solidarity among ST representatives across party lines over issues of special interest for STs—which is being observed in many urban local bodies as far as women are concerned, as shown in the paper by Tawa Lama-Rewal.

Lastly, the case of women suggests that reservations may pave the way for mobilization insofar as they legitimize gender as a new political category. Yet, the unique reluctance evoked by the notion of a women's party—as compared to Dalit parties, tribal parties and OBCs parties—reveals that gender is not as legitimate a category as caste, tribe and class in Indian politics today (Tawa Lama-Rewal, 2001).

The presentation of articles clubs them by category of beneficiaries along a rough chronological order, and shifts from the states to the local level with Xaxa's paper (even though Jain's paper is concerned with the representation of OBCs at the state level).

All papers are strongly opinionated, and as such reflect the Indian debate on reservations as much as they contribute to it. To put it simply, all authors are concerned that there is either not enough or too much of reservations, depending on the categories. Affirmative action in general and (electoral) reservations in particular are about core values of social cohesion. Indeed, reservations affect all Indian citizens, whether they are entitled to them or whether they feel deprived by them: equality of opportunity, and more generally social justice, are at stake, for all.

NOTES

1. But affirmative action in other forms dates back to 1874 (see Narayana in this volume).
2. The Kalelkar and the Mandal Commissions respectively identified 2,399 and 3,743 communities as OBCs, that is, 32 per cent and 52 per cent of the total population. Both commissions used caste, and not economic status, as the principal criteria of the social and educational status of the considered communities.
3. In the southern states, where the mobilization of non-Brahmins as such dates back to the first decades of the twentieth century, reservations for the OBCs were implemented on a large scale from the 1960s onwards, while in northern India they started being implemented only about two decades later (Jaffrelot, 2003: 237).
4. The reservation policy in institutions of higher education evoked violent protests, mostly by upper-caste students, in Gujarat in 1981 and 1985 and in north India in 1989–90, when Prime Minister V.P. Singh promised to implement the recommendations of the Mandal Commission.
5. We favour the phrase 'electoral reservations' over that of 'political reservations', in order to avoid any confusion with internal reservations of various executive positions provided for by political parties' respective constitutions—and most often only vaguely implemented.
6. The asymmetrical focus on SCs and STs as compared to OBCs and women reflects the longer history of reservations for the former two categories, and their existence at all three levels of political life in the Indian Union today.
7. See Pai's paper for a review of the results produced by studies adopting that perspective.
8. The 1935 Government of India Act marked a culminating point in the political representation of groups, since twelve groups (including Depressed Classes, women and Muslims) then benefitted from reserved seats.
9. See Louis' essay for an elaboration of the meanings of the word 'Dalit'.
10. Reservations for women in local assemblies had been implemented in a few states (notably Karnataka, Andhra Pradesh, Kerala and Maharashtra) even before the 73rd and 74th Constitutional Amendments were passed.

11. The political career of the Dalit leader Ram Vilas Paswan, as presented by Louis, shows that reservations occasionally favour the emergence of critical individuals.

REFERENCES

Beteille, André, 'Distributive Justice and Institutional Well-Being', in Gurpreet, Mahajan (ed.), *Democracy, Difference and Social Justice*, Delhi: Oxford University Press, 1998, pp. 463–88.

Dushkin, Lelah, 'Scheduled Caste Politics', in J. Michael Mahar (ed.), *The Untouchables in Contemporary India*, Delhi: Rawat, 1998, pp. 165–226.

Fraser, Nancy, 'From Redistribution to Recognition? Dilemmas of Justice in a "Post-Socialist" Age', *New Left Review*, # 212, pp. 68–93, 1995.

Galanter, Marc, *Competing Equalities: Law and the Backward Classes in India*, Delhi: Oxford University Press, 1991.

Jaffrelot, Christophe, *India's Silent Revolution: The Rise of the Low Castes in North Indian Politics*, Delhi: Permanent Black, 2003.

Michels, Roberto, *Political Parties: A Sociological Study of the Oligarchical Tendencies of Modern Democracy*, New York: Hearst's International Library Co., 1915.

Pitkin, Hannah, *The Concept of Representation*, Berkeley: University of California Press, 1972.

Tawa Lama-Rewal, Stéphanie, 'Fluctuating, Ambivalent Legitimacy of Gender as a Political Category', *Economic and Political Weekly*, 28 April 2001, pp. 1435–40.

CHAPTER 1

A Quest for Identity through Politics: The Scheduled Castes in Uttar Pradesh

SUDHA PAI

In 1950, the Indian Constitution provided protective discrimination to historically disadvantaged social groups such as the Scheduled Castes (SC). Reservations in the fields of education and employment were based upon the principle of equalization of opportunity structures and meant to improve the social and economic position of these disadvantaged groups. Electoral or political reservations, on the other hand, based on their distinct low-caste identity, were aimed at giving a hitherto excluded social group a decisive share of political power. They were the end product of the struggle for separate representation in the colonial period, based upon the consciousness of a low-caste identity distinct from the caste Hindus. The importance attached by the founding fathers of the Constitution to reserved seats can be seen from the fact that among the wide array of preferential schemes for disadvantaged groups, such as SCs, this is the only scheme that is specifically provided in the Constitution. All other constitutional provisions for preferences are merely authorizations empowering the State to make provision for disadvantaged groups (Galanter, 1984: 45). The founding fathers hoped that the provision of reserved seats would provide the SCs with an opportunity not only to enter political institutions, but to produce leaders who would devote themselves to the specific interests of the community.

While much literature exists on the effects of reservations in the fields of education and employment on the SC community, comparatively less attention has been paid to the impact of political reservations on the position and role of the SCs in the political arena. Existing studies have concentrated on the socio-economic background and the role played by the SC members holding reserved seats within the legislative institutions, in protecting the interests of their community. These studies show that in the early years of independence, SC members in reserved seats were younger, less experienced and predominantly rural as compared to their fellow legislators; few had professions (they were mostly landowners) or a formal education. They were less articulate, less assertive, less independent, and less likely to hold party office, serve on committees, contribute to debate or talk to ministers (Galanter, 1984).[1] The findings of a study on the Orissa legislature were similar (Mohapatra, 1973). However, more recent studies show that most of them are not from backgrounds of absolute poverty; rather a small, privileged section has gained a disproportionate share of the seats (Sachchidananda, 1977; Mendelsohn, 1986; Abbayasulu, 1983; Shah, 1987). Narayana's study shows that while SC workers directly dependent on agriculture constituted 72.2 per cent of the total workforce, their representation in Parliament was only 36 per cent; and while 1.2 per cent of the SC population was engaged in trade and commerce, their proportion in Parliament was 9.2 per cent (Narayana, 1978).

The studies are divided in their assessment of the role played by SC representatives. Low rates of participation, it is pointed out, do not imply an absence of effective representation of SC interests. Kochanek found SC members of Parliament (MPs) strong supporters of land and urban income ceilings and generally giving 'higher than average support for any process of levelling' (Kochanek, 1968: 48). Narayana's study, quoted by Galanter, suggests that reserved-seat legislators were active and sometimes influential in matters concerning the working of the preference policy. Between 1962 and 1971, they were successful in securing the appointment of the Elayaperumal Committee and the Joint Standing Committee on SCs and STs, and in 'killing' the 1965 Lokur Committee, which had recommended the descheduling of some SCs and STs (Galanter, 1984: 53). Galanter also refers to studies which show that in 1962, SC legislators in reserved seats gave the Congress a majority in eight of the thirteen legislatures and that in nine other states at least, the governments were dependent on the SC MLAs occupying reserved seats (ibid).

Others have pointed out that the role played by this elite group in the Central and state legislatures in protecting the interests of their own community has not been significant. While their sheer presence has helped 'to maintain support for SC development programmes at a time of rising political demands on scarce national resources from economically stronger groups', they have not acted effectively when atrocities were committed against members of their own communities or pressured the administration to implement policies for the disadvantaged sections (Joshi, 1982: 169). Mendelsohn affirms that 'they are comparatively better off than other *dalits* outside the legislative institutions, but not powerful enough to play the strong and independent political role which might more effectively promote their community's interests' (Mendelsohn, 1986). Shah notes that a number of studies on SC legislators show that despite the constitutional directive to enact laws prescribing punishment for acts contravening the rights of untouchables, they could not effectively pressure Parliament to get the Untouchability (Offences) Act passed quickly, or use their power for the effective implementation of the Act (Shah, 1997). More importantly, Saberwal in an earlier study stressed the absence of leaders who understood 'the larger institutional mechanisms which underlay and renewed the current inequalities, nor any who had the stamina for changing the larger system so that its processes would generate effective . . . equality' (Saberwal, 1972: 79).

This paper in contrast, attempts to relate the pattern of voting in reserved constituencies in the post-Independence period to SC politics. SCs have used two avenues of representation to protect their interests in post-Independence India: through a broad-based aggregative mainstream party, namely the Congress, up to the mid-1980s, and in more recent years through narrower identity-based parties such as the Bahujan Samaj Party (BSP). This paper examines the contribution of the policy of electoral reservation to both these types, but particularly to the emergence of Dalit identity and a distinct identity-based party in the state of Uttar Pradesh (UP). While such trends are visible in many states, UP provides us with an important field base for such a study, due to the emergence of a strong identity-based party. Our study shows that the Congress party won most of the reserved seats during its period of dominance, and following its decline since the late-1980s, the Bharatiya Janata Party (BJP) has won a majority of these seats, followed by the Samajwadi Party (SP), with the BSP in third position. Dalit parties, whether the Republican Party of India (RPI) in the 1960s, or the BSP since the late-1980s, have won few reserved seats in the assembly and parliamentary elections, even during periods when they have performed well in the state. They have not depended on reserved seats to either gain entry into the legislature or increase the number of their legislators.

Our study argues that the role played by the policy of electoral reservations in the construction of a Dalit identity and a Dalit party devoted exclusively to the protection of the interests of the SC community has been very limited. The emergence of a Dalit identity and party in recent years is the result of changes taking place within society; namely the impact of reservations in the fields of education and employment and the increasing democratization of society and polity since Independence. These developments have been instrumental in creating an educated, articulate middle class within the SC community, a vanguard that has, since the mid-1980s, led movements and created exclusively Dalit parties demanding respect, economic betterment and a share in the political power. The BSP, in short, is a product of the mobilization undertaken by the political leaders grounded in civil society, outside the formal legislative institutions. However, at the same time, the BSP has not been able to muster all Dalit voters, some of whom vote for the BJP and the SP in reserved constituencies, despite the existence of an exclusive Dalit party. This shows that the Dalit identity remains fragmented.

The paper is divided into three parts. The first part looks at the struggle for political reservations in the colonial period, its impact on low-caste consciousness and identity and its legacies in the post-colonial period, particularly in UP, while the second part discusses the constitutional provisions on which reserved seats are based. The third part examines the pattern of voting in reserved constituencies in the post-Independence period and its relationship to SC politics, in particular the emergence of a Dalit party in UP. In the conclusion we again discuss the issue of the relationship between reservations and the continuing search for identity by the SCs.

THE STRUGGLE FOR POLITICAL RESERVATIONS: COLONIAL LEGACIES

The struggle for electoral representation, and later for separate electorates for the Depressed Classes (DC)[2] in the colonial period, played an important role in making the DCs conscious of their low social status and distinct identity from caste Hindus. The demand for separate representation can be traced to two developments in the early twentieth century: firstly, the colonial census and secondly, the Morley–Minto reforms of 1909. These reforms, while legalizing the principle of elections to the central and provincial legislatures, granted communal electorates to the Muslims in proportion to their demographic weight. With the introduction of separate electorates, communal statistics gained importance; communities became conscious of their numbers and those of others, leading to the 'politics of numbers' (Gupta, 1985: 37). For the first time the DCs became important as the caste Hindus were keen that the former should be counted as Hindus, while the Muslims in 1909 argued that they were an independent group and should not be enrolled in the census as Hindus. The Indian National Congress, which had earlier ignored the need for reforming the position of the DCs, also began to take interest and hoped to gain their support. The issue acquired greater significance when the 1911 census for the first time attempted to list those castes that 'do not conform to certain (religious) standards or are subject to certain disabilities' (ibid.: 40). From 1917 onwards, various estimates began to be put forward by the DC associations, especially in the Madras, Bombay and Bengal Presidencies and the Central Provinces, demanding the expansion of the provincial legislative councils and a larger franchise. The grant of nominations to the DCs in the central and provincial legislatures by the 1919 Government of India Act, on the basis of their recognition as a distinct and backward group, proved to be an important step that gave the DCs the self-confidence to continue their struggle. Their separate identity was now a given constitutional fact enabling them to use the legislature to voice demands for upliftment and welfare measures on the part of the government.

However, the demand for a separate electorate persisted. In its memorandum to the Simon Commission, the Bahiskrit Hitkarini Sabha[3] from Bombay, under Ambedkar's leadership, opposed nominations and strongly pleaded for the extension of the elective principle to the DCs. On the instance of M.C. Rajah, the Madras Legislative Council of which he was a member passed a resolution asking District Collectors to nominate suitable DC candidates to the various local bodies and municipalities (Gupta, 1985: 224). The demand gathered momentum in the 1920s and representations were made before the Simon Commission, which rejected the demand for separate electorates but recommended reservation of seats for the DCs in all the provinces based upon the principle of demographic weight.

From the mid-1930s, the issue of separate electorates assumed greater significance as it became clear that independence would be granted by the British in the near future. The DCs viewed separate electorates as part of the political safeguards for the protection of their community in the future Constitution of a self-governing India. Therefore, in order to be in a position of power to influence legislative and executive action, they demanded the right to adequate representation in the legislatures, the right to elect their own men as representatives through adult suffrage and separate electorates for a period of ten years, and thereafter through joint electorates (ibid.: 270). This demand was put forward at the first Round Table Conference by Ambedkar and given sympathetic consideration by the British government, but Gandhi's opposition to separate electorates as divisive and wholly against the interests of caste Hindus and the DCs made this impossible. Initially unwilling to accept joint electorates, Ambedkar wondered: 'Will SCs be able to elect a SC candidate who has their confidence to the seat reserved for them, or will the Hindus be able to elect a SC candidate who is their tool and who has no confidence of the SCs?' (Moon, 1991: 154). But ultimately, he compromised and accepted the system of primary and secondary elections for a number of seats in the Poona Pact of 1932. The 1935 act incorporated the agreement and guaranteed reservation to SCs in the various Indian legislatures. In order to mobilize the SC voters in reserved constituencies, the Congress founded the All-India Depressed Classes League with Jagjivan Ram as president. While Ambedkar's Independent Labour Party performed well in western India in the 1937 elections, the Congress won 73 out of 151 seats in the country as a whole, a large number of them in north India (Bandyopadhyay, 2000: 898). However, the demand for separate electorates continued and was taken up by the All-India Scheduled Caste Federation (AISCF), formed by Ambedkar in 1942. It was the agitation led by the AISCF and its branches in various provinces that finally led the Constituent Assembly to provide reserved seats to the SCs.

The impact of these developments was tardy in many parts of the country, including the United Provinces. It was only in the 1930s that the 'politics of numbers' was taken up by DC leaders in this region. In contrast to southern and western India, the United Provinces did not experience a large-scale or sustained identity-based movement under the influence of Ambedkar until very late in the colonial period. Its mobilizational impact upon the vast mass of Depressed Classes in the province was limited, and came too late to have a transformative impact on society. This region came under the influence of Gandhi and the Congress, leading to the emergence of a passive Harijan identity and the idea of upliftment rather than mobilization. Moreover, in contrast to the Bombay Presidency, apart from a little commercialization of agriculture, a few sugar mills and the construction of some canals, there was little investment by the colonial government. Economic development in the United Provinces was slow, as a result of which the traditional village structure and relations between castes in the rural areas remained unchanged. The result was 'delayed development of identity consciousness' among the large mass of Depressed Classes in the state (Pai, 2001: 259). It was only in the 1940s that the United Provinces experienced the 'Ambedkar break' (Jurgensmeyer, 1988: 163) when a section of the urban, educated, SC leaders came together on a common platform, though briefly, to form the Scheduled Caste Federation of the United Provinces (UPSCF) in 1944, a branch of the AISCF. Consequently, although the Federation played a significant role in the politics of the late colonial period, its impact on the poorer sections of the SCs was limited.

During its brief life of about a decade, the UPSCF joined the AISCF in demanding reservations for the SCs in the legislatures and in government jobs, as well as special rights for them in the Constitution of independent India. The AISCF was disappointed when the Cabinet Mission and the British government did not provide separate representation for the SCs by recognizing them as a separate community (Narayan, 1996: 59). It was decided that satyagrahas would be organized throughout the country from June 1946 onwards to protest against the Cabinet Mission Award and the Congress. The AISCF had three main demands: a blue-print from the Congress on the position of SCs in independent India, abrogation of the Poona Pact, and separate electorates for SCs, recognizing them as a separate community. The agitation in the United Provinces was part of the protest.

The movement organized by the UPSCF began around the first week of June 1946 and affected 23 districts in Oudh, of which 10 witnessed a prolonged agitation from June to November 1946 (ibid.: 64). On 16 July 1946, hundreds of *satyagrahis* marched to the Legislative Assembly and courted arrest in large numbers. The AISCF suspended the agitation on 28 July, but in the United Provinces the agitation continued until 15 August when the Assembly adjourned. Apart from Lucknow, the main centres of the agitation where meetings and demonstrations were organized were the towns of Kanpur, Etah, Etawah, Faizabad, Azamgarh, Agra, Ferozabad and Farrukhabad. A second round of satyagraha was organized from September onwards by the state Federation. The leaders of the movement presented eleven demands to the provincial government in Lucknow, including one for reservation of government jobs for the SCs. It was due to this satyagraha that the SCs were awarded reservations (17 per cent) from the United Provinces' government. The latter also created a new department, the Harijan Sahayak Department, to initiate welfare measures for the SCs (ibid.: 133).

A third round of agitation, organized by the UPSCF, took place between 26 March 1947 and 14 May 1947, but proved to be shortlived and unsuccessful. It was organized independently by the UPSCF, unlike the earlier one in 1946, which was part of the agitation by the AISCF and was specifically directed against the Congress (ibid.: 109). Meanwhile, the United Provinces government decided to introduce a bill in the legislative assembly to remove the social disabilities of the SCs, such as guaranteeing their right to hold public office, or to carry on any trade or business (ibid. 110). The bill did not satisfy the UPSCF, which demanded constitutional safeguards for the SCs and decided to agitate against the Congress ministry in the province. Demonstrations were held in front of the Assembly from 25 March onwards. Some of the demonstrators, led by Manik Chand, entered the Council Chamber on 26 March, where they were arrested. The agitation continued till 25 April, after which it slowly died down, as all the important UPSCF leaders were in jail (ibid.: 114).

The agitation carried out by the UPSCF did not lead to the granting of separate electorates but it was important in making the Congress party agree to reserved seats as part of the policy of protective discrimination. The question came up again for discussion in the Constituent Assembly and Ambedkar again put forward the demand, but the Assembly rejected it and adopted the principle of joint electorates with reserved seats. In the Constituent Assembly there was little debate on the need for reservation and very few members spoke on the issue (Saksena, 1981).[4] However, the legacy of this struggle in the United Provinces must be kept in mind in the post-colonial period. The newly created SC identity, which formed the basis for the creation of the UPSCF, was neither united nor clear. Two developments show this clearly. First, the Federation, the only opposition party, was defeated by the Congress in the final elections held in 1946, despite performing well in the primaries (Reeves, 1971: 111–42). There was a clear divide between the 'Ambedkarites' and the 'Congress Harijans', the latter being more numerous. Second, once independence was declared, the UPSCF disintegrated and most of its members joined the Congress, a party they had been opposing until very recently. By May 1947 it was evident that India would gain independence. On 28 April 1947 the Constituent Assembly passed a bill abolishing untouchability, making its practice a criminal offence, and on 2 July Ambedkar was nominated to the Constituent Assembly as a Congress candidate from the Bombay Legislative Council. In this situation, prominent SC leaders in the United Provinces, such as Pyarelal Kureel, Nandlal Jaiswar and Shamlal offered their co-operation and support to the Congress. An exodus began and many leaders of the UPSCF joined the Congress (Narayan, 1996: 121). Many of these leaders fought the 1952 and 1957 general elections on a Congress ticket and won. During the transitional phase of 1945–7, the UPSCF constituted an important political force, but once independence was won its task was over. It lacked the necessary rural roots to evolve either into a broad-based social SC movement or into a political party alongside the Congress in the United Provinces.

All this shows that the grant of reserved seats was the result of an understanding between the nationalist leadership and the leaders of the SC community, leading the movement for separate electorates in the late colonial period. The great mass of the SCs in the state were not conscious of their distinct identity, and their social status, literacy levels and economic resources were much inferior compared to the caste Hindus. In addition, the Congress party, due to its seminal role in the national movement and Gandhi's leadership, had already gained the support of a large section of the SC community and won in a number of reserved seats in the province and in many other parts of the country. Moreover, the reserved seats granted by the Constitution were to operate in the post-Independence period under the system of adult franchise within a democratic framework. These factors would play an important role in the functioning of the policy of political reservation after Independence.

RESERVED SEATS: CONSTITUTIONAL PROVISIONS AND THEIR SIGNIFICANCE

The Indian Constitution provides reserved seats to SCs, in proportion to their demographic weight, in the Lower House of Parliament (the Lok Sabha) and in state Assemblies (the Vidhan Sabhas), but not in the Upper House at the Centre or in the states. Seats are reserved in the legislatures in proportion to the SC population of each state. Accordingly, under Articles 330 and 332, a total of 78 and 540 seats are 'reserved' for the SCs in the Lok Sabha and state Assemblies respectively. These seats do not involve 'separate electorates', i.e. the representation of a specific group by legislators chosen by an electorate composed solely of members of that group, a system which was demanded by the Depressed Classes in the colonial period. The seats are 'reserved' in the sense that candidates who stand for election to them must belong to the SC community, but the entire electorate votes in selecting the candidates so qualified. In fact, separate electorates are specifically outlawed by Article 325, which states that no person shall be excluded from any electoral roll on grounds of religion, race or caste. In a bid to help disadvantaged social groups, smaller election deposits are demanded of candidates to reserved seats and they are given more permissive residence requirements. Unlike other authorizations for special treatment and the provision of reserved seats in government service, under Article 334 the reserved seats in legislatures were made subject to a time limit of 10 years (Galanter, 1984: 45). However, they have been periodically extended by constitutional amendments in every decade and at present are valid until 2010.

The manner in which the constituencies are designed is important for our study as it attempts to relate the voting behaviour in these constituencies to SC politics. The demarcation of constituencies and designation of those reserved for SCs are entrusted to a Delimitation Commission and courts are specifically barred from intervening in the process of delimitation or allotment of seats.[5] Regarding the criteria used by the Commission for delimitation, in the case of the Scheduled Tribes it is simple, as they are concentrated in specific areas. For SCs the Commission is instructed to use two criteria—concentration and dispersal of reservations. The Commission does this by first reserving the constituencies with the highest concentration of SCs—usually not more than 20 per cent; and then selecting the others by the dispersal criterion. Since the SC population—unlike the Scheduled Tribe population—is evenly dispersed, the constituencies reserved for them contain far fewer SC members. Galanter's calculations show that among the 76 constituencies reserved for SCs in the 1962 elections, there were none in which they constituted a majority and only 13 in which they were as much as 30 per cent. The bulk of the constituencies contain between 10 and 30 per cent SC population. Thus, the vast majority of SCs live outside the reserved constituencies. Of the 111 constituencies in which SCs constituted more than 20 per cent of the population in 1961, only 46 were reserved, whereas 29 constituencies with less than 20 per cent were reserved. Examining the records of the Delimitation Commission, Galanter points out that while all legislators agreed in principle that reserved seats are important and must be maintained, the delimitation of a constituency usually encounters objections and suggestions, so that it may be maintained as a general constituency (Galanter, 1984: 48). However, as courts do not interfere, such objections rarely result in change.

It has been debated whether the system of reserved constituencies—which are few in number compared to the large number of general constituencies, with no more than an approximate 20 per cent of SCs in the electorate—has served any purpose. Galanter points out that SCs would not have gained entry into the legislatures, particularly in the early years of independence, if it had not been for the reserved seats. In the first six Lok Sabhas, only a handful of candidates from the SC or ST communities could win on unreserved seats—five were elected in 1971 and three in 1977 (ibid.: 49). In the lower houses of the state legislatures the situation was no better, although smaller constituencies mean that local concentrations of population and resources normally offer greater chances of success. For example, in 1970–1, there were only three SC and two ST representatives as compared to a total of 2,853 non-reserved seats in the Vidhan Sabhas (ibid.). Thus, the presence of SC members in the state legislatures, until the emergence of SC parties, such as the BSP in the 1980s, was almost entirely due to the provision of reserved seats. There is no constitutional requirement for the reservation of political appointments within the legislatures or the government, for example, cabinet ministerial berths. But it soon became the norm to have at least one SC cabinet minister at the Centre and in each of the states, who were mainly chosen from the reserved seats. Similarly, at the state level, the first extension of reservations to promotions occurred when a SC politician became Chief Minister in AP; the ascension of a SC home minister in Madras was followed by a more vigorous prosecution under the Untouchability (Offences) Act (ibid.: 54). Thus, reservations have provided a substantial quantitative presence that would otherwise be lacking.

When assessing the quality of representation of these representatives, it is necessary to remember the 'structural constraints' imposed by the arrangements for reserved seats. Reservations are designed in a manner that both 'filters and muffles' the representation of the interests of the SCs insofar as they diverge from those of other groups. On the one hand, the reserved seat legislator is responsible to a population overwhelmingly made up of non-SC persons, and on the other, he is expected to represent the interests of his own community, which is a difficult task (ibid.). Finally, Galanter points out that the importance of reserved seats is seen in the fact that the press, the public and the political parties have supported the extension of reserved seats every 10 years, as if the end of these reservations would be the end of all reservations, although there are little constitutional grounds to justify such an idea. He argues that this symbolic function tells us something important 'about the way in which political reservations function to lock into place all the other programmes for SCs and STs' (ibid.: 55).

ELECTORAL RESERVATIONS IN UP: VOTING PATTERNS AND IMPACT

Keeping in mind both the historical background which made reserved seats possible in India and the constitutional provisions under which they operate, in this section we will attempt to examine the impact on SC politics in UP of the policy of electoral reservations in the post-Independence period, particularly the rise of an identity-based party. As mentioned in section two, in any reserved constituency the percentage of SCs in the population is only between 10–30 per cent. Hence, an analysis of the electoral results of reserved seats taken alone—whether in UP or in any other state—does not help us understand the voting behaviour of SCs in such constituencies. However, what is attempted here is an analysis of long-term voting trends in the post-Independence period from 1952 to 2002 in the reserved constituencies, as compared to the voting trends of the general seats in UP.[6] Such an exercise brings out some patterns of singular importance from which conclusions can be drawn. Our analysis is divided into two periods: until the late 1980s, when the SCs agreed to let mainstream parties represent their interests, and the 1990s, when they chose to be represented through a Dalit party, the BSP. However, while the 1990s have been dealt with separately, it needs to be emphasized that despite the rise of a distinct identity-based party, some long-term trends have continued into the 1990s.

Representation through mainstream parties

Tables 1.1 to 1.3 give the electoral results of reserved seats in all the assembly elections in UP from 1952 to 2002, and all the parliamentary elections in UP during the 1990s.[7] A long-term trend which emerges is that the pattern of voting in the reserved seats throughout the post-Independence period has largely followed that of the general seats and reflects major changes in the polity, particularly the decline of the one-party system and the rise of a multi-party system. No separate pattern emerges despite the fact that UP had as many as 82 reserved seats in the state Assembly in 1952 and 91 in 2002. It is essential to note that the general electorate also preferred candidates put up by the Congress in the reserved constituencies to those of other parties, during the former's period of dominance. During the 1950s and 1960s,

TABLE 1.1: RESERVED SEATS WON BY PARTIES IN ASSEMBLY ELECTIONS IN THE 1950s AND 1960s

Year	Congress	Others	Total
1952	80	2	82
1957	60	29	89
1962	58	30	89*
1967	45	41	86
1969	43	43	86

NOTES: Distribution of seats in the 'Others' category:

1957: Independent 16, CPI 3, Jan Sangh 3, PSP 8.

1962: Jan Sangh 8, RPI 1, PSP 5, Swatantra 5, CPI 2, Independent 4, Socialist Party 6.

1967: Jan Sangh 24, Swatantra 3, SSP 10, RPI 1, CPI 1, Independent 2.

1969: BKD 21, Jan Sangh 13, SSP 5, Swatantra 2, CPM 1, Independent 1.

* Election to one seat was not held.

SOURCE: Singh and Bose, vol. 4, 1988.

TABLE 1.2: RESERVED SEATS WON BY PARTIES IN ASSEMBLY ELECTIONS IN THE 1970s AND 1980s

Year	Congress	Others	Total
1974	49	41	90
1977	8	82	90
1980	76	17	93
1985	73	20	93
1989 *	19	73	92

NOTES: Distribution of seats in the 'Others' category:

1974: BKD 24, Jan Sangh 15, CPI 2.

1977: Janata Party 81, Independent 1.

1980: Janata Party 10, BJP 3, CPI 2, Independent 1, INCU 1.

1985: LKD 15, Janata Party 1, BJP 2, Independent 2.

1989: JD 50, BJP 13, BSP 5, Independents 5.

* The source for 1989 is the Statistical Report of the Election Commission of India.

SOURCE: Same as Table 1.1

the Jan Sangh, Swatantra, Socialist and other smaller parties in UP put up candidates in the reserved constituencies, but the Congress won in a majority of them. The reserved seats were also distributed among opposition parties in proportion to their strength in the assembly: the Jan Sangh gaining the largest number, followed by the Socialist parties and by the Swatantra Party. While in 1967 it looked as if UP was moving towards a two-party contest with the Jan Sangh emerging as the largest opposition party, the emergence of the Bharatiya Kranti Dal (BKD) made it a three-cornered contest by 1969, which is faithfully reflected in the voting pattern of the reserved seats. In the 1969 assembly elections, the BKD gained 21 reserved seats, pushing the Jan Sangh, which had gained 24 seats in 1967, to third place with 13 seats.

Second, during its dominance between 1950 and the late 1980s, the Congress party gained the largest number of reserved seats compared to any other party. This pattern can be understood by examining the psychology of a minority community, who in the absence of a strong leadership felt that its interests would best be served by a mainstream party, i.e. the Congress. During this very same period, we find the Muslim community of north India thinking along similar lines. Table 1.1 shows that in the two state assembly elections held in the 1950s, the Congress won almost all the reserved seats. Moreover, it was able to gain over 40 per cent of the votes in majority of the cases.[8] Even in 1967, despite the downturn in its fortunes, the Congress gained more seats than all the other parties, although its margin of victory now fell to 30 per cent. The 1969 and 1977 assembly elections are two exceptions—the Congress' position was threatened. In both cases the Congress regained its dominant electoral position in the next election.

However, a third and more important feature is that throughout the post-Independence period, SCs have, through the medium of reserved seats, supported the dominant mainstream party at any point of time. In the 1950s, 1960s and 1980s this party was the Congress, in the mid-1970s the Janata Party, in 1989 the Janata Dal, and in the 1990s the BJP. SC voters in the reserved seats shifted to the alternative victorious party, which won a majority of the seats and received a high percentage of the votes cast for the reserved seats. Whenever the dominance of the Congress has been successfully challenged by an alternative party, reserved seats have been captured by that party. The SCs have not hesitated to desert the Congress whenever they were vexed with it or when it showed signs of weakening and decline. Unhappy with the Emergency in the 1970s, the SC did not hesitate to punish the Congress and crossed over in large numbers to the Janata Party. The latter emerged as an alternative, despite the alliance with parties such as the Jan Sangh, identified as an upper caste party, and the Bharatiya Lok Dal (BLD), identified with the middle caste, landowning classes who were the direct oppressors of the landless SCs in the countryside after the Green Revolution. In the 1977 assembly elections, the Janata party received over 50 per cent of the votes in most of the 81 reserved seats it won. In the 1980 and 1985 assembly elections, the Congress was able to regain its dominant position. It won 76 and 73 reserved seats respectively in these elections and its margin of victory in the reserved seats again rose above 40 per cent. Following the decline of the Congress in the late-1980s, the SCs crossed over to the Janata Dal, which helped it to come to power in 1989. In 1989, a new pattern became visible: the Congress gained only 19 reserved seats, the Janata Dal as the dominant party gained 50 seats, while the BJP as a party on the rise managed 13 and the BSP as a new party only 5. The Janata Dal obtained over 40 per cent—and even 50 per cent in some cases—in the majority of the reserved seats it won. With the emergence of the BJP as the largest party in the state, the SCs began to switch over from the early 1990s. In the 1991 assembly elections, when the BJP tried to create a large vote-bank across north India, including the lower castes, it was able to gain 56 reserved seats, while the Janata Dal gained 21, but the BSP did not gain a single seat. Except in the 2002 assembly elections, the BJP has gained the largest number of reserved seats since 1991.

Fourth, this pattern remains valid even when SCs have had a party of their own. In the mid-1960s, the RPI, despite being an SC party, was able to win only two reserved seats—one out of its total of eight seats in 1962, and one out of its total of 10 seats in the 1967 assembly elections. While the RPI disappeared before it could establish itself in the late-1960s, the same pattern is visible in the case of the BSP, a much stronger lower caste party based on Dalit identity. As Table 1.3 shows, the BJP has been able to gain more reserved seats than the BSP in both the assembly and the parliamentary elections during the

1990s. In the 1993 and 1996 assembly elections, the BJP was able to win 34 and 37 seats, while the BSP could only win 25 and 19 reserved seats. With the weakening of the BJP in the late-1990s, in the 1999 parliamentary and the 2002 elections, the SP gained the largest number of reserved seats, followed by the BSP. Its share of reserved seats rose from 20 in 1996 to 35 in 2002. This follows the general pattern of voting for all seats where the SP has emerged as the single largest party. Thus, the same trend has been maintained throughout the 1990s, with reserved constituencies following the pattern of non-reserved constituencies.

Two reasons underlie the above voting pattern until the late-1980s. First, the dominant position occupied by the Congress party until the 1980s in the electoral arena, except for a brief period during the Emergency. At the time of Independence, the Congress enjoyed a dominant position, being the party that had led the national movement. Equally important, in UP it was identified by the SCs as the party which under the leadership of Gandhi had improved the socio-economic conditions of their community during the colonial period. On the basis of this dominance, the Congress planned its electoral strategy in the 1940s and continued to follow it after Independence. The UPSCF, as an identity-based party, employed a communitarian strategy to mobilize the SCs, particularly for the elections to the primaries in the 1940s. The Congress on the other hand did not mobilize the SCs as a community, but co-opted local notables among them in each area, reaching out to the rest of the community through them (Duncan, 1979: 229). This proved a successful manoeuvre in a society where a large mass of the SCs were poor, illiterate and not conscious of their specific identity or interests and were, therefore, ready to copy their leaders. This strategy was later continued in the post-Independence period when selecting candidates for reserved seats. As the studies mentioned earlier have shown, SC members elected from reserved constituencies on the Congress ticket have not been from the poorer sections but constitute the elite section of the community. The Congress in short has co-opted local notables from the SC community in the reserved constituencies.

The second reason is the lack of charismatic leaders within the SC community with a clear-cut agenda, who could mobilize the SCs and use reserved seats as a rallying point for the community. At the time of Independence, SC leaders in UP were confronted with two major issues regarding their future course of struggle against the unequal social order. First, should they form a separate party or join the Congress? While a few were keen to protect their hard-won identity from caste Hindus, many of the SC leaders felt that the Congress as a mainstream party could protect their interests better. Lynch mentions that in Agra the community was torn between two groups: the 'Congress conservatives' who wanted to support a ruling party better positioned to help them, and the 'RPI leaders' who were keen to maintain a separate party based on a distinct lower-caste identity (Lynch, 1979: 111). In this situation the policy of protective discrimination set out in the Constitution played an important role. Among the small group of socially and politically aware SC leaders, many felt that political participation within the new constitutional order, was a more effective way of penetrating the new power structures and obtaining social upliftment, than leading a movement against the established social and political order. Consequently, their attitude towards the State and the ruling Congress party remained ambivalent, making it easy for the latter to absorb them. A second and related issue was what kind of party should be formed, a communitarian party for only the Scheduled Castes or one which catered to all the weaker and exploited sections? Ambedkar's conversion to Buddhism and his death soon afterwards left his followers with an 'ambiguous legacy' (Duncan, 1979: 230). On the one hand, when the SCF in UP and elsewhere failed to make a mark in the first two general elections after Independence, Ambedkar called upon his followers to form a more broad-based party, drawing support both from the Dalits and other castes/classes. On the other, his conversion to Buddhism indicated his continuing belief in the separate identity of the Dalits and a strategy for keeping it intact. (ibid.). These ambiguities were reflected within the RPI, resulting in divisions and thus making it easier for the Congress to absorb it.

Equally important, the RPI was a product of developments in the late colonial period. Its leaders consisted of a small better-off section among the SCs. Most were young, in their thirties or forties, well educated, and a number of them were lawyers, businessmen in the leather trade, or full-time political leaders. They were local notables in the western districts from where most of them were elected, being members of the municipal corporations, workers' unions, bank employees' unions, water works committees, etc. Only two of the relatively older members had been members of the Congress earlier and defected to the RPI in the 1960s. Between one-fourth and half of the members in this period were Muslims, the number rising in the mid-1960s when the RPI had an alliance going with Muslim organizations in some of the principal towns of western UP (*Who's Who*, Vidhan Sabha, 1962, 1967). Unlike the BSP members in the UP Assembly, who come from smaller towns and are still involved in land, the RPI leaders were from the bigger towns in western, and to a lesser extent eastern UP, besides which very few were from a rural background or from small-town constituencies. An urban, educated elite of the late colonial period, as part of the UPSCF they had shown little interest in mobilizing SCs in the rural areas, their area of activity remained the towns, as seen in the poor performance of the UPSCF in the 1946 elections. Hence, they had few links in the countryside and were unable to mobilize the vast mass of SCs. The social base of the party was also largely limited to the Chamars in the state. Starting from a limited social and regional base at a time when the majority remained trapped within the larger Hindu identity, before it could mobilize and improve its vote share or spread to new areas, the party disappeared.

Moreover, the existing power structure in UP, particularly in the rural areas, in the first few decades after Independence did not allow space for the development of a strong SC party. Congress party leadership came from the upper castes, while the middle castes were mobilized by the opposition parties—the Jan Sangh, Samyukta Socialist Party (SSP), Praja Socialist Party (PSP) and later the BKD/BLD. But its base in caste terms was wider; it comprised people from the top and the bottom of the hierarchy. Through patron–client relations, the upper castes were able to build their vote-banks, and thereby gain the support of the SCs. The Congress was a broad-based aggregative party. At the local level in each district, it successfully built a broad-based coalition consisting of former zamindars, the locally dominant proprietary castes of Brahmins, Rajputs, and Bhumihars, sections of the middle status cultivating castes with self-sufficient land holdings, the bulk of the lower SCs, and the Muslim minority vote (Brass, 1985: 15). In the 1960s, the Congress party also tried to mobilize through its own organization, the Dalit Varg Sangh (Depressed Classes League), which enabled it to win a chunk of the SC vote. The result was that issues relating to SCs were addressed by non-SC political leaders and became subsumed within the broader agenda of development and change. Change was also slow in coming to UP, which even today remains a conservative state. The formation of the BKD/BLD and the onset of the Emergency, which led to the formation of the Janata Party (JP), undoubtedly challenged the dominance of the Congress, thereafter weakening it. The party machinery in the districts also declined. But in electoral politics, apart from a brief interregnum between 1977 and 1980, the Congress remained the dominant majority party in the state until the late-1980s. This was faithfully reflected in the voting pattern in the reserved seats.

Representation through a Dalit party

A more complex pattern of voting in relation to reserved seats emerged in the 1990s, though long-term trends continued to show continuity. Tables 1.3 and 1.4 show that unlike the earlier period, a more differentiated pattern of voting emerged. For the first time reserved seats were divided between three distinctly opposed parties, the BJP, the SP and the BSP, a reflection of the decline of the single dominant party system and the emergence of an increasingly fragmented multi-party system. Unlike the Congress during the period of its dominance, in no election has the BJP been able to win more reserved seats than all the other parties put together. The margin of victory of the three opposing parties has also been lower, being 30 per cent in most cases, as votes have been divided between them. Nevertheless, Table 1.3, shows that except for the 1999 parliamentary and 2002 assembly elections, the BJP has won more reserved seats in every election than any other party. In the 1993 and 1996 elections it obtained 34 and 37 seats respectively, leaving the SP and the BSP far behind.

At the same time, Table 1.4 shows that the number of reserved seats won by the BSP in both the assembly and parliamentary elections in the 1990s, were in most cases half the non-reserved seats it obtained, precisely during a period of rising Dalit assertion and increase in its seat and vote share. However, in the 1999 parliamentary and 2002 assembly elections, the BSP has for the first time been able to get

TABLE 1.3: RESERVED SEATS WON BY PARTIES IN THE ASSEMBLY ELECTIONS IN THE 1990s

Party \ Year	1991	1993	1996*	2002
BJP	56	34	37	20
BSP	0	25	19	24
SP	7	22	20	35
Congress	8	7	3	2
JD	21	3	3	1
CPM	–	1	3	2
BKKGP	–	–	2	–
SJP	–	–	1	–
Ind.	–	–	3	4
RSP	–	–	–	3
Total	92	92	92	91

NOTE: * Election to one seat was not held.

TABLE 1.4: RESERVED SEATS WON BY PARTIES IN THE PARLIAMENTARY ELECTIONS IN THE 1990s

Year	BJP	BSP	SP/JP	Congress	JD	CPM	ABLTC	Total
1991	10	0	1**	0	7	0	0	18
1996	14	2	2	0	0	0	-	18
1998	11	2	5	0	0	0	-	18
1999	7	5	5	0	0	0	1	18

NOTE: ** Seat won by the JP
SOURCE: Same as the previous tables.

more reserved seats than the BJP, though the party with the largest number of reserved seats in the assembly elections is the SP. Moreover, the share of the reserved seats gained by the BJP fell sharply in the 1999 parliamentary elections and 2002 assembly elections, which reflects its declining fortunes in UP. These were largely won by the SP, which emerged as the single largest party, and to a lesser extent, by the BSP. This situation indicates continuity from the earlier period.

Our analysis indicates that beginning in the late-1980s, the SCs in UP have preferred representation through a Dalit party rather than mainstream parties as in the past. Yet the voting pattern outlined above points to the fact that reserved seats have not contributed to the rise of a separate Dalit party in the state. The BSP, formed 30 years after Independence, is not the product of electoral reservations but of two post-Independence developments: reservations in education and employment and a long-term process of democratization which has made Dalits politically aware and identity conscious. A glance at some aspects of the BSP makes this clear. It was formed by a post-Independence educated generation, an economically better off and upwardly mobile middle class that was able to mobilize the SC community, construct a unique Dalit identity and party. This new generation of SCs is a product of reservations in education and employment, seen in the fact that the BSP has its roots in the Backward and Minorities Classes Employees Federation (BAMCEF), an organization of government employees, and not in grassroots mobilization in the countryside (Pai, 2001: 269). Economic growth in UP in the 1980s, particularly in the agricultural sector, helped this class revolt against upper/middle caste domination, leading to the breakdown of patron–client relations, vote-banks and co-option by the Congress party. The literacy level among the SCs rose by a little over 4 per cent between 1971 and 1981, but between 1981 and 1991 it rose by 8 per cent points. This is still lower than the national average for SCs (30.70 per cent) but the gap has begun to narrow (Pai, 2000: 408). A small professional and entrepreneurial class has emerged, which has made use of job quotas under affirmative action to shift to non-agricultural professions, particularly in the better-off regions of the state. It is important to note that by the 1990s, the Chamars, Kureels and Jatavs holding Class I jobs in the UP government compared favourably with those from the Brahmin, Kayasth or Vaishya communities (ibid.).

It is through the mobilizational efforts of this new generation that the BSP has been able to establish itself as a Dalit party. Critical of the Indian State and the Congress party as a 'Manuvadi' or Brahmin party, they pointed to the failure of its policies to improve the socio-economic condition of their community. Through the criticism of the Congress leadership, particularly Gandhi, of its role during the national movement, of its treatment of Ambedkar and of the acceptance of the Poona Pact, a space was created for the new party. Kanshi Ram, in fact, has been very critical of the policy of reservations. In his book *The Chamcha Age: An Era of Stooges*, he points out that since in no constituency in India SCs form an absolute majority, they have to depend upon mainstream parties and maintain good relations with non-SC leaders in order to get the votes of caste Hindus. Consequently, SC leaders such as Jagjivan Ram, Buta Singh or Ram Dhan, who won on reserved seats, became *chamchas* or stooges of the Congress party which, by such methods had in the post-Independence period, monopolized Ambedkar's legacy and not allowed any 'real' Dalit leader or party to emerge. Thus, he feels that the rejection of the demand for separate electorates and the setting up of joint electorates really amounts to a Dalit defeat, the denial of social justice and the strengthening of the Brahminical order (Ram, 1982). Although Kanshi Ram is in favour of reservations in education and employment, he views them as 'crutches' used by SCs and would like to see them abandoned as soon as possible. Rather, he exhorts the SCs to vote for the BSP, which he argues would be the best method to end the upper castes' domination and political rule (ibid.).

An analysis of the socio-economic background of BSP representatives in the UP Legislative Assembly between 1989 and 1996 shows that they comprised young educated Dalits who were new entrants into politics. In the 1989 and 1991 assembly elections, all BSP representatives—except one who had earlier won on CPI ticket from eastern UP—had not been members of the legislature earlier. In 1993, out of 16 who had been elected earlier, 15 had won on BSP ticket. In 1996, for the first time a number of members drawn from other parties are seen among the representatives of the party. Out of 24 who had been elected earlier, 13 had won on BSP ticket, 11 had been elected on Congress, JD, Lok Dal (LD) or JP ticket. However, a constant influx of fresh entrants continued because the party tried to widen its support base to include Muslims and backward castes. These facts indicate that the BSP has drawn upon new entrants into politics from among the lower castes in the rural areas (Pai, 2002: 95).

BSP representatives were young, most of them 30–40 age group and some in the 40–50 age group; very few were above 50. Most of the younger representatives, particularly those who were 30 years and less or between 30–40 years, were Dalit*s*, which points to the emergence of a younger generation of leaders within this community. Representatives belonging to the BCs and Muslim community were comparatively older. There were no representatives above 60 years, except one, in 1996. Moreover, the age of members decreased over the years, indicating the influx of younger members into the party. In 1989 and 1991, most representatives were in the age group 40 to 50, but in 1993 and 1996, the majority was between 30–40 years, with some in the age group 20–30. In 1996, a majority had a college degree from the minor universities of the state. In 1993 and 1996 many were lawyers, most of whom were based in the smaller towns, owned land and still practiced agriculture. There were no small-scale entrepreneurs or industrialists among them, although a few had procured a diploma in engineering after their graduation. Considering the low level of literacy and the small number of landowners among the Dalit*s* and lower backward classes in UP, the BSP representatives are from the better-off groups among the rural lower castes (ibid.: 97).

The socio-economic background of BSP members in the ninth to the thirteenth Lok Sabha from UP shows similar picture. Their numbers in the ninth and tenth Lok Sabha were very few and consisted mainly of leaders/founders of the party, such as Mayawati, who won from Bijnor in 1989 and Kanshi Ram from Etawah in 1991. It is only in 1996 that the number of representatives increased, reaching a total of 11 members, 6 being from UP (ibid.: 99). Most of the members elected to the Lok Sabha in the late-1990s were new entrants, carefully chosen by the leadership. The BSP leader Mayawati began her parliamentary career from reserved seats, but initially was not successful. In the Lok Sabha by-election to the Bijnor (reserved) seat in December 1985, the Congress candidate Meera Kumar (the daughter of Jagjivan Ram) defeated Mayawati by a margin of 5,000 votes (ibid.: 156). In the Hardwar (reserved) Lok Sabha constituency, in a 1987 by-election, Mayawati stood second, losing by 23,000 votes against the Congress candidate (*Indian Express*, 29 March 1987). She has also stood from reserved seats such as Akbarpur and Misrikh during the 1990s, but this has been because these are constituencies with a high SC population rather than because they are reserved seats. Thus, reserved seats have not played a central role in the establishment of the BSP in UP.

The BSP has not used the reserved seat route to widen its base or increase its number of seats in the legislature. Rather, it has used two political strategies to consolidate the Dalit votes behind it:

opportunistic coalitions with the BJP in order to capture power that has had undeniable symbolic importance, and strategies of ticket distribution and electoral mobilization (Pai, 2002). In the early-1990s, the BSP was viewed as a party of the better-off Dalits, but by the end of the decade, while it has not been able to homogenize the Dalit community and factional rivalries remain among sub-castes, it has been able to unite it insofar as voting for the party is concerned. As a result, today the BSP has the support of the newly emerging small elite and middle class groups among the Dalits, as well as the poor and illiterate Dalits, from whom it gets the majority of its votes. Thus, there are two 'layers'. A small inner layer consisting of the urban, educated elite and middle class, who are fewer in number but influential within the party; and an outer layer comprising the mass of poor, illiterate Dalits, who support it in the countryside (ibid.: 189). Competitive politics in UP and the political strategies pursued by the party during the 1990s have combined to make it a strong Dalit party.

However, an important question that arises from the analysis of voting patterns related to reserved seats in the 1990s is why did the BSP not win a larger share of reserved seats in the state Assembly once its seat and vote share had steadily risen by the end of the decade. Table 1.5 shows a rise in the number of reserved seats gained by the BSP in the Assembly from 5 in 1989 to 25 in 1993, 18 in 1996 to 24 in 2002.[9] But the BJP and the SP won a larger number of seats during this period. The reasons lie in the divisions within the Dalit community. A study shows that the Ayodhya movement in the early-1990s attracted a section of the Dalits, namely the Balmikis. This was because they saw the BSP as a Chamar party and also preferred to side with a 'Hindu' party; unlike the Chamars, they had undergone a process of *Hinduization* (Pai and Singh, 1997). Factional rivalries are also seen among these two sub-castes, and the Balmikis have in recent years argued that the Chamars should no longer be provided reservations in jobs as they have become a prosperous group, unlike other poorer sections of the Dalits. The Dalit community is also divided along caste and class lines. Some of the educated, economically well off and upwardly mobile sections of the Dalits have preferred to vote for the BJP in the second half of the 1990s (Mitra, 1999) indicating that Dalit identity, despite the provision of reserved seats and mobilization by a Dalit party, remains fragmented.

TABLE 1.5: GENERAL AND RESERVED SEATS GAINED BY THE BSP IN THE 1990s

TABLE 1.5A: ASSEMBLY ELECTIONS

General					Reserved				
1989	1991	1993	1996	2002	1989	1991	1993	1996	2002
8	12	44	49	73	5	0	25	18*	24

NOTE: * In the 1996 assembly elections, Mayawati contested and won from two reserved seats: Bilsi and Harora. She resigned from one; hence, the number of reserved seats won by the BSP in 1996 is 18.

TABLE 1.5B: PARLIAMENTARY ELECTIONS

General				Reserved			
1991	1996	1998	1999	1991	1996	1998	1999
1	4	2	9	0	2	2	5

SOURCE: Same as the previous tables.

CONCLUSION

Our study has attempted to understand the role played by the policy of electoral reservations in the quest for identity of the SCs in the political arena. This process began in the colonial period when the DCs demanded separate representation from caste Hindus, based on a growing awareness of their low-caste position and distinct identity and hence of the need for adequate safeguards of their interests. At the time of Independence reserved seats were granted to a community; in which the large majority was illiterate, with little awareness of its identity as distinct from the rest of the Hindu community, and without adequate resources to win elections. Moreover, reserved seats were to operate within an unequal society and under a predominantly capitalist system. As numerous studies have shown, this created an elite SC leadership within mainstream parties, mainly the Congress. Moreover, the latter employed a strategy of selecting local notables on the basis of vote-banks in order to co-opt them. As a result, these leaders have been unable to provide effective leadership, mobilize the community, or help in building identity awareness or identity-based parties.

Our analysis shows that despite the fact that reserved seats were based upon the principle of identity, they have not impacted significantly upon electoral outcomes, or created independent voting patterns in the post-Independence period. Rather voting behaviour, both in the case of reserved as well as the non-reserved seats, has been the same and has reflected the changes taking place within the polity, particularly the realignments taking place within and between parties. The SCs, during much of the post-Independence period, cast their lot with the Congress. Much of the writing of this period describes the SCs as appendages of the Congress in north India. Paradoxically, a persistent feature has been the SC support of the dominant political party through the medium of reserved seats at any point of time, as for example its support of the Janata Party, Janata Dal or even the BJP in UP. However, they have not hesitated to stand behind other parties whenever the dominance of the Congress has been challenged or its influence curtailed. This customary support of the ruling party has persisted despite the rise of a separate Dalit party. This is because of a historically close connection between the State and the SC community. The State has always occupied a central role and been a reference point in the quest for social and economic justice of the SCs. The colonial State, sympathetic to their weak socio-economic and political position, recognizing their specific identity, provided them welfare benefits in response to their demand for separate representation. Similarly, the post-colonial State instituted protective discrimination measures and electoral representation. Consequently, the attitude of the SCs towards the State and the ruling party remained ambivalent, making it easy for mainstream parties to appropriate leaders, and at the same time making it difficult for a separate Dalit party to emerge. As the ruling party, the Congress was able to provide patronage and succeeded in absorbing the fledgling SC movement slowly emerging in UP since the late colonial period.

It was only after the democratization of both the society and the polity, the emergence of a low-caste identity, and the decline of the Congress that a new generation of educated leaders within the SC community succeeded in forming a Dalit identity and a party, which has been able to grab political power and which professes to speak on behalf of the SCs. Our study shows that the success of the BSP is not due to reserved seats, but to mobilization, based on a distinct identity, by a strong and confident leadership that can no longer be co-opted by mainstream parties as in the past. It has relied on political strategies such as opportunistic coalitions, ticket distribution to non-Dalits and electoral competition, rather than on reserved seats to enter the legislature or widen its support base. The leaders of the BSP believe that the Indian State and particularly the Congress, which was able to gain the support of the SCs for a long period of time, has failed to look after their interests. Yet, the Dalit movement in UP, under the leadership of the BSP, is a combination of State policies of protective discrimination 'from above' and changes taking place in society and in the economy. The State remains important for the Dalit movement, hence the stress on the BSP grabbing power by any means. Consequently, the rise of an exclusive SC party has introduced changes in the pattern of voting in reserved constituencies in the 1990s, but some long-term trends remain. The BJP and the SP, both avowedly upper and backward caste parties, have been able to win a large number of the reserved seats during the 1990s, precisely during the period when the seat and vote share of the BSP was rising. At the same time, the BSP has not been able to gain the support of all sections of the SC community. Dalit identity, despite mobilization by the BSP for over a decade, remains fragmented, reflecting caste and class divisions within the community. Hence, our study points to both continuity and change in the voting patterns of reserved seats.

Does this mean that the policy of granting reserved seats has been a failure? Was it merely a symbolic gesture, which legitimized the newly formed Indian State, enabling the national leadership to co-opt and gain the support of the SCs. Further, is there a strong and homogenous Dalit identity, and can such identities be adequately and effectively represented through reservations? While it is difficult in the absence of studies to assess the impact of electoral reservations, there is enough evidence to suggest that the SCs could not have penetrated the central and state legislatures in the absence of reservations. This would have otherwise led to their being further marginalized in politics, until the fairly recent advent of Dalit parties. In the first few decades only a small number of SCs were elected on general seats. Moreover, some scholars have argued that SC legislators in reserved seats have been active on issues concerning their community within the legislatures. This suggests that reserved seats have played a definite role in bringing SCs into the mainstream of political life.

However, at the same time, our study questions the effectiveness of granting reservations in formal decision-making institutions without supportive socio-economic changes within the larger society. There are limits to the role of the legislature in introducing social change as they reflect the existing power structure within society. Studies of both the background and the legislative behaviour of members of Parliament and the state legislatures have demonstrated this. On the other hand, the post-Independence experience shows that reservations in education and employment have helped SCs stand on their own feet and generated new leadership within the community. SCs were unable to make use of the reserved seats, leading to co-option, until the change in their socio-economic position provided them with the means to challenge the existing order through the formation of an exclusive Dalit party. The success of the BSP also shows that leadership and mobilization are key factors in the forging of identities and political action based upon them.

NOTES

* I would like to thank Sutapa Lahiri, a doctoral student at the Centre for Political Studies for help in collecting data and compiling the tables.

1. See Galanter's review of studies from the 1960s and 1970s: 51, footnote 47.
2. The term 'depressed classes' was used by the colonial authorities to refer to the untouchables in preference to more demeaning terms used earlier.
3. Literally 'the Association for the upliftment of the socially marginalized and excluded'.
4. Saksena's analysis of the debates of the Constituent Assembly shows that not much time was spent discussing the issue of affirmative action. The number of persons who spoke was very small. Out of a total of 324, only 103 members, i.e. 30 per cent actually participated in the debates and even out of these 103, 66 persons spoke only once or twice. (Saksena, 1981: xviii)
5. The Delimitation Commission, under the Delimitation Act (1972), consists of a retired judge of the Supreme Court, a sitting High Court judge and

the Election Commissioner. In each state the Commission is assisted by 10 non-voting associate members (5 MPs and 5 MLAs) nominated by their Speakers, who are consulted after every delimitation. After changes are made they are published and objections invited and hearings held. The location of reserved seats is the most frequent source of objections, but they are rarely shifted (Galanter, 1984: 46).

6. Ideally, empirical studies of reserved constituencies are needed to understand the impact of reserved seats on SC politics.
7. As the voting pattern for parliamentary seats is similar to that for Assembly seats, the results of the former for the period 1950–89 have not been given in the tables. The electoral results of reserved seats in the 1990 parliamentary elections have been included because this was a period of contestation between three parties. Moreover, by the end of the decade a shift is seen in the voting pattern for the parliamentary seats, which is reflected in the reserved seats in the 2002 assembly elections as well.
8. This is not given in the tables but is evident from an analysis of the reports of the Election Commission for the relevant elections.
9. The rise in 1993 is due to the alliance between the SP and the BSP that gave both a greater number of seats in the assembly.

REFERENCES

Abbayasulu, Y.B., *Scheduled Caste Elite: A Study of Scheduled Caste Elite in Andhra Pradesh.* Hyderabad: Osmania University Press, 1983.

Bandyopadhyay, Sekhar, 'Transfer of Power and the Crisis of Dalit Politics in India, 1945-47', *Modern Asian Studies*, 34, 4: 893–942, 2000.

Brass, Paul, *Caste Faction and Party in Indian Politics*, vol. 2, *Election Studies*, Delhi: Chanakya, 1985.

Duncan, R. Ian, 'Levels, the Communication of Programmes and Sectional Strategies in Indian Politics, with Reference to the BKD and the RPI in UP State and Aligarh District', unpublished Ph.D. thesis, University of Sussex, 1979.

Galanter, Marc, *Competing Equalities: Law and Backward Classes in India.* Delhi: OUP, 1984.

Gupta, S.K., *The Scheduled Castes in Modern Indian Politics: Their Emergence as a Modern Power*, Delhi, 1985.

Joshi, Barbara, *Democracy in Search of Equality: Untouchable Politics and Social Change*, Delhi: Hindustan Publishing Corporation, 1982.

Jurgensmeyer, Mark, *Religious Rebels in the Punjab: The Social Vision of Untouchables*, Delhi: Ajanta, 1988.

Kochanek, Stanley, *The Congress Party of India: The Dynamics of One-party Democracy*, Princeton: Princeton University Press, 1968.

Lynch, Owen, *Politics of Untouchability, Social Mobility and Change in a City of India*, New York: Columbia University Press, 1969.

Mendelsohn, Oliver, 'A Harijan Elite? The Lives of Some Untouchable Politicians', *Economic and Political Weekly*, 22 March 1986, pp. 501–9.

Mitra, Subrata K., *Democracy and Social Change in India: A Cross-Sectional Analysis of the National Electorate*, Delhi: Sage, 1999.

Mohapatra, M.K., 'The SCs and the Tribal Political Elites: An Empirical Exploration of the Attributes, Ascent and Role Perceptions of "Token Elites" in an Indian state', *International Behavioural Scientist*, 5(4): 1–23, 1973.

Moon, Vasant, *Dr. Babasaheb Ambedkar: Writings and Speeches*, vol. 10. Mumbai: Govt. of Maharashtra, Education Department, 1991.

Narayan, Ram, 'The Making of the Scheduled Caste Community in Uttar Pradesh: A Study of the SCF and Dalit Politics 1946–48', M. Phil. thesis, Department of History, University of Delhi, 1996.

Narayana, G., 'Social Background of Lok Sabha Members 1962-71', *Economic and Political Weekly*, 16 September 1978, p. 1603.

Pai, Sudha and Jagpal Singh, 'Politicisation of Dalits and Most Backward Castes: Study of Social Conflict and Political Preferences in Four Villages of Meerut District', *Economic and Political Weekly*, XXXII, no. 23, 7 June 1997, pp. 1358–61.

Pai, Sudha, 'Changing Socio-Economic and Political Profile of Scheduled Castes in Uttar Pradesh', *Journal of Indian School of Political Economy*, XII, nos 3 & 4, special issue on *The Scheduled Castes: An Inter-Regional Perspective*, 2000, pp. 405–22.

———, 'From Harijans to Dalits: Identity Formation, Political Consciousness and Electoral Mobilisation of the Scheduled Castes in Uttar Pradesh', in Ghanshyam Shah (ed.) *Dalit Identity and Politics*, Delhi: Sage, 2001, pp. 258–87.

———, *Dalit Assertion and the Unfinished Democratic Revolution: The BSP in Uttar Pradesh*, vol. 3 in the Sage series: *Cultural Subordination and the Dalit Challenge*, Delhi: Sage, 2002.

Ram, Kanshi, *The Chamcha Age: An Era of Stooges*, privately printed, New Delhi, 1982.

Reeves, Peter, 'Changing Pattern of Political Alignments in the GEs to the UP Legislative Assembly, 1937 and 1946', *Modern Asian Studies*, vol. 5, no. 2, 1971, pp. 111–42.

Saberwal, Satish, 'The Reserved Constituencies: Candidates and Consequences', *Economic and Political Weekly*, 1972, pp. 7, 71–80.

Sachchidananda, *The Harijan Elite*, Thomson, 1972.

Saksena, H.S., *Safeguards for Scheduled Castes and Scheduled Tribes: Founding Fathers Views*, Delhi: Uppal, 1981.

Shah, Ghanshyam, 'Congress and the Deprived Communities', in Ram Joshi and R.K. Hebsur (eds), *Congress in Indian Politics: A Centenary Perspective*, Mumbai: Popular, 1987.

———, 'Untouchability Revisited', in Ghanshyam Shah (ed.), *Dalits and the State*, Delhi: Sage, 1997.

Singh, V.B. and Shankar Bose, *State Elections in India: Data Handbook on Vidhan Sabha Elections 1952–85*, vol. 4, 'The North' (part 2: Bihar and UP), Delhi: Sage, 1988.

REPORTS

Election Commission of India:

1. *Statistical Report on the General Elections to the Legislative Assemblies 1989–90*, vol. II, New Delhi.
2. *Statistical Report on the General Elections to the Legislative Assemblies held in 1993*, New Delhi.
3. *Statistical Report on General Elections 1996 to the Legislative Assembly of UP*, New Delhi.
4. *Statistical Reports on the Ninth (1989), Tenth (1991), Eleventh (1996) and Twelfth (1998) Lok Sabha Elections*, New Delhi.
5. *UP Vidhan Sabha Who's Who, 1962, 1967.*

CHAPTER 2

Safeguards or Segregation? Reservations for the Scheduled Castes in Bihar

PRAKASH LOUIS

Over the last five decades, India's political establishment has espoused affirmative action in favour of the country's marginalized and vulnerable communities. These groups are usually referred to as 'educationally and socially backward classes'. The ruling castes/ classes enacted various policies, plans and schemes that were supposed to provide this segment of the population with opportunities to overcome the disadvantages they had perforce been subjected to for centuries. The basic argument was that these communities were socially, economically and politically dispossessed within the Indian social order. Further, since they were the objects of discrimination, they were incapable of faring well in open competition. Affirmative action or positive discrimination in favour of the backward social groups was a means to ensure their mobility. This mobility would in turn contribute to nation building.

This effort by the dominant castes and ruling classes was generally termed 'reservation'. Over the years various expressions were used to describe the process of extending special provisions to the disadvantaged segments of the population. These terms, like 'affirmative action', 'positive discrimination programme', 'protective discrimination', and 'compensatory discrimination' affirm the central fact that special provisions are in place to enable those at the bottom rung of society to rise above their situation.

Reservation is also seen as an effort to right a historical wrong. It is argued that the lower castes not only suffered social and economic discrimination but were also subjected to psycho-social exclusion and segregation. Reservation is a move to include the excluded. In a sense it is a restoration of the rightful place and role of weaker sections in the Indian polity and society.

While these ideals are publicly pronounced at regular intervals, the ground reality remains unchanged as far as the lives and opportunities of the victims of prejudice are concerned. A careful examination of the social conditions of the poor and the downtrodden in general, and of the Scheduled Castes and Scheduled Tribes in particular, reveals that their life situation has been worsening in Bihar despite reservation and other welfare measures that are supposed to lead to their upliftment.

RESERVATION: THE CONCEPTUAL FRAMEWORK

The concept of reservation did not emerge out of the blue. The framers of the Constitution realized that if Indian independence was to succeed, enhancing the social and economic power of the marginalized communities was imperative. Article 46 of the Constitution of India states that 'The State shall promote with special care the educational and economic interests of the weaker sections of the people and, in particular, of the Scheduled Castes and the Scheduled Tribes, and shall protect them from social injustice and all forms of exploitation'. While the Constitution upholds the right of all to equal treatment before law, it allows protective discrimination towards the Scheduled Castes and Scheduled Tribes.

The provision of reservations for the weaker sections has not escaped controversy. There are some who consider reservations as a compensation for historical and institutional disadvantages. They see policies and programmes geared towards reserved preference as distributive strategies. Against this view are others who argue that reservation would only perpetuate the caste system. They also reason that reservation diminishes the importance of merit.[1]

With the announcement in August 1990 by the National Front Government, of its decision to implement the Mandal Commission Recommendations[2] to accord 27 per cent reservations to the Other Backward Castes, the issue took centrestage once again. This move not only raked up bitter controversy among different sections of the population but also caused a grave law and order problem. Interestingly, the anti-Mandal agitations were more pronounced in northern India, especially Gujarat, Bihar and Uttar Pradesh, than in the southern parts of the country. While the upper castes formed a broader alliance to counter the National Front Government's move, the Other Backward Castes also aligned themselves to meet the challenge[3]. While part of the recommendation is being enacted and part is pending the decision of the Supreme Court of India, the process itself has changed the political sociology of India.

Reservation *per se* was envisaged to build an egalitarian society that would replace the stratified caste-based social order. The constitutional provisions conceived for the well-being of the Scheduled Castes and Scheduled Tribes[4] can be grouped under three heads: developmental measures; protective measures; and positive discrimination measures.

DEVELOPMENTAL MEASURES

The developmental measures with regard to the weaker sections can be further clubbed under educational benefits, financial intervention, and liberating activities. To begin with, the most important scheme introduced by the Government of India was the Centrally Sponsored Post-Matric Scholarship to Students Belonging to Scheduled Castes. This was introduced in 1944-5 to help students from the Scheduled Castes (and extended to the Scheduled Tribes in 1948-9). In the beginning this scheme covered 114 students, but at present over 20 lakh students are benefitting from it. In the same vein, the National Overseas Scholarship for Scheduled Caste Students for Higher Studies was established as early as 1954-5. This scholarship was planned exclusively to provide financial assistance to students who wished to pursue advanced studies abroad in highly technical fields.

In 1977-8, the Centrally Sponsored Pre-Matric Scholarship to Students Belonging to Scheduled Castes scheme was also introduced. The basic objective of this scheme was to provide financial assistance to children of scavengers, sweepers, tanners, and so on to pursue pre-matric education. The scholarship is provided for 10 months in a year. In addition to this each student also receives a sum of Rs 50 per annum. About 2.05 lakh students were expected to benefit from this scheme annually. In June 1996, a new Central scheme to establish free residential schools for Scheduled Caste girls below the poverty line was launched through the Zilla Parishad (District Assemblies) in 48 districts[5] where the female literacy rate among Scheduled Castes was less than 2 per cent. This was a way of removing them from social surroundings that were not conducive to formal education.

From 1979–80 onwards, the Special Component Plan (SCP) was adopted. Its objective was to provide direct financial assistance for the development and welfare of the Scheduled Castes. The SCP was designed to canalize the flow of outlays and benefits from general sectors in state and Central ministry plans to Scheduled Caste development schemes. State governments look after the welfare and development of the Scheduled Castes through their respective special component plans, with the support of Special Central Assistance provided by the Central Government. Moreover, the Scheduled Castes Development Corporations (SCDCs) were established in March 1979. The SCDCs were expected to interface between poor Scheduled Caste entrepreneurs and the financial institutions with regard to bankable schemes for economic development. To avoid undue delay, it was decided that from 1994 onwards, the Central share would be released to the SCDCs directly instead of through the state governments.

The National Scheduled Castes and Scheduled Tribes Finance and Development Corporation (NSFDC) was established in February 1989 to promote self-employment and develop entrepreneurial and skilled abilities among the Scheduled Castes. According to the Report of the Ministry of Social Justice and Empowerment, financial assistance is provided for the following: agriculture and allied activities; horticulture, animal husbandry and dairying; minor irrigation; small industries and trade services and transport. It also states that disbursements have risen substantially, from Rs 35 lakh in 1989–90, to Rs 409.15 crore as of March 1998.[6] The National Safai Karmacharis Finance and Development Corporation (NSKFDC) was made operative in January 1997 to promote economic development/self-employment for the economic rehabilitation of *Safai Karmacharis*, besides providing training in technical and entrepreneurial skills and extending loans to students from the *Safai Karmachari* community for pursuing higher education.[7]

The National Scheme of Liberation and Rehabilitation of Scavengers and Their Dependants, which was launched in March 1992, has been extended up to the end of the Eleventh Plan period. This scheme was launched in pursuance of government's commitment to eradicate the inhuman practice of manual handling of night soil and refuse by the end of Eighth Plan period. This scheme has three components: (a) a rapid survey to identify scavengers and their dependents and their aptitude for alternative trades and professions; (b) training of scavengers and their dependents; (c) rehabilitation of scavengers through projects with a prescribed funding pattern.

In addition to the programmes already mentioned, the Ministry of Social Justice and Empowerment is entrusted with the task of economic welfare, social justice and empowerment of disadvantaged and marginalized sections of society, viz., Scheduled Castes and Scheduled Tribes. The Scheduled Castes Development Bureau has been created within the ministry to deal with all matters related to their development.[8]

Even a cursory glance reveals that the theory underlying these schemes in particular and reservation in general, was compensatory discrimination in favour of the weaker sections. The political motivation behind these provisions was to open the path to social mobility, which had been so far closed to members of the weaker sections by the historical and social denial of access to education. These schemes were aimed at providing Scheduled Castes and Scheduled Tribes the opportunity for education, which is the key to social mobility.

These schemes and provisions addressed the specific needs of different categories within the weaker sections. For example, the National Scheme of Liberation and Rehabilitation of Scavengers and Their Dependants has specific and definite provisions such as (1) the prohibition of employment of manual scavengers and construction of dry latrines; (2) the regulation of construction and maintenance of water-seal latrines; (3) schemes for the rehabilitation of manual scavengers.

An objective examination of the success rate of these schemes reveals that the bias against the weaker sections has rendered their implementation nugatory. Since education proved a powerful tool for upward mobility, the implementing agents of these schemes, who were from the dominant castes, put off their implementation. Since the caste system itself was anti-weaker section, these schemes could make only a nominal change in their condition. The Scheduled Castes and Scheduled Tribes Commission, while making an examination of the overall impact of these schemes highlights the fact that, 'Though the SCs and the STs have benefited from 50 years of planning and development, it has been far less than what was intended or expected. The inequality between the SCs and the STs and others has been persisting. Problems have further accentuated as inequality intra SCs and STs has also been growing. Here there is an outcry among the SCs and STs against the others as also different SC and ST communities for not having their fair share in governance and administration of the country.'[9]

Legal measures

One can identify at least three key legal measures for the protection of the rights of the Scheduled Castes and Scheduled Tribes. The Protection of Civil Rights Act, 1955 [formerly known as Untouchability (Offences) Act, 1955] was enacted in line with Article 17 of the Constitution. By this Act 'untouchability' was abolished and its practice in any form was forbidden under the threat of punishment.[10] This act clearly and categorically states that denial of entry to members of Scheduled Castes into public utilities and places of assembly is an offence and calls for punishment.

Going beyond the provisions of the Protection of Civil Rights Act, the political establishment of this country enacted the Scheduled Castes and Scheduled Tribes (Prevention of Atrocities) Act, 1989 from January 1990. Interestingly, the statement of objectives spells out the reasons behind the introduction of this Act: 'Despite various measures to improve the socio-economic conditions of the Scheduled Castes and Scheduled Tribes, they remain vulnerable. They are denied a number of civil rights. They are subjected to various offences, indignities, humiliation and harassment. They have, in several brutal incidents, been deprived of their life, and property. Serious crimes are committed against them for various historical, social and economic reasons'.[11]

In pursuance of the Constitution's 65th Amendment Act, 1990, the National Commission for Scheduled Castes and Scheduled Tribes was established in March 1992 with wide-ranging powers and functions. Some of the functions of the Commission are: (a) to investigate and monitor all matters relating to the safeguards provided for Scheduled Castes and Scheduled Tribes under the Constitution or under any order of the Government and to evaluate the working of such safeguards; (b) to enquire into specific complaints with respect to the deprivation of rights and safeguards of the Scheduled Castes and Scheduled Tribes, etc.[12]

The legal measures presented above are once again in line with safeguarding the interests of the weaker sections. Moreover, with the human rights approach becoming a dominant discourse within civil society, the National Commission for Scheduled Castes and Scheduled Tribes was constituted to address specific rights of the weaker sections and also to protect their rights from being violated. The National Crimes Record Bureau in its annual reports establishes the fact that even today discriminatory behaviours are aggressively pursued by the dominant castes. This is a nightmare for the powerless among the weaker sections.

Positive discrimination measures

The positive discrimination measures, usually known as the provisions of reservation, are seen as the mainstay of Indian democracy. There are three types of provisions: (a) reservation in educational institutions; (b) reservation of services and posts in the government services; (c) reservation of seats in the legislatures. These three areas where reservation has been provided are interconnected. Reservation of services and posts can be utilized only if the Scheduled Castes and Tribes who were denied access to education can be provided the opportunity to educate themselves and become socially mobile. Only when these communities are represented in the legislatures will a serious demand for reservation be forthcoming. Thus, the positive discrimination provisions are aimed at bridging the gap between the Scheduled Caste/Tribe population and the non-Scheduled Caste/Tribe population.

The intent to provide representation to the Scheduled Castes and Scheduled Tribes in educational, professional and political institutions was clearly spelt out by Dr B.R. Ambedkar who is usually credited with being the architect of the Indian Constitution. He is also remembered as a person who overcame his Scheduled Caste origins to achieve greatness. But not many remember his efforts to build a better social order. The social order he envisaged was based on the principles of equality, liberty and fraternity. But within this social order, he called for safeguards to the dignity and freedom of the individual. His contribution to the emancipation and liberation of India's weaker sections is immeasurable. 'There shall be no disabilities attached to anyone on the ground of his being a member of the Depressed Classes in regard to any elections to local bodies or appointment to Public Services. Every endeavour shall be made to secure fair representation of the Depressed Classes in these respects subject to such educational qualifications as may be laid down for appointment to the Public Services'.[13]

Dr Ambedkar's one-point agenda was to ensure the inalienable rights of the individual, which are guaranteed through political democracy. His concept of political democracy rests on four premises: (1) the individual is an end in himself; (2) the individual has certain inalienable rights which must be guaranteed by the Constitution; (3) the individual shall not be required to relinquish any of his constitutional rights as the price for any privilege; (4) the state shall not delegate power to private persons to govern others.[14] The political leaders involved in the freedom struggle and in nation building stressed the need for cooperative development, sacrificing the interests of the individual for the welfare of all. But Dr Ambedkar, keeping in mind the deplorable conditions of the weaker sections, demanded safeguards for the inalienable rights of individuals from these groups. He was also a proponent of the casteless and classless society. But from the perspective of the Scheduled Castes and the Scheduled Tribes, he wanted to ensure their rights and hence fought relentlessly for affirmative action.

The immediacy of reservation for the marginalized communities is clearly stated in the Constitution. According to Article 16(4), 'Nothing in this article shall prevent the State from making any provision for the reservation of appointments or posts in favour of any backward class of citizens which in the opinion of the State, is not adequately represented in the services under the state.' Article 335 declares, 'The claims of the members of the Scheduled Castes and the Scheduled Tribes shall be taken into consideration, consistently with the maintenance of efficiency of administration in the making of appointments to services and posts in connection with the affairs of the Union or of a State.' These provisions have the objective of ensuring the right to equality before law, and right to equal protection of the law. Keeping this reality in mind, in September 1947, immediately after Independence, instructions were issued to implement reservation.[15]

Taken together, the three measures listed above were expected to herald a change in the lives and conditions of the weaker sections of Indian society. Even a cursory glance at the various schemes envisaged by the country's administration shows that there was no dearth of projects and programmes meant to alleviate the misery of the Scheduled Castes and Scheduled Tribes. But what 'affirmative action' or the 'positive discrimination programme', or reservation for the weaker sections achieved in reality fell far short of these objectives. This is not only from the point of view of social mobility gained by the Scheduled Castes and the Scheduled Tribes, but the manner in which allocations were made also presents a sorry picture. For instance, the allocation for SCP in the Sixth Plan was 7.67 per cent and in the Seventh Plan was 8.31 per cent against the total State plan outlay. While this is normally the case, the Ministry of Social Justice and Empowerment has consistently insisted that allocation of funds should be in proportion to the Scheduled Caste population; the Ministry demanded that a separate budget head for SCP be opened, to prevent diversion, under-utilization, and misutilization of funds earmarked for the Scheduled Castes; and that the allocation of funds be in line with the specific needs and priorities of the Scheduled Castes.[16]

Education is considered both by the policy makers and the weaker sections as the key to social mobility. Hence, many policy perspectives have been introduced during the last five decades. The 1986 National Policy on Education (NPE) aimed at universal enrolment of all Dalit children in the 6–11 age group and 75 per cent enrolment in the 11–14 age group as well as their successful completion of primary and middle school stages by 1990. The targets were reiterated in the revised programme of action in 1992. The educational scene in the 1990s was dominated by the District Primary Education Programme (DPEP), which placed special emphasis on improved access, participation, and achievement of children from marginalized groups. In addition, the 'Sarva Shiksha Abhiyan' (Universalization of Education Campaign) announced in 2000 emphasizes the involvement of Dalit communities in the ownership of school committees, setting up of alternative schooling facilities in unoccupied habitations, using community teachers, monitoring attendance and retention of Dalit children.

Strategies laid down to universalize primary/elementary education among Dalits are concerned with:

- Expanding school provisioning at primary and middle stages. In predominantly Dalit habitations, distance norms are relaxed so as to facilitate easy access to elementary education. Hostel facilities are also recommended to facilitate learning.
- Subsidized costs and providing incentives; abolishing tuition fees and providing incentives such as free books, uniforms, school bags and midday meals; scholarship to children from Scheduled Castes, financial assistance for children of indigent groups and attendance scholarships for girls.
- Recruitment of teachers from within these communities by relaxing qualifications, if necessary.
- Providing non-formal and alternative/innovative programmes for children who are seen as unable to access formal schooling.[17]

If one examines the resources set aside for the development of this marginalized group against this policy perspective, it becomes clear that the implementation of policy was at best confined to public pronouncements. According to the National Commission for Scheduled Castes and Scheduled Tribes, 'The most important cause for non-development of SC/STs is non-allocation of resources for their development on a priority'.[18] The Commission goes on to argue that resources equivalent to the population percentage of SC/STs should be set apart and transferred to a national level development authority, which would focus attention on the development of SC/STs.

Irrespective of innumerable provisions made to improve the educational status of the Scheduled Caste community, there has been no tangible change in literacy or educational levels. Even if we analyse one indicator, that is, the school attendance of Dalit[19] children in schools, it becomes clear that the Scheduled Castes have remained 'untouched' even after four decades of the enrolment drive. Leaving out the regional variations, if one examines the increase in enrolment from 1987–88 to 1993–94 (Table 2.1) it becomes absolutely clear

TABLE 2.1: SCHOOL ATTENDANCE RATES (%) AMONG CHILDREN BETWEEN 5-14 YEARS[20]

States/Union Territories	% of SC population to total population, 1991	1987–8				1993–4			
		SCs		Others		SCs		Others	
		M	F	M	F	M	F	M	F
Andhra Pradesh	15.93	55.1	32.1	63.9	42.3	64.3	44.5	71.7	56.0
Assam	7.40	69.9	70.5	63.2	58.7	75.4	70.8	75.9	71.7
Bihar	14.55	24.1	9.3	46.9	27.3	46.0	22.5	63.5	44.1
Gujarat	7.41	70.3	48.6	68.1	53.9	77.5	65.3	78.6	62.6
Haryana	19.75	63.1	49.0	76.9	54.9	76.6	56.6	85.0	71.7
HP	25.34	76.5	59.6	83.9	69.3	87.6	82.1	91.8	83.9
J&K	8.31	70.2	53.4	63.3	40.9	87.5	63.9	85.0	75.7
Karnataka	16.38	47.5	29.4	62.5	50.8	65.7	50.5	76.2	67.6
Kerala	9.92	86.1	81.9	89.7	87.5	96.0	88.5	92.9	94.0
Madhya Pradesh	14.55	48.2	25.7	63.0	34.0	57.6	37.0	70.4	52.5
Maharashtra	11.09	66.0	43.1	77.1	62.5	83.8	72.8	86.4	76.7
Orissa	16.20	46.7	30.9	66.1	51.5	67.9	43.9	76.5	68.0
Punjab	28.31	50.5	41.3	76.3	69.3	68.6	59.2	88.4	83.6
Rajasthan	19.29	49.8	12.3	65.5	27.9	58.1	21.5	76.8	41.1
Sikkim	5.93	60.3	57.3	77.1	74.2	100.0	64.7	89.6	88.4
Tamil Nadu	19.18	72.4	58.1	79.6	63.7	76.9	71.2	85.6	76.6
Tripura	16.36	65.7	63.0	70.6	68.8	87.9	83.2	86.7	86.6
Uttar Pradesh	21.05	43.6	15.1	57.0	33.6	59.7	31.5	69.9	49.4
West Bengal	23.62	47.3	39.0	56.6	52.4	67.9	56.9	71.1	65.9
Chandigarh	16.51	*	*	75.5	98.0	94.8	66.0	99.8	91.4
Delhi	19.05	*	*	88.7	90.1	*	*	89.4	96.2
Pondicherry	16.25	64.7	71.3	89.3	74.3	95.7	100.0	80.5	100.0
All-India **	16.37	49.8	33.1	63.4	45.8	64.3	46.2	74.9	61.0

NOTES: * Results not presented, as the number of sample households was less than 20.

** All-India figure includes states that have not been listed as their SC population is very small.

SOURCES: *Census of India 1991*; National Sample Survey Organisation (1990), 'Employment and Unemployment Situation of Scheduled Caste and Scheduled Tribe Population During the Late Eighties'. NSSO 43rd Round, July 1987–June 1988. NSSO, Department of Statistics, Government of India, New Delhi; National Sample Survey Organisation (1997), 'Economic Activities and School Attendance by Children of India. NSS 50th Round, Report No. 412, Fifth Quinquennial Survey, Department of Statistics, Government of India', New Delhi.

that the growth is not substantial. In comparison to male enrolment, female enrolment among the Dalits is pitiably low. This is all the more disheartening, as most of the educational schemes were directed towards the weaker section with special emphasis on the educational mobility of the girl child. When we compare the female enrolment of Dalits with the female enrolment of the general population in states like Bihar, we find that the situation is deplorable.

On the whole, reservation for the weaker sections was designed to protect them from historically determined forms of oppression, exploitation and segregation. The socio-political objective behind the reservation policy is to bring the downtrodden at par with members of other communities. Reservation as a national affirmative action policy became a contentious issue, subject to a variety of interpretations. But while the policy itself remained controversial, its implementation led to an enormous crisis. The powerful support received by anti-reservation agitators over five decades indicates that protective discrimination has become an electoral weapon in the hands of India's ruling elite. They exploit it for electoral gains while using the force of their power to resist the equality that they aim to ensure through reservation.

SCHEDULED CASTES OF BIHAR

Scheduled Castes constitute about 14.56 per cent of Bihar's population (Table 2.2), which is lower than the national average of 16.37 per cent. In terms of spatial distribution, about 91 per cent of Bihar's Scheduled Castes live in villages. The majority is dependent upon agriculture for its livelihood. It is clear from the table that only about 15.63 per cent are cultivators, while over 72.25 per cent are landless agricultural labourers. Since Dalit families are entirely dependent upon agriculture and allied activities, it becomes impossible for them to provide educational opportunities for their children. Thus, the literacy rate of the Dalit population in Bihar is only 19.49 per cent, while the female literacy rate is just 7.07 per cent.[21] The anomaly becomes all the more glaring if we consider that in the year 1992–3 over Rs 1,200 crore were spent under the now famous 'Bihar Education Project' (BEP).

The reservation system includes provisions for obtaining services

TABLE 2.2: A PROFILE OF SCHEDULED CASTES OF BIHAR

Area		
Total population—General	Total	8,28,78,796
	Males	4,31,53,964
	Females	3,97,24,832
Literacy—General [% of the total state's population]	Persons	47.53
	Males	60.32
	Females	33.57
Scheduled Caste population [% of the total state's population]		14.56
Literacy—Scheduled Castes [%]*	Persons	19.49
	Males	30.64
	Females	7.07
Scheduled Caste cultivators [% of the SC population]		15.63
Scheduled Caste agricultural labourers [% of the SC population]		72.25
Scheduled Caste household industries [% of the SC population]		1.77
Scheduled Caste other works [% of the SC population]		4.56
District with lowest female literacy rate [%]	Kishanganj	3.40
Male enrolment [1993–4]	-	46.0
Female enrolment [1993–4]	-	22.5
Scheduled Caste total drop out class I–VIII	-	84.47
Scheduled Caste girls drop out class I–VIII	-	89.05
Scheduled Caste teachers [1993]	-	9.49

SOURCES: Provisional Population Totals; Paper 1 of 2001. Bihar; * *1991 Census Report, Elementary Education in the State of Bihar: A Statistical Report,* 1993.

and posts in the public sector. But the stark reality is that one has to be educated to avail of the benefits of education.[22] Table 2.2 clearly indicates that over 84 per cent of the Dalit students drop out by the VIII standard. The situation appears more dismal when we note that over 99 per cent of Dalit girls drop out by the XII standard. It is a proven fact that due to economic deprivation, social segregation, cultural discrimination and political subjugation, the Dalits are excluded from every sector of human growth and development. And in this regard it is pertinent to state that these girls are not 'drop outs' but are 'pushed out' by the system.

Over five decades of educational provisions, geared in many ways exclusively towards the uplift of the Scheduled Castes, present another harsh reality. Even at the primary level only about 15 per cent of Scheduled Caste children are getting education (Table 2.3). But as one proceeds to the higher levels there is a further decline in numbers which proves that dropping out is a permanent reality as far as the Scheduled Castes are concerned. At the M.Com. level the presence of Scheduled Caste students is almost nil. But once again it is the marginal presence of girls from the Scheduled Caste community in the educational institutions in Bihar, which proves every plan and policy redundant insofar as the Scheduled Caste community is concerned. The deplorable socio-economic and political state to which the Dalit community is reduced to does not even enable them to make

TABLE 2.3: BIHAR SC STUDENTS AT VARIOUS STAGES OF EDUCATION DURING 1995–6

Stage of Education	Boys	Girls	Total
Pre-primary	700 (6.83)	540 (5.60)	1,240 (6.24)
Primary (I–V)	9,34,509 (15.90)	4,31,483 (9.25)	13,65,992 (15.02)
Middle (VI–VIII)	1,94,108 (11.65)	65,584 (9.25)	2,59,692 (19.94)
High school(IX–X)	72,016 (9.90)	16,840 (6.90)	88,856 (9.14)
Intermediate	5,959 (11.81)	2,124 (11.17)	8,083 (11.63)
B.A.	10,899 (7.81)	1,104 (2.78)	12,003 (6.69)
B.Sc.	2,605 (4.72)	286 (3.64)	2,891 (4.59)
B.Com.	1,391 (0.70)	64 (0.14)	1,455 (0.60)
B.E. (Eng.)	275 (4.62)	12 (3.63)	287 (4.57)
M.B.B.S., Ayurveda	1,085 (8.63)	205 (13.02)	1,290 (9.14)
B.Ed., B.T	142 (10.26)	47 (5.21)	189 (8.40)
M.A.	548 (6.90)	93 (3.32)	641 (5.97)
M.Sc.	63 (2.78)	21 (3.67)	84 (2.96)
M.Com.	41 (0.37)	15 (0.44)	56 (0.39)
Ph.D.	34 (5.64)	25 (16.55)	59 (7.83)
TTC	114 (6.73)	49 (5.96)	163 (6.48)
Polytechnic	554 (14.07)	12 (8.63)	566 (13.88)
ITI/Arts & Crafts	1,539 (15.03)	82 (8.96)	1,621 (14.53)

NOTES: Figures in brackets indicate percentage of SC students to corresponding total enrolment.

SOURCE: Table compiled by PSC on data supplied by Ministry of HRD (Department of Education), Government of India.

use of some of the provisions which could induce a change in their circumstances.

One can identify a few valid reasons behind the appalling and deteriorating condition of the Dalits. Jose Vadasery argues that 'Problems like dropout, stagnation and failure in competitive examinations lead to further inferiorization of the Dalits. The dominant castes, especially in the rural areas, are generally contemptuous of the education of the Dalit children. They have their own vested interest in keeping the Dalit illiterate. The same attitude is reflected among the teachers especially of the dominant castes who are entrusted with the job of teaching the Dalit children'.[23] In the present context, even if a Dalit student has the necessary qualification and is also meritorious, unless his family is capable of greasing the palms of recruiting officials, his chances of securing a job are very bleak. Thus, the denial of the right to benefit from the provisions available for this community almost closes the door to any further exploration.

It is significant to note that like other Scheduled Castes throughout India, the Scheduled Castes of Bihar are not a homogeneous social category. This heterogeneous nature of the Scheduled Castes should be borne in mind during any discussion on reservation. There are about 17 sub-castes among the Scheduled Castes of Bihar (Table 2.4). Among the 17 sub-castes, 5 sub-castes, i.e. the Ravidas, Dusadhs, Musahars, Bhuiyans and Dhobis constitute more than 88 per cent of the total Scheduled Caste population. Thus these sub-castes are numerically powerful. They have also appropriated most of the benefits of reservation. For example, the Ravidas and Dusadhs constitute 29.37 and 26.19 per cent respectively of the population. These two sub-groups have utilized their numerical strength to control the reserved constituencies.

Hajipur is a Scheduled Caste reserved Lok Sabha constituency in Bihar. The dominant social groups are Scheduled Castes (22 per cent); Yadavs (13 per cent) and Muslims (9 per cent). Among the Scheduled Castes, the Dusadhs constitute 12 per cent and Ravidas about 7 per cent. As shown in Table 2.5, the main contest in the last eight general elections has been between the Dusadhs and Ravidas. This demonstrates the fact that in this reserved constituency, it is these two sub-castes that matter. But even here, it is Ram Vilas Paswan who

TABLE 2.4: SCHEDULED CASTES OF BIHAR: POPULATION, TRADITIONAL OCCUPATION, DIVISION OF LABOUR, AREA OF HABITATION AND LITERACY

Caste (%)	Traditional Occupation and Distribution of Labour	Area of Habitation	Literacy %
Bantar 66,025 (0.65)	Bamboo basketry, thatching. (84.11% agricultural labourers, 12.6% cultivators, 1.34 % household industries).	Samastipur, Darbhanga, Saharsa, Purnea, Madhubani, Madhepura.	9.61
Bhuiya 8,50,469 (8.39)	Agricultural labour, bricklaying. (75.55% agricultural labourers, 14.21% cultivators, 5.06% household industries).	Gaya, Nawada, Aurangabad, Munger, Bhagalpur.	6.78
Chamar/ Ravidas 29,78,562 (29.37)	Leatherwork, skin and hide work, agricultural labourer. (77.11% agricultural labourers, 13.33% cultivators, 3.49% household industries, 6.7% other services).	Whole State	16.96
Chaupal 44,372 (0.44)	Weaving, cultivation and agricultural labour (74.4% agricultural labourers, 15% cultivators, 4.89% household industries).	Purnea and Katihar	14.77
Dhobi 5,53,380 (5.46)	Washing clothes (39.87% agricultural labourers, 28.16% cultivators, 22.96% household industries, 9.01% other services).	Whole state	25.56
Dom, Dhangad (also known as	Offering fire, cremating the dead, grave digging,	Doms primarily reside on the	13.62

(contd.)

TABLE 2.4 (contd.)

Oraon) 2,00,828 (1.98)	bamboo basketry (28.53% agricultural labourers, 10.12% cultivators, 37.37% household industries).	banks of river Ganges.	
Dusadh, Dhari, Dharhi 26,55,832 (26.19)	Village guards, cultivation, agricultural labour, palanquin bearers. (74.79% agricultural labourers, 15.21% cultivators, 10% other services)	Whole state.	17.77
Ghasi 84,760 (0.84)	Fishing, collection of forest produce, basketry, drum beating. (41.22% agricultural labourers, 20.23% cultivators, 7.42% household industries).	Near forest areas.	20.14
Halalkhor 5,463 (0.05)	Scavenging (Details not available)	Bihar Sharif and adjoining areas.	20.87
Hari, Mehtar, Bhangi 1,56,349 (1.54)	Scavenging, basketry, drum beating, bone collection. (40.12% agricultural labourers, 6.26% cultivators, 8.28% household industries, 45.34% other services).	Whole state.	21.02
Kanjar 1,781 (0.02)	Trapping and selling forest animals: mostly live monkeys, snake skin, rabbit skin, etc. (25.79% agricultural labourers, 2.16% cultivators, 45.59% household industries).	Semi-nomadic, mainly in Purnea, Saharsa and Madhubani districts.	8.42
Kurariar 4,449 (0.04)	Honey collection, herbs, hunting, trapping birds and small animals, etc. (64.99% agricultural labourers, 15.08% cultivators, 8.65% household industries, 10.38% other services).	Semi-nomadic, mostly in Darbhanga, Samastipur, Begusarai, Madhepura, Saharsa, Siwan, Muzaffarpur, and Vaishali.	15.07

(contd.)

TABLE 2.4 (contd.)

Lalbegi (Originally Balmikis but after becoming Kabirpanthis, they call themselves Lalbegi.) 933 (0.01)	Scavenging (30.64% agricultural labourers, 6.73% cultivators, 8.76% household industries, 53.07% other services)	Hazaribagh, Jharia, Dhanbad, Sindri, Giridih, Ranchi.	17.24
Musahar 1,391,000 (13.71)	Agricultural labourer, rat trapping. (95.34% agricultural labourers, 2.52% cultivators, 2.14% other occupations).	Bhagalpur, Champaran, Munger, Purnea, Gaya, Saran, Darbhanga, and in other districts.	3.58
Nat (Believed to be migrants from Rajasthan) 2,4,897 (0.25)	Acrobats, snake-catching, rope trick performers. (69.8% agricultural labourers, 8.79% cultivators, 7.65% household industries).	Gaya, Jehanabad, Aurangabad, Bhojpur, Rohtas.	10.44
Pasi 4,63,601 (4.57)	Toddy tapping (41.81% agricultural labourers, 17.72% cultivators, 15.87% household industries, 24.6% other services).	Patna, Gaya, Nalanda, Munger, Aurangabad, Bhagalpur, Muzaffarpur, Rohtas, Bhojpur, Darbhanga.	22.88
Rajwar 2,37,369 (2.34)	Cultivation. They are considered to be expert bricklayers. (71.78% agricultural labourers, 17.06% cultivators, 4.58% household industries)	Whole state	13.93

NOTE: Figures below the caste title indicate the population in absolute numbers of the caste. Figures in brackets indicate the percentage of the total Scheduled Caste population, Census 1981. Some of the districts mentioned here are now in Jharkhand, a state created in 2000.

SOURCES: K.S. Singh, *The Scheduled Castes*, 1999; P.C. Pathak, 'Scheduled Castes of Bihar', in B. Pathak (ed.), *Continuity and Change in Indian Society*, Concept, 1998; Census Report 1981; data on literacy rate is taken from the CD of the Registrar General's Office, New Delhi, for the year 1991.

TABLE 2.5: ELECTION RESULTS OF HAJIPUR, RESERVED LOK SABHA CONSTITUENCY

Year	Winner	Party	Caste	Runner-up	Party	Caste
1977	Ram Vilas Paswan	BLD	Dusadh	Baleshwar Ram	INC	Ravidas
1980	-do-	JPS	-do-	Medni Paswan	JP	Dusadh
1984	Ram Ratan Ram	INC	Ravidas	Ram Vilas Paswan	LKD	-do-
1989	Ram Vilas Paswan	JD	Dusadh	Mahabir Paswan	INC	Dusadh
1991	Ram Sundar Das	-do-	Ravidas	Dasai Chaudhary	JP	Pasi
1996	Ram Vilas Paswan	-do	Dusadh	Ram Sundar Das	SAP	Ravidas
1998	-do	-do-	-do-	-do-	SJP	-do-
1999	-do-	JD(U)	-do-	Ramai Ram	RJD	-do-

SOURCES: H.D. Singh, *543 Faces of India*, Delhi: Newsmen Publishers, 1996, pp. 54-77; David Butler et al., *India Decides: Elections 1952-1995*, Delhi: Books and Things, 1995, pp. 154-68; *Statistical Report on General Elections, 1996 to the Eleventh Lok Sabha*, vol. II, Delhi: Election Commission of India, 1996, pp. 59-112.

has dominated, regardless of party affiliation. Table 2.5 bears testimony to the fact that Mr Paswan has lost only once in eight elections. In the 1991 elections he moved to the Rosera constituency and won from there.

A brief analysis of Mr Paswan's electoral success reveals that electoral reservation can occasionally become a powerful weapon for social mobility. Ram Vilas Paswan began his political career as a cadre of the Socialist Party[24] and was soon elected as a Member of the Bihar Legislative Assembly from the Hajipur constituency in 1962. He also won the election in 1967 and as a member of the Socialist Party served in the Samyukt Vidhayak Dal government. From 1977 onwards he made impressive progress, winning the Parliamentary elections. Under the Janata Dal banner he won the Hajipur parliamentary constituency and was made Welfare Minister with cabinet rank under Prime Minister V.P. Singh. When the Janata Dal broke up into many splinter parties, he moved from one alliance to another, but continued to maintain his political ascendancy. As a member of the Janata Dal (U), which was a partner in the National Democratic Alliance (NDA), he was made first Railway Minister and subsequently Minister of Communications. Though Mr Paswan is now out of the NDA, he still continues to be a political force in Scheduled Caste politics at the national level, under the banner of the Lok Jan Shakti Party. Two related social facts must be stated here. Mr Paswan is one of those who has made use of the provisions of reservation and attained the highest social mobility, not only in electoral politics but also economically and socially. The only other such success story has been that of Mr Jagjivan Ram, who also hailed from Bihar and remained in the Congress fold throughout his life. While reservation provided the necessary conditions for Mr Paswan's social mobility, he also continued to maintain his mass base through the youth organization named Dalit Sena, that is, the Scheduled Caste Army.[25]

This goes to establish that while reservation is a necessary condition for the uplift of the weaker sections, it is not a sufficient condition. While there are some sub-castes among the Dalits who have made a mark for themselves by making the most of reservation in electoral politics, there are others who have progressed well in the field of education. For instance, the literacy rate among the Dhobis is 25.56 per cent, the highest among the 17 Scheduled Caste sub-castes (Table 2.4). Since they are the most educated, it is not surprising that one can find members from this community gainfully employed. Thus, the Dhobis have made the best use of reservation in services and posts. But the plight of other sub-castes like the Musahars and the Bhuiyans is beyond description. Over 95.34 per cent of the Musahars are returned as landless agricultural labourers. Just 3.58 per cent among them are educated and only about 2.14 per cent are in service. Thus, affirmative action has not made any inroads into the lives of this community and hence sub-castes like them are doubly discriminated against. They face discrimination from the upper castes and classes—and ironically, they are also denied their legitimate place by other Scheduled Caste sub-castes.

At this juncture a brief note on the impact of the reservation policy on the Panchayati Raj system would throw more light on the participation of Scheduled Castes in local governance. By passing the Bihar Panchayati Raj Act in 1947, Bihar was the first state to introduce local self-government in India. But a review of the performance and progress of Panchayati Raj Institutions (PRI) reveals the abysmal failure of decentralization. One can clearly identify three issues which have affected the participation of the Scheduled Castes in these local governing bodies.

First, with the introduction of PRIs, the dominant castes, i.e. the landed gentry controlled the Panchayats through the office of the *mukhiya* (chairperson of the village council). Thus, political power was added to the socio-economic power of the dominant castes. Sumita Mishra states that the election trend shows that during the first election, competition for panchayat posts was minimal. During this election one-third of the panchayat *mukhiyas* declared elected were chosen unanimously. Most of them were from the upper castes (Rajput and Bhumihars).[26]

Second, after the first few elections, the Scheduled Castes began to assert themselves in the PRIs. But from 1978 to 2001 elections to the 11,740 gram panchayats (village councils) were not held. A time lag of more than two decades denied the Scheduled Castes their right of participation in local governance. With the promulgation of the 73rd Amendment of the Constitution in 1993, seats were reserved in the PRIs for the Scheduled Castes, Scheduled Tribes and women. Panchayati Raj elections were held in April 2001 and this provided opportunity for the Scheduled Castes to get elected as members of local governing units. Thus out of 1,11,023 village council members, 33,307 belong to the Scheduled Castes (30 per cent of seats are reserved for them in village councils). Out of these 33,307 Scheduled Castes members, 9,993 are women, since 30 per cent of seats reserved for the Scheduled Castes are sub-reserved for women. This shows that if there is a strong political will to enact legislations, the weaker sections would benefit from the reservation policy.

Third, though reservation was provided for the Scheduled Castes, no other mechanism was worked out to enhance their power to utilize these provisions. This is clearly seen in a document published by the Bihar government,[27] which says a great deal about the duties of the panchayats but very little about their powers. This would deter marginalized communities from participating in local self-government, even though they are provided with reservation. This goes to establish the central argument of this discussion that reservation alone would not have any lasting impact on the lives of the Scheduled Castes, unless other support systems were also provided.

While Panchayat elections are fought on local issues and personalities, parliamentary elections are contested on national and international issues. But it is the assembly elections which are most keenly contested, since they lead to the formation of the state government, the ultimate power at the state level. While elections in all lead constituencies are keenly contested, those in reserved constituencies once again bring to focus not only the caste alignments but also sub-caste and party alliances and fragmentation. When the 2000 elections took place, there were 46 Scheduled Caste and 28 Scheduled Tribe reserved constituencies in Bihar (Table 2.6). Out of these, the RJD registered the greatest presence both in the number of seats won and in those where it secured the second place.[28] The BJP and JD (U) followed suit. But significantly, even among the Scheduled Castes, out of the 17 sub-castes, it is the Ravidas and the Paswans who had the largest share in the reserved seats. For instance, out of the 16 Scheduled Caste reserved seats contested by the JD (U), Ram Vilas Paswan had given tickets to 10 candidates from the Paswan sub-caste. Laloo Prasad Yadav had tried to accommodate as many sub-castes as possible. As argued in the preceding pages, if reservation in electoral politics has opened up avenues for the emergence of leadership among the Scheduled Castes and Scheduled Tribes, it has also given rise to intra-caste/intra-tribe contradictions.

The politics of reservation

The reservation policy has been in effect for more than five decades now. But there seem to be lacunae in two regards. On the one hand, no serious discourse has evolved over the years, regarding the criteria for identifying the weaker sections, the modalities of implementing the policies of reservation, the process of evaluating the impact of positive discrimination and the mechanism for denying reservation to those who do not fall into the protective discrimination category. On the other hand, the reservation agenda itself seems to have been hijacked for political manipulation. This has diminished the value of any contribution reservations could have made to the uplift of the weaker sections. Dharma Kumar opines that other countries also have reservation policies, but in striking contrast to India, in some of them at least, the issues are openly discussed.[30] While a considered debate

TABLE 2.6: ASSEMBLY ELECTION RESULTS OF SC & ST RESERVED CONSTITUENCIES 2000.[29]

	Result	RJD	Congress	BJP	Samata	JD(U)	CPI(ML)	BSP	JMM	Ind. & Others	Total
SC reserved	Won	25	2	7	2	3	2	2	2	1	46
	Runner-up	12	5	7	4	13	0	0	0	5	46
ST reserved	Won	0	6	14	1	0	0	0	6	1	28
	Runner-up	1	10	9	0	0	0	0	7	1	28

SOURCE: Collated from Election Commission Report and other reports.

on reservations has been eluding this country, anti-reservation and pro-reservation movements have been on the rise right from the introduction of this policy. As stated above, the announcement of the government's intention to implement the Mandal Commission recommendations led to a warlike situation in some parts of the country.[31]

Yet, it is of seminal consequence to note that anti-reservation and pro-reservation movements are not new to Bihar. The year 1978 witnessed widespread anti-reservation agitations when the Karpoori Thakur government introduced reservations for the backward castes. But even in the late-1930s there were pro-reservation rumblings in Bihar. As the author has written elsewhere,

> [B]y 1939, the Triveni Sangh and other backward caste associations demanded job reservation for backward castes and the Dalits. Significantly, the term Triveni Sangh means the meeting point of three streams, referring to the upper layer of the backward castes, that is, the Yadavs, Kurmis and Koeris. The impetus for demanding reservation for backward castes came from the realisation that though the backward castes and the Dalits constituted about 90 per cent of the population, they were nowhere in the reckoning, in terms of benefiting from this numerical strength. In 1952 a bill was introduced in the Bihar Legislative Assembly to provide reservations to the backward castes.[32]

Writing about the anti-reservation movement in Bihar, Indu Bharati observes,

> Violent anti-reservation agitation broke out in Bihar during the third week of December 1989 after the announcement of implementation of Mandal Commission's Recommendations. The Bihar Rajya Arakshan Virodhi Manch (Bihar Anti-Reservation Forum) came into existence overnight. Though the agitation was directed against the recommendations of Mandal Commission, the anti-reservationists broadened their movement by demanding the scrapping of the system of reservations altogether.[33]

Bharati goes on to argue that as the stir began to spread, with reports of arson and ransacking of government property and offices from various parts of the state, the National Students Union of India (NSUI), the student wing of the Congress(I), claimed responsibility for the protest. Interestingly, Bihar police personnel, otherwise well known for their harsh methods of tackling agitations, made little attempt to restrain them. Only a few months earlier, the Bihar police had brutally lathi-charged a peaceful but massive demonstration of students, organized by leftist and other student organizations, against the induction of MLAs with known records of crime and corruption into the state Assembly. Thus, for their own political benefit members of the ruling castes and classes mobilize and organize themselves against those who ask for a share of the pie.

The reason for this violent agitation against reservation for the OBCs was that while reservations for the Dalits did not pose any challenge to the hold of the upper castes over the state bureaucracy and hence over government supplies of seeds, fertilizers, etc., as well as government contracts, reservations for the backward castes would lead to their increasing entry into the state bureaucracy. Another factor behind the rabid anti-backward classes agitation at the time was that the Janata Party's coming to power epitomized the rise of the backward classes in politics. In the 1967 and 1977 elections, the backward-caste candidates had won in large numbers and this enabled them to form the government in coalition with other parties. In terms of caste, it was the Rajputs, the Kayasths and the Bhumihars, i.e. the traditional vote-bank of the Congress, who were at the forefront of the anti-reservation agitation. They were supported by the BJP, also an upper caste-based party.[34] Thus, cutting across party lines, the ruling elite of Bihar opposed the implementation of reservation for the backward classes. But this did not mean that they were in favour of reservations for the Dalits and tribals. The truth is that they resent reservations, but since it is enshrined in the Constitution they cannot easily scrap it.

It is significant that anti-reservation movements have been initiated whenever some measure of affirmative action is introduced. Moreover, upper castes have tried every strategy to thwart the efforts of members of the Scheduled Caste and Scheduled Tribe communities. For instance, indisputably honest high court judges have been denied extensions because they come from Scheduled Caste or Tribe communities in Bihar. Here, once again, the entire debate on merit stands exposed. In a state like Bihar where identities based on caste, class and region play a powerful role in acceding or denying favour, merit remains only a point of academic discussion.[35]

In fact the debate on reservation and Scheduled Castes should search for other avenues. One recommendation of the Scheduled Castes and Scheduled Tribes Commission needs to be explored in particular: 'So far, reservations have been provided only in Government service. There is no reservation in Defense forces, scientific establishments, the judiciary, etc. After 50 years of Independence, when enough qualified SC/ST candidates are available, the Commission sees no reason for keeping these sectors out of the purview of reservations, denying opportunities to SCs/STs.'[36]

Finally, it is in the fitness of things to state that reservation has not ushered in a social revolution. On the contrary, it has been used with a view to short-term political gains, like garnering more votes during elections. While this is the limited objective of the ruling castes and classes, for the Dalits and the tribals, reservation is a means of identity formation. Affirmative action in a sense is enslaving the Scheduled Castes and Scheduled Tribes into an exploitative caste system; but this is also the plank on which they have enhanced their bargaining power. The Scheduled Castes and Scheduled Tribes leadership must now seriously address the issue of appropriation of the benefits of reservation by a small minority within their ranks, otherwise reservations may not be considered by the tribals and the Dalits as their safeguard, but only as a mechanism of segregation between the vast majority of these communities and those who have benefited from reservation. Any attempt to stall this process would only provide fodder for the dominant castes and classes to engage in the 'divide and rule' policy. Hence, as argued by many Dalit and tribal intellectuals and activists, exploited masses must go beyond reservation and use it to restructure the oppressive Indian social order.

NOTES

1. For further discussion on this refer to 'Reservation', *Seminar* 268, December 1981, and 'Reservation', *Seminar* 375, November 1990; the list of articles published in *Economic and Political Weekly* beginning 1981; V.A. Pai Panandiker, *The Politics of Backwardness: Reservation Policy in India*, Delhi: Konark, 1997; and A.K. Lal (ed.), *Protective Discrimination: Ideology and Praxis*, Allahabad: G.B. Pant Social Science Institute, 2002; Prakash Louis, 'Scheduled Castes and Tribes: The Reservation Debate', *Economic and Political Weekly*, vol. XXXVIII, no. 25, 21–7 June 2003, pp. 2475–8.
2. *Reservation for Backward Classes: Mandal Commission Report of the Backward Class Commission*, Delhi: Alankar, 1980.

3. For personal testimony on the benefits of reservation refer to Kancha Ilaiah, 'Reservation: Experience as Framework of Debate', *Economic and Political Weekly*, vol. XXV, no. 41, 1990, p. 2307.
4. Under the reservation scheme both the Scheduled Castes and Scheduled Tribes are counted. But this paper deals mainly with the Scheduled Castes, since after the separation of Jharkhand from Bihar, Bihar has only a small tribal population.
5. According to the 1991 census, the female literacy rate was less than 10 per cent in 32 out of the 42 districts in Bihar.
6. *Annual Report 1997–98*, Ministry of Social Justice and Empowerment, Government of India, p. 22.
7. *Annual Report, 1996–97*, Ministry of Welfare, Government of India, p. 21.
8. Only a few schemes are presented here to give a glimpse of the programmes initiated for the development of the Scheduled Castes.
9. *National Commission for Scheduled Castes and Scheduled Tribes, Fifth Report 1998–99*, p. 9.
10. *The Protection of Civil Rights Act, 1955*, Ministry of Social Justice, Government of India.
11. *The Scheduled Castes and Scheduled Tribes (Prevention of Atrocities) Act 1989*, Law Publishers, p. 1.
12. The Ministry of Law and Justice, Government of India, 8 June 1990.
13. B.R. Ambedkar, *What Congress and Gandhi have Done to the Untouchables*, Bombay: Thacker, 1946, p. 88.
14. 'States and Minorities', in *Dr. Babasaheb Ambedkar: Writings and Speeches*, vol. 1, Education Department, Government of Maharashtra, 1979, p. 409.
15. *Brochure on Reservation for Scheduled Castes and Scheduled Tribes in Services*, New Delhi: Ministry of Personnel, Public Grievances and Pensions, Government of India, 1993.
16. *Annual Report 1997–98*, Ministry of Social Justice and Empowerment, Government of India, p. 11.
17. Geeta B. Nambissan and Mona Sedwal, 'Education for All: The Situation of Dalit Children in India', in R. Govinda, *India Education Report: A Profile of Basic Education*, Delhi: National Institute of Educational Planning and Administration, Oxford University Press, 2002, p. 76.
18. *The National Commission for Scheduled Castes and Scheduled Tribe. Fourth Report, 1996–97 & 1997–98*, p. 20.
19. The term 'Dalit' is usually used to refer to the Scheduled Castes and thus it is exclusive. But there is another view which is inclusive in nature and considers all the exploited as Dalits. The term Dalit comes from the Sanskrit root *dalna* which means to be crushed, broken,

oppressed and excluded. The nomenclature of the erstwhile untouchable castes in India also presents the trajectory this community has undertaken over the years. One can identify the following terminologies in this regard: *achut* = untouchables; *avarnas* = colourless people, which means people who were not part of the society; *panchama* = the fifth caste; *harijans* = the children of God, a term supposed to have been popularised by M.K. Gandhi but now rejected by the Scheduled Castes due to the negative connotation the term carries; Scheduled Castes = a term given by the colonial administrators who 'scheduled' the weaker sections for positive discrimination and finally, Dalits = the broken people. In the present context, the term Dalit has two connotations. (1) Yes, we are broken and outcast people; (2) But now we will not allow you to break and crush us. It is this latter aspect which has given a liberational potential to the Dalit movement. Mahatma Jyotirao Phule and Dr. B.R. Ambedkar are credited for having given the term and the Dalit movement this assertive thrust.

20. Geeta B. Nambissan and Mona Sedwal, 2002, ibid., p. 75.
21. For more details refer to Prakash Louis, 'Scheduled Castes of Bihar "Untouched" by Education: Issues and Perspectives'. A Paper presented at the National Seminar on Educational Progress of the Scheduled Castes and Scheduled Tribes Since Independence: A State Level Scenario organized by Dr Ambedkar Institute of Social and Economic Change, University of Mumbai on 14–15 May 2002.
22. Jose Vadasery, 'Dalit Literacy Education and Education in Bihar', in A.K. Lal (ed.), *Protective Discrimination: Ideology and Praxis*, Allahabad: G.B. Pant Social Science Institute, 2002, pp. 108–19.
23. Ibid., p. 115.
24. A.R. Desai, *Agrarian Struggles in India after Independence*, Delhi: Oxford University Press, 1986, p. 93.
25. The Dalit Sena was a mass-based youth organization which neither became a political party nor part of any political party. Though Mr Ram Vilas Paswan changed his party affiliation from Socialist Party to Janata Party to Janata Dal to Janata Dal (United) to Lok Shakti party, the Dalit Sena remained a mass support base for his political engagements but he did not bring it under the control of any political party or formation.
26. Sumita Mishra, *Grassroot Politics in India*, Delhi: Mittal, 2000, p. 65.
27. *The Powers and Functions of Three-tier Panchayats*. Rural Development Ministry, Government of Bihar, 2001.
28. For more on this refer to Prakash Louis, 'Fractured Mandate for Social Change in Bihar', *Economic and Political Weekly*, 18 March 2000, p. 978.

29. Ibid. From November 2000, the Jharkhand region of Bihar state was bifurcated from Bihar and constituted into a separate state.
30. Dharma Kumar, 'The Problem', *Seminar* 375, November 1990, p. 12.
31. On this subject, see *Seminar* 375, November 1990, and more particularly articles by Sachchidananda on 'The tacit reservation for high castes', by A.N. Das on 'The issue of merit against preferential treatment', and of Madhu Limaye on 'The launching of a vicious and destructive campaign'.
32. Prakash Louis, *People Power: The Naxalite Movement in Central Bihar*, Delhi: Wordsmith, 2002, pp. 129–31.
33. Indu Bharati, 'Politics of Anti-Reservation Stir', *Economic and Political Weekly*, 10 February 1990, p. 309.
34. Ibid., p. 310.
35. In the field of education, it is often argued that parents from the weaker sections of society do not encourage their children towards education. But the crux of the matter is that the parents of Dalit children yearn for education and especially quality education: they are aware of the fact that education is the only key that will open the door to social mobility. In contrast, even at the primary and middle school levels, the attitude of the teachers towards children from Scheduled Caste backgrounds is negative, to say the least. A study conducted by M.K. Jabbi and C. Rajyalakshmi states that 'Both women and children complained about the teacher's irregularity, absenteeism, negligence and utilising services of children for their personal work, poor quality of teaching, lack of physical facilities, erratic distribution of educational materials, uniforms and discontinuances of the same, and corruption at various levels' (M.K. Jabbi and C. Rajyalakshmi, 'Education of Marginalized Social Groups in Bihar', in A. Vaidyanathan and P.R. Gopinathan Nair [eds], *Elementary Education in Rural India: A Grassroots View*, Delhi: Sage, 2001, p. 448). Teachers who understand the social stigma and constraints that these children suffer enhance the ability of the children to come out of these societal constraints. But these are only exceptions and not the order of the day.
36. *National Commission for Scheduled Castes and Scheduled Tribes, Fourth Report 1996–97 & 1997–98*, p. 20.

CHAPTER 3

Reservations and Social Change: The Case of the North-East

WALTER FERNANDES

The failure of the Indian Parliament to pass the Women's Reservation Bill since its first introduction in 1996 has revived the controversy over reservations, highlighted earlier by the 1985 Gujarat riots, the 1990 anti-Mandal agitation and the demand by several groups for inclusion in the Schedule. The discussion around the issue has shown that today reservations are primarily a question of power. Members from the dominant castes claim that they go against the principle of equality or that they lower the standards. Others say that the dominants monopolize all the benefits of development, set the standards and use education, high status, jobs and other tools of upward mobility to keep themselves in power. So they demand positive discrimination in favour of those who have hitherto been excluded from these benefits.

Some people believe that these arguments concern mostly Dalits. They feel that reservations in education and jobs are inadequate for the tribals, whose priority is to protect their livelihood, which includes land and forests, culture and the identity they have built around these resources. We believe that reservations have at best given tribals some relief after being deprived of their livelihood. Besides, the literacy status of the tribals (and Dalits) remains low, except in regions such as Jharkhand and the north-east where private voluntary efforts have helped. The poor educational status of the majority precludes the possibility of their getting jobs other than low-status ones. So reservations as they exist today serve a small minority that has access to education and exclude the majority.

The question we are asking is whether reservations in their present form are a solution to the ongoing marginalization of the subalterns who have been discriminated against for centuries. We begin by rejecting the position of those who claim that they go against the principle of equality because inequality is basic to the present social system. The issue at stake is not whether reverse discrimination is required but whether reservations as implemented today are adequate for changing an unjust system. We shall study their history from this perspective. Our focus being the tribes, we shall refer only in passing to the Dalits and to issues such as the guilt felt by the dominant castes and their fear that the Dalits will convert to other religions—which is one of the origins of the reservation policy.

THE HISTORICAL BACKGROUND

Tribal communities are not homogeneous. Even from a legal perspective they live in three distinct administrative situations, some in the Fifth Schedule areas, others in the Sixth Schedule regions of the north-east and the rest in States with no Schedule.[1] Besides, to understand the impact of reservations we need to go beyond them and look at positive discrimination in its totality. So we shall situate tribal reservations within the totality of the protective laws, such as the Scheduled Areas, prohibiting tribal land alienation and the customary laws in the north-east. Common to the three administrative systems mentioned above is the fact that the protective laws were a response to tribal struggles and resurgence witnessed in the nineteenth and early twentieth century India, in defence of their livelihood and identity, both of which came under attack from the colonialist. The myth of the foreigner's civilizing mission, propagated in fact for the purpose of legitimizing colonial occupation for economic exploitation, had special implications for the tribal areas.

The land, forests and other natural resources that were the sustenance of the tribal communities were merely economic commodities to the colonialist, who needed to change the Indian economy to suit the needs of the British industrial revolution. So, after occupying tribal regions, the British began to eye the former's livelihood for profit. They made a direct attack on those resources that were at the centre of tribal religious beliefs, culture, economy and social system—in short, their very identity. So an attack on them was bound to cause a complete crisis in their life (de Sa, 1975: 55). In addition, North-eastern India was considered a buffer zone by the British. They, therefore, decided to treat much of it as 'unadministered' territory in order to protect its people from external influences (Fernandes, 1999: 3,580).

A major step in ensuring control over these resources was to change the land and forest laws so as to make it easy for British mining and tea companies to acquire land at a low price. The British had also enacted several social reform laws but did not implement them for fear of losing the cooperation of the upper classes and castes, whose collaboration they required for the success of their economic enterprise. The laws concerning land and forests were the real kernel of colonialism (Rothermund, 1992: 7–8).

Intrinsic to these laws was individual ownership. It conferred on the owner the right to use the property according to his/her will, with no obligation to anyone else unless it impinged on the rights of another individual. The changeover to individual ownership was based on the principle of eminent domain, called *terra nullius* (nobody's land) in Australia. The European colonization of the Americas, Australia, New Zealand and southern Africa was based on the principle that anyone could occupy land that belonged to no one. The Australian judiciary has declared it null and void, but it continues to be the basis of Indian land laws. Its first facet is that natural resources such as forests and land with no individual title, belong to the State. Its second facet is that the State alone has the right to define a public purpose and deprive individuals of their assets for it (Ramanathan, 1999: 19-20).

These laws had a profound impact both on the community-resource based tribals and on the Dalits, who sustained themselves on land owned by others. Resistance was bound to follow and one saw revolts against them in all three tribal situations. Such uprisings eventually forced the decision-makers to enact protective laws. However, their context as well as implications differed from region to region. Since 'mainland India' felt the impact of the colonial policies before the north-east did, we shall begin with the tribal communities of the former.

THE TRIBALS IN MAINLAND INDIA

In order to make colonial economies serve the interests of the industrial revolution, the colonies had to be turned into suppliers of capital and raw materials. Trade and land tax were integral to the effort to generate capital (Rothermund, 1992: 10–12). The first to feel the impact of such a strategy were Jharkhand and Orissa, which were integrated with the Bengal Presidency. These regions were rich in the resources that the British needed as raw material. Jharkhand, for example, accounts for 48 per cent of India's coal, 100 per cent of its mica and about a third of all the other minerals in the country. The tool used by the colonialist was *Permanent Settlement 1793.* Meant to make tax collection easy, the Permanent Settlement depended on individual land ownership and landlordism. These concepts were new to the tribals. Their ignorance of the system made it easy for the landlords to exploit them. The Jharkhand tribes had some individual components in their *khuntkhatti* rights, which gave those families whose forebears had founded the village the right to cultivate land in the village. This right was not entirely individual. It had a communitarian foundation. Land was community based in most other tribal areas, including in the Jharkhand forests (Sarkar, 1996: 100–2).

Through the twin measures of individual ownership and landlordism, the British obtained the cooperation of the Indian upper classes to control the tribal livelihood and communities on their behalf. Whether they intended it or not, this strategy also had the effect of diverting attention and tribal discontent from the foreign ruler to the local landlords and the Indian upper classes. To ensure that these classes controlled the resources on their behalf, the British colonialist turned those whom the earlier local kings and chieftains had appointed as tax collectors, into landlords. The colonialist also presented control over land and other resources through their Indian collaborators as a process of State formation, thus further legitimizing colonialism. (Schverin, 1987: 30–8)

The tribals were thus deprived of their livelihood, impoverished and forced to become tenants or sharecroppers or migrate to Assam and North Bengal as tea labourers. The Forest Act, 1867 marginalized them further. The principle of eminent domain that turned all the natural resources into State property denied them some of their customary rights over the forests and made them encroachers in their own habitat, where they had been living for several centuries. Its outcome was their impoverishment through massive land alienation. (Munshi Saldanha, 1993: 71-2)

In reaction some of them, for example the Kols of Mayurbhanj in

Orissa, took to crime for sheer survival. The British declared them 'criminal tribes' (Praharaj, 1988: 72-4). Many others revolted against the loss of resources since their alienation resulted in a total crisis in their life. Struggles followed in Jharkhand, Himachal Pradesh (Mehta, 1998), western India (Shah and Patel, 1998) and elsewhere. Most such movements before the 1830s were local in nature, but with the intensification of Company rule they were slowly transformed into a general insurgency, both against the British and the zamindars, since the tribals perceived both as their exploiters (Das Gupta, 1991: 116). The fact that they were also against the Indian upper classes is probably the reason why official histories have not recognized them as part of the freedom movement led by sections of the same class that collaborated with the colonialist.

However, through these uprisings tribal communities extracted concessions from the British, such as the Chotanagpur Tenancy Act, 1908, the Wilkinson Rules governing Kolhan and the Agency Areas Act in Andhra Pradesh. The British administrators and industrialists aligned with the Indian upper classes to subvert these laws. However, a section of the missionaries who had experienced the egalitarian ideology of the European political revolutions, and a small minority of administrators with an anthropological background, worked for reforms favouring tribals.[2] Though the British merchants and their Indian collaborators opposed these Acts, the colonial rule had no choice but to implement them in order to protect commercial interests and prevent unrest that could cause loss of revenue (Sharma, 1978: 38). Thus, the humanitarian concern of some missionaries and administrators coincided with the British need to maintain peace in the resource rich regions to ensure regular supply of raw material. This led to the land protection and other laws in the tribal regions. The Fifth Schedule applied in 10 states emerged as a result of tribal resistance to their exploiters (Fernandes and Roy Choudhury, 1993: 14-15).

THE TRIBAL COMMUNITIES OF THE NORTH-EAST

Around 12 per cent of India's tribals live in the 'Seven Sisters' of the north-east. A few of them, for example the Bodo, Mishing and Tiwa, are plains tribes of Assam. Most others inhabit the hills. The plains are dominated by non-tribals, for example the Meitei in Manipur, Bengali in Tripura and Assomiya in Assam. In the hill states of Meghalaya, Mizoram and Nagaland, the tribals constitute more than 80 per cent of the population and in Arunachal Pradesh they are around two-thirds. But their proportion is small in the populous states of Assam, Manipur and Tripura. The Bodo-Kachari, numerically a third of the tribals in the north-east, constitute only 3.7 per cent of Assam's population. Besides, because of the ongoing immigration of Hindus from Bangladesh (erstwhile East Pakistan), the proportion of tribals has declined in Tripura from 56 per cent in 1951 to around 30 per cent today.

Several north-eastern tribes come under the Sixth Schedule. Under it, the village court or the District Autonomous Council deals with civil offences. It also recognizes community ownership of land or forests, in conformity with their tradition. Such Autonomous Councils exist in two districts of Assam, the whole of Meghalaya, Mizoram and Tripura. Arunachal Pradesh does not come under it but continues to follow the administrative system that evolved under the British. Nagaland has never had district councils, but a constitutional amendment in 1963 (Article 371A) enabled it to follow the customary law in place of the Sixth Schedule. Manipur does not have Sixth Schedule areas but has specific laws governing its hill areas (Barooah, 2002: 99–100).

The Sixth Schedule too evolved as a protective measure, amid the unequal power relations and conflicts between the tribal and non-tribal communities, as well as between various tribes. The effort to control resources is basic to the conflicts in the region. But unlike the rest of India, struggles have taken the overt form of ethnic consciousness, emerging from the encounter with the dominant cultures. The land issue is present in these struggles, though in a covert form, because these tribes feel the impact of resource depletion caused by the commercialization of forest and agricultural produce. Unable to cope with it, they have joined hands to safeguard their livelihood or to take advantage of modernization, although they give it a cultural veneer.

The main reason why even land agitation took the form of ethnic and identity conflicts is that the British required the hill areas more for trade than for land. In Assam, which had been earmarked for tea and later petroleum production, they acquired land from the Ahom, Koch, Bodo and other tribes on extremely exploitative terms. In the rest of the north-east they needed to popularize the finished products of the industrial revolution. To achieve this they had to destroy or commercialize tribal craft to ensure that it did not compete with the Manchester textiles. Thus, in most of the north-east, colonialism represented new forms of trade based on a monetary economy. Most tribals, used to a barter system, were not familiar with money and lost out to the merchants. For example, since the Bodo-Kachari were not familiar with money, merchants from Tezpur, Barpeta and elsewhere in Lower Assam took control of trade and also came to control Bodo cultivation, since much of the trade was in agricultural produce. It increased land alienation, which had started after the Permanent Settlement, 1793 and the 1834 Assam Land Act. Then came the move to settle Bengali peasants on 'wasteland' that was their livelihood (Roy, 1995: 24–31).

One can give similar examples from other states too. Since the hill areas of the north-east were only required for the commercialization of tribal crafts and not for land, they were left 'unadministered'. As a result, they had very limited contact with outsiders. When resentment grew, the British way of ensuring commercial peace was to isolate them further through the introduction of the Inner Line Permit, which was a more stringent measure than the laws banning tribal land alienation in the rest of India. Besides, the British came to consider the north-east a buffer zone against China and Burma. As such it was kept isolated (Doley, 1998: 15–16). Colonial intervention also involved the destabilization of tribals' lifestyle. This created awareness among them so that in the north-east too most tribal communities resisted British intrusion, though very few of their revolts have been recorded in the official histories of the freedom movement. In the nineteenth century one hears of resistance from the Akas, Miris, Mishmis, Nagas and others (Mackenzie, 1995).

The tribals viewed the dual process of deprivation of their livelihood and the imposition of what they considered an alien culture as an attack on their identity. It resulted in many struggles, both against the British and their Indian collaborators. Conversions were the outcome of their efforts to protect their identity against both. Initially, they converted to Christianity. Very few missionaries understood tribal culture, but the tribes used the organizational base the missionaries had established to evangelize the tribals, for their own purpose of protecting and expanding their identity. For example, the missionaries introduced Sunday worship, Sunday school and educational institutions that brought many tribes under one roof. They started the process of eliminating divisions between tribes that were at war with each other. Gradually, the tribals came to think of themselves as one. This brought about an expansion of identity and a feeling of strength against the outsiders. Among the Nagas, the turning point was the Japanese invasion, when Z.A. Phizo brought 27 tribes together under one umbrella. British inputs also resulted in competition between various groups to get the benefits of education and jobs. From the 1930s, the desire to appropriate these benefits expressed itself in the form of new organizations. For example, many Naga organizations emerged that helped to make the Naga voice heard (Sanyu, 1996: 115–26).

But conversions were not to Christianity alone. The Bodos converted to a reformist Brahmo Hindu sect, to which their leader Kallicharan Brahma had been introduced in Kolkata. What they needed was social reform together with the protection of their identity. They were ready to accept any alternative that was available, and the Brahmo reformist sect was one of them (Roy, 1995: 90-5). After their conversion, like the Nagas, the Bodos too tried to build organizations for their development or emulate the Assomiya institutions that had helped the latter to make advances in education. The Bodo Chhatra Sammilani (Bodo Youth Association) and literary associations were created in the 1930s for the purpose of education, welfare and the standardization of language. However, indebtedness and land alienation were major problems. The Notified Areas Act, enacted in the 1930s and amended in 1947 to prevent land alienation, did not improve the situation because of malpractice (ibid.: 41–57).

To commercialize the handicrafts of the hill areas and collect taxes, the British required the cooperation of the traditional leaders. But new leaders emerged from the education process introduced by the missionaries. These were a threat both to the traditional chiefs and to the British who depended on them and as a result, both opposed the missionaries. The new leaders were sympathetic to the freedom movement and were ready to cooperate with national leaders, while retaining their identity (Sharma Barkataki, 1985: 86–8). However, the failure of the national leaders to grasp the diversity of this region made it difficult for them to cooperate with the new tribal leaders. The latter in turn felt that the national leadership was unable to comprehend and respect their cultural and ethnic identity or even accept the fact that they had a culture and a religion of their own. So the situation of conflict continued (Acharya, 1990: 71–95).

The conflict also strengthened the process of cultural revival. The missionary infrastructure of schools and Sunday worship, which brought tribes together, enabled several to merge and expand their identity, without giving up their individuality. Unity also enabled them to resist the homogenizing bias of the dominant 'one State one nation' thinking propounded by the Indian State, and its tendency 'to take the degree of Aryanisation as a measure of Indianisation' (Datta, 1990: 41). In colonial times they reacted to such attacks through religious conversion. After 1947, through their revolts, they amalgamated three steps in pursuit of their aims, namely, defending their livelihood, protecting their identity and propounding a sub-nationalism specific to a cultural and ethnic group. The official reaction was similar to what happened in the rest of tribal India. Its first stage was repression. Once the unrest spread to Nagaland, Mizoram and other states, compromises followed. At the same time, new tribal leaders slowly led the region towards the Sixth Schedule and other protective measures. Another compromise was the formation of new states and constitutional amendments in recognition of the tribals' customary laws.

RESERVATIONS TODAY

Reservations in education, the legislature and public employment need to be placed in the context of tribal and Dalit resistance. In fact, reservations were a response more to the Dalit leader Dr B.R. Ambedkar than to the tribals. After the Morley–Minto reforms (1909) granted a separate electorate to Muslims, many subaltern groups that wanted a share in power independently of the dominant castes felt that they too could lay claim to this autonomous arrangement. Hence, Dr B.R. Ambedkar's demand that Dalits be considered a minority and granted a separate electorate and reservations. But Mahatma Gandhi was not ready to countenance a separate 'low caste' electorate, since numbers would have a considerable say in the competition between religious groups through separate electorates. He needed them in the Hindu electorate. Eventually, a compromise was reached. The Dalits had no choice but to accept a certain number of elective posts reserved for them within the Hindu electorate (Dass, 1996: 241–4).

Tribal reservations were an appendix to the concessions made to the Dalits. The dominant-class leaders who led the freedom struggle had very little understanding of tribal issues, so the concessions granted to the Dalits were simply extended to them. Thus, the basic feature of the present reservation policy is that it originated more out of the dominant class' need for numbers than as a response to subaltern demands. This policy is welfare or relief oriented, it is based not on the questioning of the basis of inequality but on the project of assimilating the subalterns into the 'mainstream'. So power relations did not change.

The implementation of reservations has to be studied in this context. Some people think that reservations have been instrumental in stifling subaltern protest by co-opting the Dalit and tribal elite into the dominant system. Others feel that reservations have raised hopes of social transformation among the scheduled classes. Thus, though reservations have benefitted a small minority which threatens to appropriate them at the expense of the majority, they have also been instrumental in making many subalterns aware of their rights as citizens.

Yet, what the tribal leaders were demanding was not reservations but acceptance of their right to a livelihood and to an identity, instead of which they were given concessions in education and jobs. The eminent domain principle and the colonial laws that had endangered their livelihood were not questioned. Rather, the approach to national development, which considered common property resources as State property, was strengthened. At the time of the promulgation of the Constitution in 1950, the assumption was that these classes would reach the standard of the high castes within a decade. Thus, the dominant thinking was assimilationist. Instead of recognizing a separate tribal identity it was assumed that the tribals would be assimilated into the system. This thinking, which was also reflected in the ILO Convention 109 of 1956, conditioned the implementation of the reservation policy.

Thus, rose a contradiction in the reservation policy and protective legislation. Central to it was the ideology of the decision-makers and the post-Independence pattern of development. On the attainment of Independence, power was transferred to the bourgeoisie that had led the freedom struggle. This class lacked the ideology required for social transformation. The new capitalists who had funded the movement viewed it as a long-term investment in the economic future of independent India (Shankardass, 1982). This class viewed the Western form of development as the only one possible. Its focus was on economic growth through capital-intensive inputs and sophisticated technologies. It was assumed that such a process of modernization and technological progress would solve the social problems of illiteracy, ill-health and unemployment. But this required persons with high educational skills, which the Scheduled Classes lacked because of their limited access to schools. The main thrust was on industrial infrastructure development and economic growth. Investment was also made in health and educational institutions. But for such investment to be effective, it was necessary to guarantee access to these institutions to groups that till then had been repressed by the dominant classes. In reality no effort was made to transform the imbalance in society. It was not realized that modernization introduced in an unequal society does not reduce inequalities but intensifies them (Kurien, 1996: 36–8).

Far from being effective, the system has worked against Dalits and tribals in general, and women in particular. It has strengthened inequalities in education, health care and nutrition. Access to it is conditioned by a caste- and class-based socio-economic hierarchy. On top of it is the urban dominant-caste upper-class male, followed by the urban upper-class woman, the rural dominant-caste male and female and finally the rural low-caste or tribal male followed by the female. This hierarchy conditions economic, political and social power as well as access to services like education and health and to high-status jobs. The scheduled classes, particularly women, are the most illiterate and malnourished, and have the least hope of improving their status. Illiteracy, but also malnutrition, infant and child mortality, bondage and child labour, which are well-known indicators of the neglect of the social sector, are the highest among the scheduled classes. Thus the reservation policy that was meant to close the gap between the dominants and the subalterns has failed in the case of a majority of the tribals and Dalits.[3]

PROTECTIVE MEASURES AND LIVELIHOODS IN MAINLAND INDIA

Tribal leaders were concerned with their identity and the struggle for autonomy and not with reservations. Jaipal Singh, the Jharkhand leader, demanded a separate state for the tribals. He did not demand reservations because he was convinced that autonomy would give them control over their livelihood and bring them up to the standard of the dominant classes (Minz,1992: 360). When statehood was denied and reservations were thrust upon tribals, they followed the logic of a patriarchal society. The few who could afford education sent only boys to school, resulting in lower rates in literacy, access to jobs and other tools of upward mobility among women than men.

The neglect of the social sector combined with the pattern of development resulted in the transfer of tribals' livelihood to the corporate sector and the middle class through deforestation and displacement due to development projects. Indeed the main resource under attack in the name of national development is land. Whether private or common, it is the livelihood not merely of its *patta* owner but also of the landless service classes such as the Dalit labourers. Most tribals are community resource users. Traditionally, forests met more than 50 per cent of their food, fodder, medicinal and other needs. To the economic planner forests are only a raw material used for producing consumer goods for the middle class and securing profits for the industrialist. Deforestation is its consequence. This approach deprives the forest-dependent communities of their sustenance. Similarly, at least 30 million people have been displaced without their consent or deprived of livelihood because of the development projects implemented in the last 50 years. Around 40 per cent of them are tribals, another 20 per cent Dalits and a large but unspecified number are from other poor rural communities. Less than a third of these displaced have been resettled. The rest are left with no economic, social or cultural support (Fernandes, 1998: 251 and 265). Even among them, women are the worst hit. Given their low literacy and lack of exposure to urban reality, at most they can get unskilled jobs in the informal sector. Their nutritional and health status has declined because of deforestation and displacement, as seen in the studies conducted in Orissa (Fernandes and Raj, 1992: 45–6), Kerala (Muricken et al., 2003) and elsewhere.

Thus, while the protective laws are meant to protect the livelihood of tribals, the policies pursued in the name of national development deprive them of their sustenance. The benefits of development reach the middle and upper classes but the tribals are impoverished. Reservations are based on the assumption of equal access to institutions. Their impoverishment denies them such access. As we noticed in many of our studies in Orissa, Chhattisgarh, West Bengal and Andhra Pradesh, deforestation and displacement deprive children of the possibility of education. In the former case, resource depletion forced children to spend much of their time looking after the home and the siblings, as women have to travel longer distances than in the past to collect food from the forest. For example, in Orissa and Chhattisgarh the distance between the forest and the home has increased from less than a kilometre in the 1960s to more than 7 km in the 1980s. Besides, with resource depletion many have made the transition from constructive to destructive dependence on forests. In Orissa, for example, in our sample of 272 families, the number depending on the sale of fuel wood as the main source of income had grown from 18 in the early 1960s to 77 two decades later. Men cut fuel wood in the forest, children get it ready for the market and women carry the bundles to the town to sell (Fernandes, Menon and Viegas, 1988: 175–7).

Besides, tribals make very little money from selling forest produce and as daily wage earners once they lose their livelihood. So the possibility of sending their children to school is very slim. In the above circumstances, children represent two additional hands rather than a mouth to feed. Moreover, the culture imparted in schools is urban middle class oriented and does not respect the tribal ethos. As a result, tribal children who go to school become misfits in their own society and at the same time are not accepted by the dominant classes. Thus, the present type of education results in double alienation (Sharma, 1978).

In fact, for the reservation policy to become effective, the focus should be on protective laws designed to safeguard the common property resources. However, as stated above, land and forest laws based on the eminent domain fail to do this. Other protective laws are not of much use either. For example, the law banning tribal land alienation is based on individual ownership, whereas the tribal ethos favours community assets. As a result tribals find it difficult to understand the norms of the formal sector on which these laws are based. Besides, the administrative system is controlled by the dominant classes with a vested interest in their poverty. Studies show that powerful outsiders manipulate land records in their own favour. The powerless tribals are unable to stop this. Official data shows that 48 per cent of land in the tribal districts of Andhra Pradesh are in non-tribal hands, and the reality is even worse (Laya, 1998). The situation is the same in Orissa (Pradhan and Stanley, 1999), Madhya Pradhesh (Mander, 1998) and elsewhere.

PROTECTIVE LAWS AND THE SIXTH SCHEDULE

The Sixth Schedule in the north-east was designed to protect the community's assets. In reality, it is implemented in such a way that it supports both class formation and gender-based discrimination. Exceptions apart, the type of impoverishment observed in the middle India tribal belt has not yet reached the north-east. However, the process leading to it is visible even today. For example, natural resources are supposed to belong to the whole community but the State treats the *gaonburah* (village head) as the landowner. Community assets can be turned into individual land or alienated to outsiders with his permission and without the consent of the whole village, and he can be influenced. As a result, in many Sixth Schedule tribal areas, one sees individuals owning several hundred acres, while others have no land (Barbora, 2002).

This policy also has a gender bias. Among the Garo and other matrilineal tribes the female landowner's husband is taking charge of all land transactions because he has better exposure to the outside world. In parts of the East Garo hills there has been a slow transition to growing cash crops, supported by the State. But for the implementation of this policy the State deals only with the heads of families (loans and subsidies for commercial crops are given only to individual owners). In practice it means dealing only with the men. As a result, land and power in the family are passing from the woman to the man (Fernandes and Barbora, 2002: 114–18).

The reservation policy (in education and public jobs) has to be situated in this context. A society reacts to external inputs according to its internal organization. That is what the scheduled classes have done. To limit ourselves to the north-east, a recent comparative study of six tribes showed that most of them have given priority to boys' education.

A comparison between the matrilineal Garos of Meghalaya and the patrilineal Angamis of Nagaland is particularly interesting. In common with the Nagas, a majority of Garos became Christians as a result of a social process after the 1950s. The Church introduced schools to them. Being a male-dominated structure, the Church provided schools to both boys and girls, but did not introduce measures to ensure their equal access to these institutions. The reaction of Garos and Angamis to education as a social input has been very different.

In both traditions the woman is in charge of the family economy and decision making and the man represents the family in society and controls the resources. Thus, both tribes observe the male–female division between the social and family spheres.

The Garo are matrilocal and inheritance is through the woman. Yet girls are discriminated against when it comes to education.[4] For example, our sample of 200 Garo families has 173 girls in the 10–19 age group. 12.14 per cent of them are illiterate, as against 9.2 per cent of boys, and the male-female difference grows as one goes up the age ladder.[5]

The Angamis, a patrilineal tribe, were at the forefront of the Naga nationalist struggle. A large number of their young men went underground or were killed in the struggle. As a result, there is a high male deficiency in the above 40 age group. In the absence of men, women were left in charge both of the family and society. Consequently, a large number of them developed ideas about gender equity. That is when many schools came into their region, which they frequented. Thus, the tribal tradition of a divide between the family and social spheres was weakened because of the absence of men, which made it easier for women to transcend tradition. Almost all Angami boys and girls below 20 are in school or college. Illiteracy is around 5 per cent in this age group; in the above 40 age group, it is 18.07 per cent among men and 17.07 per cent among women.

However, even when a political process facilitates change, community traditions and State policies can subvert it. In the case of the Angami, for example, the women's high educational status is not reflected in the reserved employment quota. Because of their high educational status, as many as 22.75 per cent of Angamis above

15 have salaried jobs, most of them in the reserved category, and 5.18 per cent are in business. However, only 22.16 per cent of the salaried individuals and 18.42 per cent of the people involved in business, are women. It shows a gender bias, although women are better educated. Similarly, while the number of Garo males and females involved in agriculture is almost equal, the other occupations show a male bias. There are only 26.51 per cent of women holding salaried jobs; 19.74 per cent of family members above 15 live on daily wages, 36.36 per cent of them women. As a result, 71.68 per cent of unemployed persons are women (ibid: 114–18).

The Christian and Hindu male-dominated structures are only one explanation. Other reasons can be found in tradition and in the nature of reservations. Tribal tradition is one of male control over community resources and society. Even though, through an amendment to the Constitution, the Nagas have won the right to follow their customary laws, they have not brought in reforms to introduce gender equity. As pointed out earlier, this is compounded by the fact that the State supports individual property and deals only with the head of the family, usually a male. Thus, the administration and the market forces effect a series of transformations on the social structure. In such a situation, traditional institutions are so transformed that patriarchal rules get strengthened. For example, in the traditionally matrilineal Garo society, the question of a woman's status has to be read alongside that of other male kin, who wield considerably more economic and political power today than in the past. Although a woman is the heiress, her husband manages the inheritance (Marak, 1997: 58–61). Since the State recognizes him as the head of the family, decisions on land transactions and transfers have to be routed through him.

The predominance of men in employment follows from this slant. The State considers it a male domain and gives them preference. As a result, despite education, property relations have not changed among the Angami; the man remains the head of the family. Thus, both laws meant to protect tribals' livelihood and jobs under the reservations policy reinforce male domination.

THE SEARCH FOR ALTERNATIVES

It was hoped that reservations would provide equal opportunities to the communities that had been neglected for centuries. In reality this objective of creating an egalitarian society has not been achieved because Indian society in general and its decision-makers in particular have been ambiguous on the issue of inequality. While reservations offer tribals free education and jobs, the pattern of development deprives them of access to schools. Their livelihood has been alienated from them. The literacy, health, mortality and child labour data show that their situation has deteriorated. Thus, though a small section has benefitted from reservations, the policy has not dealt with the basic issue of inequality. As a result, class and gender inequalities have been intensified to some extent.

It is in this context that one has to search for solutions. This is where India can learn a lesson from the 'Asian tigers'. They have been presented to the world as a success story of capitalism, and mainland China as a case of 'socialist success'. Studies indicate that their success lies in their approach to development. According to analysts like Jean Dreze and Amartya Sen, for economic benefits to reach the masses not less that 10 per cent of the GNP has to be invested in the social sector. That is what South and North Korea, Malaysia, Indonesia under Soekarno, Singapore and the two Chinas have done. On the one hand, the State supported the building of an infrastructure either through the public sector or through private investors. On the other, these countries invested 8 to 15 per cent of their GDP on these components. One may state that actually countries such as South Korea and Taiwan created a class of consumers, but they did it through social investment that qualified the masses for jobs in the system and thereby gain access to the benefits of economic development (Colonel-Ferer, 1998). In mainland China, the endeavour to raise the masses from misery to poverty rather than focusing on the prosperity of a few reduced inequality. This approach provided the masses with access to educational, health and other institutions.

Another example is Malaysia's *Bhumiputra* policy. Reservations as they exist in India are only one of its components. Malaysia went far beyond in its endeavour to remedy the social and political causes of inequality. An important reason for this difference is its very origin. Unlike the Indian policy, the Malaysian one was initiated after the traumatic independence of Singapore in 1966, and the Malay–Chinese riots of 1969. The Malaysian decision-makers realized that these events were caused by social injustice that the Malays suffered from. Although they formed 60 per cent of the population, people of Chinese origin controlled the economy and jobs were to a great extent cornered by persons of Indian descent. The Malays were excluded from the benefits of development. In that sense their situation was not much different from that of the Dalits in India.

The leaders, therefore, did not stop at instituting relief measure, as India's reservations policy has done. They turned the *Bhumiputra* policy into a response not to the trauma of Singapore's independence or to the riots but to the causes of these events. Within its framework they combined an industrial with a social infrastructure. Unlike India, Malaysian reservations are not limited to the public sector but extend also to the private sector at every level. Besides, Malaysia made massive investments in the fields of education, health, nutrition and hygiene, thus preparing Malays both for jobs and as consumers.

This is the lesson that India needs to learn from the 'Asian Tigers' in general and Malaysia in particular. India should look beyond the physical infrastructure and make massive investments in the social infrastructure of primary education, community health, nutrition and hygiene. It is not just material investment that is important, but also giving the subalterns hope in their future. As things stand, the dominant classes are not ready to share power with the subalterns but are only prepared to provide relief to a few and co-opt them into the mainstream. In some cases such relief itself helps the subalterns to become aware of their rights and that becomes a threat to the dominants and they react as they did in Gujarat in 1985. In other cases, reservations themselves have fallen prey to vested interests, allowing a minority to corner the benefits. The masses are excluded from it. This vicious circle can be broken not through relief but through a combination of economic, social and political inputs.

CONCLUSION

This paper has looked beyond the history of tribal reservations at the role of other protective laws that were meant to protect the tribals' livelihood. We have seen that those with clout refused to part with the advantages they possessed. So the subalterns have been forced to fight for their rights. In reaction to their revolt, the ruling classes have tried to provide them relief but have not taken steps to arrest the process of transferring their sustenance to another class nor the ensuing impoverishment. The dominant classes, to whom power was transferred after Independence, took it for granted that some sops to the subalterns in the form of reservations would help them reach their own standards. But the social system did not change. A small group among the subalterns has gained access to education, and has got most jobs under the reserved category.

We have also seen that the main reason is that India lacked the social infrastructure that would have made reservations accessible to all. Globalization further intensifies this process. We shall not analyse it here for lack of space, except to say that with economic liberalization the social consciousness of the middle class has all but died out, as one saw in the Gujarat caste riots and the anti-Mandal uprising. It should be clear that to break this vicious circle, one cannot depend on relief measures alone. They have to be combined with social investment. It does not mean that reservations should be abandoned. Communities that have been discriminated against for centuries cannot be expected to compete as equals with those who have had access to education and social services for several generations. However, the benefits cannot reach them until they become a part of a composite policy of economic investment combined with social investment aimed at social transformation.

NOTES

1. Scheduled areas are defined in the Indian Constitution as 'such areas as the President may by order declare to be Scheduled Areas'; they are meant to benefit from special administrative arrangements. 'The criteria followed for declaring an area as Scheduled Area are preponderance of tribal population; compactness and reasonable size of the area; under-developed nature of the area; and marked disparity in economic standard of the people' (Menon and Sinha, 2003: 7). Fifth Schedule Areas are said to be 'tribal dominated areas', and include areas located in ten states, stretching from Gujarat to Orissa. Sixth Schedule Areas are said to be 'tribal areas' and concern four states of the Northeast (Assam, Tripura, Mizoram and Meghalaya).
2. John Baptist Hoffmann, a German missionary, drafted the *Chotanagpur Tenancy Act, 1908*, while some others worked on similar lines elsewhere.
3. The number of jobs provided through reservations should be seen in this context. Official data give global figures on the number of tribals and Dalits in employment, but do not mention that a large number of reserved posts remain unfilled because the subalterns lack access to education.

4. Garo families have an equal number of boys and girls.
5. 17.56 per cent women in the 20–9 cohorts are illiterate as against 11.72 per cent men. Their number goes up to 45.45 per cent women as against 32.89 per cent men in the above 30 age group. In the over 40 cohort, 49.12 per cent women and 40 per cent men are illiterate. The male–female ratio for graduates is 2:1.

REFERENCES

Acharya, S.K., 'Ethnic Processes in North-Eastern India', in D. Pakem (ed.), *Nationality, Ethnicity and Cultural Identity in North-East India*, Delhi: Omsons, 1990, pp. 69–108.

Barbora, Sanjay, 'Ethnic Politics and Land Use: Genesis of Conflicts in India's North-East', *Economic and Political Weekly*, vol. 37, no. 13, 30 March 2002, pp. 1285–92.

Barooah, Jeuti, 'Property and Women's Inheritance Rights in the Tribal Areas of the North East', in Walter Fernandes and Sanjay Barbora (eds), *Changing Women's Status in India: Focus on the Northeast*, Guwahati: North Eastern Social Research Centre, 2002, pp. 99–113.

Colonel-Ferrer, Miriam, 'Emulating South-East Asian Development: The Neo-Liberal Tale of Two Studies', paper presented at the International Conference on Colonialism to Globalisation: Five Centuries after Vasco da Gama, Delhi: Indian Social Institute, 2–6 February 1998.

Das Gupta, Malabika, *The Impact of Land Reforms on North East India*, Delhi: Omsons, 1991.

Dass, Bhagwan, 'Reservations Today and Tomorrow', in Walter Fernandes (ed.), *The Emerging Dalit Identity: The Re-Awakening of the Subalterns*, Delhi: Indian Social Institute, 1996, pp. 234–57.

Datta, Brijendranath, 'Ethnicity, Nationalism and Sub-Nationalism, With Special Reference to North-East India', in D. Pakem (ed.), op. cit., pp. 36–44.

de Sa, Fidelis, *Crisis in Chotanagpur*, Bangalore: Redemptorist, 1975.

Doley, D., 'Tribal Movements in the North Eastern Region', in K.S. Singh (ed.), *Antiquity to Modernity in Tribal India*, vol. IV: *Tribal Movements in India*, Delhi: Inter-India, 1998, pp. 14–49.

Dreze, Jean and Amartya Sen, *Hunger and Public Action*, Oxford: Clarendon Press, 1989.

Fernandes, Walter, 'Development-Induced Displacement in Eastern India', in S.C. Dube (ed.), *Antiquity and Modernity in Tribal India*, vol. I: *Continuity and Change Among Indian Tribals*, Delhi: Inter-India, 1998, pp. 217–300.

Fernandes, Walter, 'Conflict in North-East: A Historical Perspective', *Economic and Political Weekly*, vol. 34, no. 51, 18-24 December 1999, pp. 3579–82.

———, Geeta Menon and Philip Viegas, *Forests, Environment and Tribal Economy: Deforestation, Impoverishment and Marginalisation in Orissa*, Delhi: Indian Social Institute, 1988.

——— and S. Anthony Raj, *Development, Displacement and Rehabilitation in the Tribal Areas of Orissa*, Delhi: Indian Social Institute, 1992.

——— and Arundhati Roy Choudhury, 'Search for a Tribal Identity: The Dominant and the Subaltern', in Walter Fernandes (ed.), *The Indigenous Question: Search for an Identity*, Delhi: Indian Social Institute, 1993, pp. 9–22.

——— and Sanjay Barbora, *Modernisation and Women's Status in North Eastern India: A Comparative Study of Six Tribes*, Guwahati: North Eastern Social Research Centre, 2002.

Kurien, C.T., *Global Capitalism and the Indian Economy*, Delhi: Orient Longman, 1996.

Laya, *Land Alienation in Tribal Andhra Pradesh: A Preliminary Report*, Vishakhapatnam: Laya, 1998.

Mackenzie, A., *The North-East Frontier of India*, Delhi: Mittal, 1995.

Mander, Harsh, *Tribal Land Alienation in Madhya Pradesh: A Brief Review of Problem and The Efficacy of Legislative Remedies*, Bhopal: Government of Madhya Pradesh, 1998.

Marak, Caroline, 'Status of Women in Garo Culture', in Soumen Sen (ed.), *Women in Meghalaya*, Delhi: Omsons, 1997, pp. 56–72.

Mehta, Shalina, 'Tribal Movements in Himachal Pradesh and Jammu and Kashmir', in K.S. Singh (ed.), op. cit., pp. 149–71.

Menon, P.S.K. and Bakshi D. Sinha, *Panchayati Raj in Scheduled Areas*, Delhi: Concept, 2003.

Minz, Boniface, 'The Jharkhand Movement', in Walter Fernandes (ed.), *National Development and Tribal Deprivation*, Delhi: Indian Social Institute, 1992, pp. 345–71.

Munshi Saldanha, Indra, 'Customary Rights and Colonial Regulations: Thana Forests in the 19th Century', in Mrinal Miri (ed.), *Continuity and Change in Tribal Society*, Shimla: Indian Institute of Advanced Study, 1993, pp. 70-83.

Muricken, Jose, M.K. George, K.A. Emmanuel, Boban K. Jose and Prakash Pillai, *Development-Induced Displacement: Case of Kerala*, Jaipur: Rawat, 1993.

Pradhan, Manoj and William Stanley, *Land Alienation in the Tribal Areas of Orissa*, Bhubaneswar and Semiliguda: CPSW and WIDA, 1999.

Praharaj, Debebdra Mohan. *Tribal Movements and Political History in India: A Case Study from Orissa 1803-1949*, Delhi: Inter-India, 1988.

Ramanathan, Usha, 'Public Purpose: Points for Discussion', in Walter Fernandes (ed.), *The Land Acquisition (Amendment) Bill 1998*, Delhi: Indian Social Institute, 1999, pp. 19–24.

Rothermund, Dietmar, '500 Years of Colonialism', *Social Action*, vol. 42, no. 1, January–March 1992, pp. 1–15.

Roy, Ajay, *The Boro Imbroglio*, Guwahati: Spectrum, 1995.

Sanyu, Visier, *A History of Nagas and Nagaland: Dynamics of Traditional Village Formation*, Delhi: Commonwealth Publishers, 1996.

Sarkar, M.C., 'Customary Rights in Land and Forest of the Tribals of Chotanagpur-Santal-Parganas Region', in Mrinal Miri (ed.), op. cit., pp. 97–108.

Schverin, Detlef, 'The Control of Land and Labour in Chotanagpur, 1853-1948', in Dietmar Rothermund and D.C. Wadhwa (eds), *Zamindars, Mines and Peasants: Studies in the History of an Indian Coalfield and Its Rural Hinterland*, Delhi: Manohar, 1987, pp. 21–68.

Shah, Ghanshyam and Arjun Patel, 'Tribal Movements in Western India', in K.S. Singh (ed.), op. cit., pp. 172–204.

Shankardass, Rani Dhavan, *The First Congress Raj*, Delhi: Macmillan, 1982.

Sharma, B.D., *Tribal Development: The Concept and the Frame*, Delhi: Prachi, 1978.

Sharma, Barkataki Meena, *British Administration in North East India 1826–74*, Delhi: Mittal, 1985.

CHAPTER 4

The Policy of Reservations for Scheduled Tribes

BHUPINDER SINGH

The scriptures-ordained caste system of the Indian society has for centuries been responsible for the social discrimination, economic exploitation and moral degradation of the lower castes, notably the Shudras. Religious and social reformers have appeared on the Indian scene from time to time, but the impact of their teaching has not penetrated deep enough to liberate it adequately from these ills. So far as the Scheduled Tribes (ST) are concerned, their remote habitat may have occluded even their presence till the recent centuries. Straggler tribal groups or individual members of such groups were treated no better than Shudras. Early reformers like Jyotirao Phule and Narayana Guru did splendid welfare work among the depressed classes, particularly in the educational field. Their dedication to the cause of the oppressed people did not fail to move others of their own as well as succeeding generations.

THE COMMUNAL AWARD AND THE POONA ACCORD

Undivided Bombay and the southern states were the first to recognize the claim of representation for backward classes in public services. In 1906, the British Government introduced communal representation in the administration for Muslims, Sikhs and Anglo-Indians. It was only in 1919 that the Franchise Committee recognized the claim of the Depressed Classes as a separate entity, favouring their nomination, and the Government of India nominated one of their members to the Central Assembly. At about this time, Dr B.R. Ambedkar appeared on the political scene. His contribution to the cause of Scheduled Castes (SC) in general and reservations in the legislatures as well as public services in particular, was to come in the following decades.

From the beginning, Dr Ambedkar was of the view that the problem of the Depressed Classes was a political one. At the Round Table Conference in 1930, he was emphatic that the problem of the Depressed Classes was not merely a social one and that it could never be solved unless they got political power. As a result of his advocacy, the Conference decided in principle to treat the untouchables as a separate unit and to give them special representation in the future set-up of India. But the matter could not be finalized as the Indian National Congress did not participate in the first session of the Round Table Conference. In the second session held on 15 September 1931, as the sole representative of the Congress, M.K. Gandhi opposed special treatment for the untouchables, saying that their interests were as dear to the Congress as the interests of any other body or any other individual and, further, special representation in the legislatures was totally unnecessary. Nevertheless, the British Government recognized the untouchables as a separate entity and granted them, along with other minorities, separate electorates in the Communal Award announced by the British Prime Minister in 1932.

In September 1932, Gandhi resorted to a fast unto death against the Award. The result was the Gandhi–Ambedkar Poona Pact signed in 1932, in tune with which Gandhi conceded 'reservation of seats' for the Depressed Classes. He then went further. While the Communal Award allowed them 71 seats, the accord at Poona yielded 148 seats. In return, Dr Ambedkar gave up his insistence on separate electorates for the Depressed Classes and accepted what has remained the core of the present system of electoral safeguards: joint electorates with reserved seats. The terms of the Poona Pact were brought into effect by the British Government by incorporating them in the Government of India Act, 1935. The 1935 Act, therefore, for the first time provided political reservations to the Scheduled Castes, as the Depressed Classes came to be known under this act. Also, for the first time, the Scheduled Castes took part in the 1937 elections and participated in the government machinery. In 1942, Dr Ambedkar was appointed the Labour Member of the Viceroy's Executive Council. He secured 8.5 per cent reservations for the Scheduled Castes.

CONSTITUTIONAL PROVISIONS

In charting the course towards social, economic and political justice for all the citizens of the Indian Republic, the framers of the Constitution had to raise two sign-posts: one, for steps against continuation of inequality among equal people, for which purpose they inscribed provisions like equality of opportunity [clauses (1) and (2) of Article 16] and prohibition of discrimination on grounds of religion, race, caste, sex or place of birth [clauses (1) and (2) of Article 15]. The second sign-post was for favoured treatment of unequal people, i.e. depressed and disadvantaged people, towards which end was incorporated clause (4) in Article 16 and clause (4) in Article 15 as well as Articles 330 and 332. The principle of reservation flows out of the resolve to remove 'unjust, undeserved and unjustified inequalities' among people. Article 14 irradiates the majesty of equality before the law and equal protection of the laws of the land to all, having been designed to extend universal benign protection. Political reservations were conceived as a time-bound measure, subject to periodic appraisals. It seems that it was visualized that in free India, the Depressed Classes would be empowered to make rapid progress. Further, perhaps the Constitution framers wished individual self-reliance and entrepreneurship among them to develop apace. Expectations with regard to both having been inadequately fulfilled, political reservations have been extended from decade to decade. But the question remains moot as to whether the SCs and STs would have continued to remain the beneficiaries of the reservation policy had the reports of the Mandal Commission at the Centre and numerous commission/committees at the states level not spurred the respective ruling parties to enact the populist legislative devices of reservations for 'other backward classes' (OBCs), i.e. other than the SCs and STs. Thereafter, the OBCs acquired a vested interest in the reservation policy as it helped to consolidate their politico-economic clout. As a corollary, its continued application to the two Scheduled Classes became unquestionable. Nevertheless, in a way, the original concept of reservation as a prescription for the advancement of the really downtrodden SCs and STs stood hijacked.

POST-1950 FUNCTIONING OF RESERVATIONS FOR STs

A study of the post-1950 functioning of legislatures in India, at the state or central levels, is liable to convince a scholar that reservations for STs did create ST lobbies. The strength of the lobby has varied from state to state and from time to time. The educational level of the non-ST members of legislatures, generally speaking, has been lower than that of the ST legislators. The hiatus has been narrower in states such as Andhra Pradesh, Maharashtra and Gujarat, with the consequence that the ST lobby has been able to exert more pressure here than in states like Orissa and Madhya Pradesh, where the hiatus has been sharper. During the course of the author's experience of over four decades, it found that countrywide, the ST legislators have been less articulate than their non-ST peers. So much so that even when an ST MLA has risen to be minister, he has not asserted himself adequately and has been easily brow-beaten by his colleagues.

Now let us take the other ST institutions. The Tribes Advisory Councils (TAC) are the offspring of the Fifth Schedule of the Constitution. Despite the fact that not less than three-fourths of a TAC's total of not more than 20 members have to be representatives of the STs in the Legislative Assembly of the concerned state, no TAC can be credited with having conducted regular meetings. Initiatives for generating a positive record of safeguard and promotion of tribal interests, even those guaranteed in the Constitution, have not been many. Not many TACs can be identified, which courageously having taken up cudgels, have succeeded in combating (a) alienation of tribal land, (b) dispossession of forest and water resources, and (c) displacement. During my long stint in the tribal development field in the government, I did not come across proposals for strengthening TAC's constitutional sinews in case it felt itself ill equipped to protect tribal interests.

Secondly, in states having a sizeable ST population, there are the SC and ST Welfare Committees of the legislatures. At the Centre, Parliament has constituted one such committee. It makes valuable suggestions for looking after tribal interests and keeps the administration on its toes. There is need for closer scrutiny of their recommendations for action.

A third institution is the recently formed National Commission for the Scheduled Tribes, comprising a chairperson and four members. Under Article 338, its chief task is to make recommendations as to the steps that should be taken by the Union or any state for effective implementation of safeguards and other measures for the protection, welfare and socio-economic development of the STs. While inquiring into a specific complaint of deprivation of rights and safeguards, the Commission enjoys the powers of a civil court.

RESERVATIONS IN PANCHAYATS

An event of far-reaching importance relating to the basic law of the land has been an amendment in the Constitution to give a place to panchayats. Passed in December 1996, Article 243 mandates constitutional sanction to village, intermediate and district panchayats as the third tier of the federal structure, below the national and state tiers. It provides for reservation of seats for STs in panchayats. As per Clause 4(b) of Article 243M, Parliament enacted the Provisions of the Panchayats (Extension to Scheduled Areas) Act, PESA for short. In conformity with the recommendations of the report (1995) of the Committee of Members of Parliament and Experts, in the drafting of which the present writer played a major role, the Act calls upon the states to ensure that in the Scheduled Areas, the gram sabhas and the panchayats at the appropriate level are endowed, *inter alia*, with the power (a) of control over local plans and resources, (b) of ownership of minor forest produce, (c) to prevent alienation of land in Scheduled Areas, (d) to exercise control over money-lending, (e) of control over institutions and functionaries in all social sectors, (f) of identification or selection of beneficiaries of poverty alleviation and other programmes by the gram sabha, and (g) of certification of utilization of funds. Further, PESA contains the injunction that the state legislatures shall make laws (i) after prior consultation with gram sabhas or the panchayats at the appropriate level before proceeding with the acquisition of land in Scheduled Areas and before resettling or rehabilitating persons affected, and (ii) the laws are in consonance with the customary law, social and religious practices and traditional management practices of community resources. To cap it all, PESA calls for state legislations endowing 'Panchayats with powers and authority as may be necessary to enable them to function as institutions of self-government' and containing 'safeguards to ensure that Panchayats at the higher level do not assume the powers and authority of any Panchayat at the lower level or Gram Sabha'. Taken as a whole, one may describe its total design as a Magna Carta of democratic empowerment of the lower rungs of federal representative hierarchy. Even though it is still early, as expected, available accounts of the performance of the panchayats vary. Some show them in good light, the performance of others may be indifferent. The record may improve as the Gram Sabha and panchayat executives acquire experience and confidence. But an important factor here is how the political executive and the bureaucracy view the constitution-backed panchayats. Not with equanimity. For the state and district tiers have been noticed to perceive the new institutions as upstart sharers of their resources and patronage. It should cause no surprise to anyone that, in consequence, their interest lies in creating impediments and ensuring their dysfunction.

RESERVATIONS AND POLITICAL MORES

Reservations in legislatures and in panchayats may be the sheet anchor for the entry of STs, but political dynamics and governance paradigms are influenced, not inconsiderably, by the current mores in the larger society. Witness, for example, that in practice, the dominant political culture pervades even the new 'tribal states' like Chhattisgarh and Jharkhand.

Looking back, a couple of decades preceding Independence, the tribal communities in Central India brought forth Jaipal Singh, a leader the like of whom had not been witnessed since Birsa Munda of the late nineteenth and early twentieth centuries. Charismatic in appeal, he was essentially a product of the pre-1947 climes. Independence of mind and passionate devotion to the tribal cause characterize his speeches in the Constituent Assembly, leaving an indelible impression for posterity. Jaipal Singh inspired his followers towards the goal of a separate tribal state of Jharkhand. However, subsequently falling in line with post-Independence values, he capitulated to co-option in the then political monolith, the Indian National Congress. That he had been swept to power by a largely Jharkhand tribal electorate in a reserved seat acted as no deterrent.

It may be beyond the experience and even imagination of many of us that the administration can be so high-handed in its attitude towards the panchayats as in the Chhattisgarh case, which I will briefly narrate, based on a fairly reliable version. This happened in recent months in the Bastar district. The state administration had been interested in setting up a steel plant in the Gram Panchayat Nagarnar, gram sabhas of Amaguda, Kasturi and Maganpur. As mentioned earlier, under PESA, prior consultation with the Gram Panchayat is required. The concerned gram sabhas and gram panchayat in their meetings demurred and asked for time to consider the matter. Ignoring their views, the collector issued a notification under Section 4(1) of the Land Acquisition Act, 1894. It is alleged that in order to show compliance with the provisions of the Act and rules, the administrative authorities tampered with the gram sabha's records and fabricated false records. On the basis of the fabricated records, notification under Section 6 was also issued a month later by the collector. When the people protested against the illegalities, repression and terror were unleashed on them. Villagers refusing to accept the compensation invited the wrath of the administration.

The people lodged a complaint with the constitutionally-established SC & ST Commission. After an enquiry under Article 338, the Commission came to the conclusion that (i) the provisions of Section 4(1) of PESA regarding prior consultation with gram sabhas had not been followed; (ii) there were reasonable grounds to believe that official records had been tampered with and false records had been fabricated, attracting criminal liability; (iii) since the actions of the concerned officials denied the tribal people the protection of law concerning their lands, it also attracted the provisions of Section 3(v) of the SCs and STs (Prevention of Atrocities) Act, 1989. The Commission made the significant observation that 'scant regard has been shown to the principle of natural justice and the dignity of the Gram Sabhas which have the central position in all affairs at the village level in Scheduled Areas'. Copies of the findings were sent to the chief secretary to the Government of Chhattisgarh, the chairman-cum-director of the National Mineral Development Corporation (a public sector enterprise for whom the land was sought to be acquired), and the district collector, Bastar, 'for initiating necessary action'. Thus, action for justice has been entrusted to those in authority against whom allegations have been levelled.

This episode is symbolic. It is noteworthy that it occurred in the 'tribal state' of Chhattisgarh which was expected to be zealously protective of tribal interests. Secondly, it also highlights the limitation of the erstwhile National Commission for SCs and STs for, beyond forwarding copies of the report to the Government of Chhattisgarh, the collector of Bastar and other state officials, many of whom were alleged accomplices, it found itself powerless to initiate steps so that the appropriate authorities could proceed further in the matter. In a sense, the enquiry reached a *cul-de-sac*. That being the case, one feels that the tribal people and tribal representatives, as also guardian institutions like the Commission stand discounted. Even the rule of law has been contravened.

Where does redress lie? Law courts are, from the tribal point of view, inaccessible and dilatory. One is hesitant to suggest a measure that might contribute to multiplying institutions in a matrix already riddled with them. It is, however, tempting to advocate a totally autonomous watchdog authority at the central and state levels vested with adequate power and manned by independent and outstanding personalities. At the present moment, I would content myself with proposing that some thought be devoted to better arming the new ST Commission.

THE CREDIT SIDE

If I have tilted more on the shortcomings of political reservations, it is with a view to direct attention towards their reformation. But lest it be thought that the policy of reservations has nothing to its credit, I have much to add.

In the first instance, we need to acknowledge that the policy has enabled gifted men and women to rise in public life. In the political field, they have become members of state legislatures and Parliament. I have already spoken of Jaipal Singh. T. Sanganna of Orissa rose from an excise sub-inspector to become a state minister. In the last two decades, through the medium of reservations, the tribal communities have contributed Amar Singh Choudhury who became Chief Minister of Gujarat, Giridhar Gomango who became Chief Minister of Orissa, P.A. Sangma who did the STs proud by becoming the first minister of cabinet rank at the Centre, as also speaker of the Lok Sabha.

Three recent additions in the field of institutions have been: (i) a separate Ministry of Tribal Affairs at the centre with an ST minister of cabinet rank; (ii) the National Commission for Scheduled Tribes under Article 338, split from the erstwhile single National Commission for SCs and STs; and (iii) the creation under Article 339(1) in 2002 for a two-year term of the Second Commission for Scheduled Areas and Scheduled Tribes, entrusted with the task of projecting a vision for tribals for the coming decades, the first such Commission having placed such a blue-print before the nation in 1961.

There was also the singular instance when one ST vote in Parliament in 1999 brought down an elected government. Apart from these eminent personalities and institutions, the pressure of the ST lobby in the Parliament brought forth the Protection of Civil Rights Act, 1995 the Scheduled Castes and Scheduled Tribes (Prevention of Atrocities) Act, 1989; the Provision of Panchayat (Extension of Scheduled Areas) Act, 1996, and several other measures. That implementation of these enactments has not resonated with the spirit of their framers in the ST reserved lobby does not detract from their concern and perseverance. The establishment of the new states of Jharkhand and Chhattisgarh also testifies to their strength of purpose.

Those who have been a part of tribal development administration are so engrossed in efforts at tribal socio-economic improvement that they underrate the value of political reservations. But without political reservations, ST lobbies in legislatures would have been smaller or even non-existent, with the consequence that their influence would have been weaker. A further consequence would have been that the pace of development among tribals would have been even slower.

Sub-reservations

One matter which has sometimes figured in discussions in the sphere of reservations in public services, but which has seldom culminated in firm conclusions, is the skewed representation among ST legislators of different Scheduled Tribe communities in the country. It is well known that some tribal communities are comparatively advanced and others extremely backward, one obvious factor being their proximity to the rest of society in the case of the former and relative isolation in the case of the latter. Among the more than 400 officially recognized ST communities in India, 75 have been categorized by the Government of India as 'primitive', a term which not only does them socio-cultural injustice but seems also otherwise pejorative. Examples of differentially-developed ST communities are legion. Members of the more developed category may have the distinction of representing all the ST communities in their respective constituencies, including the less advanced and more backward communities. It is doubtful that the interests of the more disadvantaged are equally protected. It looks like the scenario in representation may persist for some time to come, long enough for the backward groups to rise in education and awareness. The issue is: is it possible to provide, without further delay, some opportunity to members of the second category? The answer may lie in sub-reservation. But one result of sub-reservation could be that so long as it lasts, ST representation in the concerned legislature may not be as vocal, strong and articulate as when members of the former communities only are voted in. Some tribal leaders fear that the proposal may dent pan-tribal unity. A balance has to be struck somewhere.

A CRITIQUE OF THE RESERVATION POLICY

Critics of reservation hold strong views: that the policy has been responsible for creating fissures in society; that it strikes at the concept of merit in democratic governance; that, in any event, reservations act as crutches and crutches are, in the long run, inimical to healthy growth. To an extent, there is substance in these arguments. More importantly, some prominent and successful members of tribal societies subscribe to them.

But, looked at from a different perspective, reservations have helped tribal growth and development. Not a few members of the earlier ST generations after Independence were products of Ashram schools, i.e. residential schools providing free education and upkeep for tribal students run by governments and NGOs and gained entry into the portals of legislatures through electoral reservations. Among many tribes, their example served as a trailblazer, inspiring generations, creating first ripples, then waves. But for reservations, many tribal societies would have remained stagnant even to this day.

As for fissures, the ancient caste system had already ensured a well-stratified general society. Electoral politics during the past five decades has contributed to its further fragmentation. As Justice Douglas pointed out in his Tagore Law lectures: 'The Supreme Court of India has struck . . . telling blows at attempts to divide the community among cases based on races, caste, or religion.' The part played by the higher judiciary in the reining in of runaway reservations has controlled the damage to an extent. If reservations for Scheduled Tribes has to share the blame, it may be in a small way and for a worthwhile cause.

The votaries of a meritocratic republic have a point in their favour. In the Indian context, it is conceivable that in the operation of the principle of reservations, merit and efficiency stand compromised to an extent in the short run. But we have to take a long-range holistic view. For the long term, the nation stands to gain in the elimination of weakness of any segment and emergence of a fully advanced society. In any case, the purpose would have been better served had the state and society paid adequate attention to providing to the unprivileged sections quality primary, secondary and tertiary education, beginning right after Independence. They would long ago have been prepared for the competitive world. This has been a serious lapse and should be tackled even now.

It is generally felt that the idea of reservation has become diluted, some would say vitiated, because of its populist expansion tendencies, beyond the 50 per cent limit prescribed by the Supreme Court in the *M.R. Balaji* v. *State of Mysore* (1963) case. It is lamentable that the public mind persists in the impression of the 50 per cent Rubicon, though the Court observed that while it is not possible to predicate the exact permissible percentage of reservations, it can be said in a general and broad way that they should be less than 50 per cent. Its concern was that the reservations should be limited so as not to be detrimental to the larger interest of society. The Court reiterated the same view in *D.N. Chanchala* v. *State of Mysore* (1971) stating that reservation for the weaker sections should ordinarily be less than 50 per cent although no firm percentage could be fixed and the actual reservation must depend upon the relevant prevailing circumstances in each case. The principle was followed by the Court in *Chakradhar* v. *State of Bihar* (1988). In any event, caution must be exercised against the whole falling short of the sum of its parts. This applies more to reservations in services, but the notice in general terms to the other types of reservations as well may not be irrelevant for the future.

THE BALANCE SHEET

There are two ways of looking at the balance sheet of reservations: first, from the point of view of the framers of the Constitution and second, from the point of view of the targetted beneficiaries. From what can be gleaned from the debates in the Constituent Assembly, it appears that the founding fathers, having such stalwarts among them as A.V. Thakkar, Jaipal Singh and J.J.M. Nichols Roy, were imbued more with idealistic impulses of empathy and advancement of the inarticulate tribals, and fearing their inability to put forward their case for representation, promoted the idea of reservations. Reservations seemed to present a means of drawing tribals into the orbit of the larger society and forging links between the two. Reservations would also hone the socio-political faculties of the tribal leadership on the one hand and facilitate their integration with society on the other. In fact, largely through the efforts of Dr Ambedkar, the principle and practice of reservations had already been established for the Scheduled Castes. It is not clear whether the framers were also aiming at implicit reiteration of the State's writ over the tribal areas implying explicit control over their abundant natural resources, like minerals, land, forests, water, though such underlying considerations cannot be ruled out. Prima facie, it did not seem necessary at that stage, for independent India had inherited all that was British and princely India. Further, except for the North-east, all other tribal areas lay passive and quiescent. It is no doubt recorded history that the British power's exercise of the doctrine of *res regius,* extending their control over forests, had met with stiff resistance from the central Indian tribes, since the doctrine was in conflict with the perceived tribal notion of forests as a common community resource, i.e. *res communis*, free of external interference. There were several uprisings against the colonial regime in the nineteenth century on this and other grounds and they were quelled with a heavy hand. Peace descended at the turn of the century and quite a few tribes took to education and constitutional means for the redress of their grievances as well as advancement.

In the foregoing context, the policy of reservations may be weighed on a scale that posits benefits accruing to tribals against what they have lost. In material terms, they have lost a lot. Since territorial occupation denotes rights over natural resources like land, forest, water and minerals found therein, the Indian State, earlier in colonial times through its imperial fiats and subsequently through cavalier measures, has encroached upon and appropriated a good part of the resources. The processes of dispossession, displacement and deprivation_continue. A large number of opportunities opening up with the harnessing of the plentiful natural resources of tribal areas have been usurped by non-tribals and outsiders, marginalizing the tribals economically as well as socially. Thus, so far, political empowerment has not translated adequately into socio-economic clout. On the contrary, association with the so-called mainstream has signalled the appearance on-stage of hegemonic segments in the tribals' midst. The reserved lobbies have been unable to address these concerns sufficiently. On the positive side, a larger share of the gains currently appears intangible. They lie mainly in the participation of tribal leadership in the political processes and, to a lesser extent, in the political discourse of civil society. Further, a number of young tribal men and women have been able to enter and make their mark in the political arena. The exercise of franchise in general, and in the reserved constituencies in particular, has been a good political training ground for the tribal communities. Of more tangible character have been reservations in the employment and educational sectors, leading them to professional fields: the aspirations of the tribal middle class have risen.

One event that appears to hold the potential to close the gap between political empowerment and economic improvement for the tribal people has been the passage of the 73rd and 74th Constitutional Amendments, leading to their insertion in the Constitution as Article 243, as well as the PESA Act cited earlier. However, three aspects need to be noted here. Firstly, the tribal communities are no strangers to self-governance; having lived in isolation for centuries, they were obliged to manage themselves and their affairs with their own informal, traditional, mainly unwritten devices. Secondly, since for the first time in the matter of governance, they will be having an interface with a formal, modern, settled bureaucratic administration, their apprehensions and misgivings are not misplaced. Thirdly, should the possibility of implementing fairly the constitutionally mandated grassroots three-tier panchayats materialize in its fullness, along with the requisite educational advancement, in the context of adequate powers of planned development as well as control over resources flowing from the PESA Act, there is reason to hope that tribals will register significant progress. Nevertheless, among the many ifs and buts punctuating this discourse, two more will have to be entered here. First, that over the decades and in diverse legislatures, the ST legislators seem to have distinguished themselves more in the matter of party loyalties than in upholding tribal interests. The consequence has been that tribal interests have been subordinated and sometimes even ignored. This may not be unexpected in a multi-party system of democracy. But the case of tribals should be considered on a different footing. Much more than for any other segment, severe economic competition puts a question mark on the survival of individual tribals, calling for introspection of political ethos. Second, no tribal leader can be unaware that the approximately 400 Scheduled Tribe communities are not only hugely diverse in character but are also very tenuously bound to each other. Comparisons may be drawn between the north-eastern and the central Indian tribes. This casts a special responsibility on the tribal leadership of the various communities to band together for the common purpose of preserving and promoting tribal interests.

Political reservations have been beneficial, but they still have some way to go. Reservations in the services and educational institutions complement political reservations. Planned socio-economic development may further help. But the goal of catching up with the modern world is still distant. It can become attainable only if there is a conscious realization among members of tribes that they must help themselves.

CHAPTER 5

Electoral Reservations for Scheduled Tribes: The Legitimization of Domination

VIRGINIUS XAXA

Groups and communities identified as tribes during the British rule had been at different levels of polity formation prior to the coming of the British. A large number of tribes had a village council only. Some of them coupled it with the institution of chieftainship, which was broadly of two types. Either the chiefs could not go against the will of the village councils, or they were all-powerful and autocratic. In some cases, villages formed confederations under a chief, known as 'raja' or such similar names. In a few cases, tribes had even evolved into principality/kingdoms and had a form of centralized authority structure.

The British brought these diverse tribes under one political structure. They had earlier done the same with the dominant and larger Indian population. Following this, a process of integration of the tribes with the larger social system was set in motion. Tribes/tribal areas began to be integrated not only with the uniform civil law and administration of the British rule but also with the land, credit and labour markets. This had devastating consequences, leading to a series of revolts and rebellions in different parts of the country. It is against this backdrop that the British initiative for a tribal system of administration, which was somewhat different from that of the larger Indian population, should be seen. Such an arrangement did provide some space, although limited, for tribes to be governed by their own traditions and customary practices. To this extent tribes had some autonomy even under the colonial administration. It is a different matter that such autonomy had much more to do with political expediency than with a genuine interest in protecting the tribal people.

Notwithstanding the fact of British subjugation, the general Indian population did succeed in carving out a limited share of power towards self-rule and governance in the form of some control over the colonial state. Tribes remained outside such decision-making bodies and processes, largely due to the policy of the colonial government. It was the considered view of the colonial government that tribes were not politically ready to represent themselves and their interests. Hence, instead of facilitating their integration into State power, they were excluded from it. Laws, rules and regulations formulated by the State for the general population were not applicable to tribes. In addition, regulations and special administrative measures were worked out, which aimed at preventing tribes from social interaction with non-tribes. In this sense the British followed a policy of isolation where the tribes were concerned. However, the process of integration that was set in motion continued unabated, with varying pace, scale and intensity in the tribal areas.

RESERVATION IN PARLIAMENT AND STATE LEGISLATURES

As observed earlier, though tribes were brought under one single political authority, they had almost no role in regulating and influencing this larger political authority. It is only after Independence that tribes were given the space to participate in the State structure of the Indian society into which they had already been drawn during colonial rule. Until then, their integration with the State and society at large was through such means as law and administration, land and revenue settlement, roads and railways and trade and commerce. Their political, social and cultural integration was conspicuous by its absence. Hence, the general thrust of orientation in respect of the tribal population in the post-Independence era has been one of integration into the domains referred to above. At least this seems to be the general ethos of the Indian Constitution if one carefully examines the provisions for the tribes laid down therein. It is a different matter that the actual policy and practice pursued has been one of assimilation. It is important to note that till date there has been no formal statement of policy for tribes in India.

Many provisions have been made in the Indian Constitution for protecting and promoting the interests of the tribal population. One such provision is reservations, which has been provided in the domain of politics (Parliament and state legislatures), employment (government and semi-government sector) and education (especially in the institutions of higher education and learning). A lot has been written on reservations in educational institutions and employment, especially regarding issues such as the merits and demerits of the reservation policy, the implications for building a casteless and classless society and aspects of implementation in different segments of the State and State-sponsored institutions. In all these concerns regarding the reservation policy, the specificity of reservations in the political domain has somehow remained unexplored and unexamined.

The constitutional provision of reservations for the Scheduled Tribes and Scheduled Castes in Parliament and the state legislatures was initially made for a period of 10 years.[1] It has been extended for a further 10-year term after expiry of each period. The last extension was in October 1999.

LOCAL GOVERNANCE AND RESERVATION: PRE-73RD AMENDMENT

Reservations for the Scheduled Tribes as for the Scheduled Castes in Parliament and state legislatures is a constitutional obligation. However, no such stipulation was attached when local self-government institutions were introduced in the country. It was left to the states to enact laws and regulations, as they deemed fit. The result was that hardly any state in India, with the exception of Maharashtra, made provisions for reservations for Scheduled Castes and Scheduled Tribes in local self-governing institutions. Some states did it much later, through amendments to their Panchayati Raj Institutions acts. The provisions made were, however, far from uniform.

In Assam, as per the Act enacted in 1986, there was provision for representation of SCs/STs in gram panchayats (i.e. village councils) if they formed less than 33.33 per cent of the local population. In case the SC/ST population was more than 33.33 per cent, then the gram panchayat president and *anchalik*[2] panchayat member as also the anchalik pradhan were to be elected from amongst SCs /STs (RGF, 2000: 158; Thapliyal, 1999: 79). The provision of reservation in this case is not separate for SCs and STs. Rather the two categories are combined for the purpose of extending reservation to them. In Andhra Pradesh 6 per cent reservation was provided in offices to STs as against 15 per cent for SCs, both at the level of district and mandal parishads.

For the office of sarpanch, 15 per cent reservation was provided for the SCs. In the case of the STs, 6 per cent reservation was provided if the office of sarpanch held by the tribes in scheduled areas and other areas together fell short of 6 per cent of the total (Subrahmanyam et al., 1995: 3–4). At the gram panchayat level, reservation for SCs/STs was decided on the basis of their population, subject to a minimum of one seat in all panchayats where their combined population was not more than 50 per cent of the total population. No reservation was provided in villages where their combined population was more than 50 per cent. In Tripura, under the Tripura Panchayati Raj Act, 1983, provision was made for the representation of SCs and STs in the gram panchayats, but there was no mandatory provision for women's representation (Dutta, 1999: 758). In Madhya Pradesh (MP) and Uttar Pradesh (UP), statutory provisions for representation of SCs, STs and women in village panchayats were made in 1988 (Jain, 1999: 810; Vithal, 1999: 394). In Karnataka, reservation in proportion to SC/ST population was provided only at the district level. In Gujarat also there was provision for representation at the taluka and district panchayat levels (Durgaprasad et al., 1995: 44–5). In some states like Rajasthan and Himachal Pradesh there were no reservations, but a provision for co-option. In Rajasthan, one person each from SC and ST categories was co-opted if the category was not represented among sarpanchs at the samiti panchayat, and it was the same for the zilla parishads, if their population was 50 per cent of the total or more (Srivastava 1995: 642–3). In Himachal Pradesh, provision for co-option of one or two SC/ST members existed at the village and samiti panchayat levels. At the latter level, the co-option seems to be confined to the SCs alone (Reddi, 1999: 261–2).

Other states also took initiatives in this direction but they all came close to the enactment of the 73rd Constitutional Amendment in 1992. In Orissa, the reservation was extended to SCs and STs in the gram panchayats in proportion to their population at the ward level only since 1991 (RGF, 2000; Meher, 2001). In West Bengal, the 1992 Amendment of the State Act provided for reservation in all tiers, in proportion to the percentage of the population in the area. Rajasthan and Bihar also made provisions but in these states reservation was yet to be implemented when the 73rd Constitutional Amendment Act was passed.

PROVISION OF RESERVATIONS UNDER THE 73RD AMENDMENT

There is little information as to how the provision of reservations before the 73rd Amendment came to be implemented. One of the reasons may be that institutions of local self-government had become almost defunct in many of the states by the time reservations began to be introduced. Often representation of STs was ensured through co-option or nomination. In this sense, the 73rd Amendment 1992 and the Panchayat Act (Extension to Scheduled Areas), 1996 are a revolutionary shift from the past.

The 73rd Amendment makes the reservation of seats for SCs, STs and women in the Panchayati Raj Institutions mandatory. What is more, it also provides for reservations both at the level of seats and at the level of offices. The reservation of seats in these bodies is provided in proportion to the respective size of the population of the SCs and STs in the concerned areas. Such seats are to be allotted by rotation to different constituencies in a panchayat. Further, one-third of the seats from within all categories (i.e. SCs, STs, general) are to be reserved for women. As for the offices, which are stipulated in the form of chair of locally elected Assemblies at different levels, the reservation is provided at each level in proportion of the size of population of the SCs and STs to the total population of the state [The Constitution (73rd Amendment) Act, 1992].

As stated earlier, provisions made under these two Acts were constitutionally binding. Hence, those states which had not provided for reservations in their earlier acts, were not only obliged to make provisions for the same, but also do so in conformity with the stipulations of the 73rd Amendment. As regards the states that already had such a provision at some level before the 73rd Amendment, measures were taken to revamp reservations in conformity with the provisions.

THE 73RD AMENDMENT AND STATE ENACTMENTS

In all states, enactments have been passed in conformity with the 73rd Amendment and reservations for STs and others in all three tiers of the Panchayati Raj Institutions (PRI) have been provided for. However, there have been some variations, both with respect to provisions and to modes of operation/implementation. And this is so in reference to both seats and offices. Broadly speaking, there are two patterns. One, states that have exactly followed the provisions laid down in the 73rd Amendment—no more, no less. The majority of states fall in this category. In these states the number of reserved seats is determined on the basis of the SC/ST population in the area. Such seats are allotted by rotation to different constituencies in the respective tiers. One-third of seats so reserved are further reserved for women of that category. Office is confined to that of a chairperson at each level, and reservation in each is provided in direct proportion of the size of the SC and ST population to the total population of the state.

Two, some states have worked out the implementation of reservations somewhat differently. In MP for example, while seat reservation is in accordance with Article 243D, in the case of chairpersons, the post of block sarpanch is reserved in proportion to the SC/ST population within the block and similarly the post of president of janpad panchayats, in proportion to their population in the district. Only in the case of zilla panchayat presidents are reservations in proportion to SC/ST population in the state. This has resulted in certain unevenness in the number of such positions reserved at different levels. The benefit of such unevenness has gone in favour of the STs. On the basis of the above criteria, the posts earmarked for the SCs and STs stand respectively at 14.62 and 29.20 per cent in the gram panchayats, 13.94 and 32.03 per cent in the janpad and 15.5 and 23.27 per cent in the district panchayats (RGF, 2000). In making the provisions referred to above, the state of MP does provide certain advantages to the tribal communities. In addition to the reservation for the chairperson's post, the state law requires that where the panchayat chairperson is not an SC, ST or OBC, the vice-chairperson must be chosen from one of these categories. One-third of seats and chairpersons' posts are reserved for women in all these categories. The law provides for selecting posts for reservation by draw of lots. It should also to be noted that in the case of panchayat seats, the rotation of SC, ST reservation has been removed by an amendment in March 1999 (RGF, 2000).

In Maharashtra, the provision is largely in conformity with the provisions of the 73rd Amendment. Yet, there are some variations in the way these are being implemented, especially with respect to posts. The state follows a system of rotation by lots for deciding the reserved categories in the posts or offices. For example, though the reservation is for the full term of the panchayat in a village panchayat, it is not the same in the case of panchayat samitis and zilla parishads, where reservation is for a period of one year only. On completion of the year the post goes to another category by rotation (RGF, 2000: 143).

The 73rd Amendment requires that reservations be provided for the office of the chairperson of locally elected bodies. The Amendment does not provide for the post of vice-chairperson. Yet some states have made a provision for the post in all three tiers in their respective state laws. In West Bengal, for example, the Amendment in 1994 provided for reservations for the office of both chairperson and vice-chairperson in all three tiers of the PRIs. Further, as in the case of chairperson, so also in the case of deputy chairperson, reservations are implemented on a rotation basis. The rotation system stipulates that if the post of pradhan at the gram panchayat level is reserved, then the post of deputy stays open and vice versa. This system is followed in all three tiers. The enactment in Orissa also makes provisions for the post of vice-chairperson in all three tiers of the panchayat. However, unlike West Bengal there is no reservation as such for this post, except that in the event of the gram panchayat sarpanch not being a woman, the naib (deputy) sarpanch position will be deemed to be reserved for women. Similar provisions exist at the levels of zilla and samiti panchayat (Rao, 1999: 561).

THE WORKING AND IMPACT OF RESERVATIONS

Reservation in Parliament and the state legislatures has been in force for over five decades. One cannot say the same with regard to the PRIs. In the new form in which reservation in local self-governing bodies has become constitutionally mandatory, the institution has been in operation for only about 10 years.[3] Hence, in keeping with this Amendment, the states either drew up new Acts or made the necessary amendments to acts that were already operative. In the case of the tribal population, these state Acts were in force only in areas that were outside the purview of the Fifth and Sixth Schedules. The Sixth Schedule areas make provision for the establishment of an autonomous district council for the purpose of local governance. There has been no such provision for local governance in the Fifth Schedule areas. At the same time, the 73rd Constitutional Amendment exempts the Fifth Schedule areas from the mandatory provisions of Part IX of the Constitution with the hope that these areas could be left free to either evolve their own system of self-government or to continue with traditional panchayats or similar bodies. Accordingly, the provision of the Panchayats (Extension to the Scheduled Areas) Act, 1996 came into force in the Fifth Schedule areas from December 1996.

It is worthwhile then to take stock of the gains and losses that have accrued to the tribes from this measure. Such an assessment could be made in terms of gain and loss to the Indian State or the unity of India on the one hand and to the tribes on the other.

Had there been no policy of reservation for tribes, would they have been able to represent themselves? It is unlikely, at least in the earlier phase of electoral politics. The participation of tribals in the freedom struggle through involvement in the activities of political parties was marginal if not rare. Neither would there have been a serious and systematic effort to recruit tribals into party cadres. It was only due to the constitutional compulsion of reservations that most political parties were constrained to build their cadres from within the tribes. And even then, the tribals have on the whole been excluded from holding important party positions. This situation cuts across all party lines, regardless of their persuasion.

Interestingly, this attitude is not confined to political parties alone, but is present in organizations like trade unions as well. For instance, the tea garden labour force in West Bengal and Assam is comprised primarily of tribals.[4] At present there are a large number of trade unions affiliated to various political parties that have been working among the tea garden population. Yet the leadership of the trade unions, even at the block level, has always remained in the hands of people from outside the tribes and outside of the labour force. It is only in very recent years that one can see some shift in the social composition of the trade union leadership in the tea gardens of Assam and Bengal. But again, this shift has only been at the local level. The scenario is similar in the case of political parties. Had there not been obligation of political reservation, the tribals would have by and large been represented by non-tribals.

This is not to say that only tribals can represent tribal interests. Even non-tribals can do so and probably do it more effectively than the tribals because of their better articulation, networking and capacity to mobilize and maneuver. More often than not, however, there has been a wedge (social, political, economic, and cultural) between tribes and non-tribes and the interests of tribes have often been sacrificed in the interest of others or in the general interest. At least that is the history of reservations for tribes over the last 50 years. There is not one single political party that has produced leadership of a national stature from within the tribes. It is doubtful if the majority of national parties can make such a claim even at a regional level.

If this is the scenario after 50 years of reservations, one can well imagine what would have happened had there been no reservations. There are two possibilities. There may have been an intense and widespread demand for separation from India among the north-eastern tribes, especially those with a sizeable population and a higher level of development. The fact that the Indian State has been able to contain such demands on the part of tribes has partly to do with the policy of reservation in politics as well as other domains. At the same time, it is worth noting that despite the provision of reservations, the integration of tribes from the region with the so-called mainstream has been extremely weak and tenuous. Elsewhere in the country, despite increasing geographical, political and economic integration, the emotional integration of tribes with the rest of the population has been far from smooth. This has been largely due to the economic and political subjugation of tribes by non-tribes. The emotional alienation especially of the emerging middle class from within the tribal society has been partly alleviated by reservation.

The Indian State made a big gain in another sense—for in extending political reservations, it also legitimized its rule over the tribes, especially over their lands and resources. Without the provision of reservations, total State control over the tribes' resources would have looked more like plundering. Industries, dams, hydraulic projects have been set up in tribal areas. Minerals and forests therein have been exploited. Yet the resultant benefits have not gone to the tribes. Rather it has led to their displacement and impoverishment. In fact, a larger proportion of tribal people live below the poverty line than any other social category in India. The number of tribal people living below the poverty line in rural areas in 1993–4 was as high as 51.9 per cent as against 37.3 per cent for the general population. As for people affected by displacement, up to 40 per cent of the tribal population is affected, as per Planning Commission figures (Planning Commission, 2000). Tribes then have lost much more than they have gained from the reservations extended to them.

The extension of reservations enabled tribes to share and participate in the State decision-making process. However, one wonders if their participation in Parliament and the state legislatures has not been merely formal and symbolic. Have they made any contribution in terms of raising questions and participating in the debates on issues or enactments? In the event they did, has their contribution been effective and substantive? It is somewhat difficult to offer definitive answers on these fronts, but whatever information and accounts we have of tribal parliamentarians and legislators invariably suggest the contrary.

Besides that, one could also pose a question regarding the extent of the tribal legislators' ability to effectively address and articulate the interests and problems of the tribes—whether pertaining to tribes as a whole, tribes of a given region/constituency, or a specific group/community. Have they been able to initiate and pursue a single bill towards the welfare and protection of the tribes and the promotion of their interests? Have they been able to stall any bill or project that had the potential to adversely affect the tribes? If such projects (Narmada, Netarhat Field and Firing, Koel Karo projects, etc.) have been stalled at all, it has been due more to peoples' mobilization than to any political initiative on the part of the legislators.

Various factors are responsible for this. The principal factor is the size of the tribal population. The share of 7.5 per cent seats in Parliament or the state legislatures is hardly significant where decisions are made on the basis of a majority vote. Even on issues that have adversely affected the tribes, such as displacement and land alienation, tribes could hardly have altered the situation because of their small demographic weight in Parliament and the legislatures. Tribes invariably have to sacrifice their own welfare and interests for the sake of national development or the general good of the people. There has been yet another factor, emerging from the morphology of the tribal society in India. The category called 'tribes' comprises over

400 distinct communities. They inhabit different parts of the country, possess different physical features, speak different languages and are at different levels of development. Hence, there is a problem of unity and cohesiveness among them and even among their political representatives. In the absence of unity, they are unable to act as a cohesive force in protecting and promoting the interests of all tribal communities. Besides, electoral politics invariably occurs along political party lines. The fragmentation of tribes according to party loyalty and ideology has often been counterproductive to the collective interests of the tribes (Xaxa, 2001).

Have there then been no benefits or gains arising from the policy of reservation in politics? There have surely been some, but not in the area of protecting the tribes' interests regarding lands, forests and other resources. For the tribes the gains from political reservation have been in another direction—that of expanding the catchments of tribal leadership. Electoral politics has raised a new, young and modern leadership in place of the old, traditional leadership. There has also been a circulation of leadership in the form of parliamentarians and state legislators. Individual legislators have been able to make gains both in terms of prestige and status on the one hand and material benefits on the other, although the material gains have been of a very limited nature. Their role as parliamentarians and legislators has expanded their knowledge and understanding of how the larger political system and politics work. They have been able to extend some benefits to members of their community/constituency by initiating some small and micro development projects or infrastructure facilities in the constituency. Of course, their support has generally not moved beyond the ethnic or religious community of which they are members. It is worth noting that there is hardly a constituency which is inhabited by a single community. Often tribal elected representatives forget this and tend to focus on their own community.

On the whole, reservations did not contribute much towards the protection of the interests of the tribes, even though they did serve some kind of purpose both for the State and for the tribes. For the State, it was a way to integrate tribes with its institutions and the larger Indian society. Indeed, this has been the avowed objective of the Indian State in regard to tribes in the post-Independence era. In this the Indian State has been fairly successful. For tribes, the consequence of political reservations has been the heightening of their political consciousness and aspirations. It is very doubtful that tribes in India, excepting perhaps those from the north-east, would have had such consciousness and aspirations had there been no reservations for them. Even after they entered political organizations as a result of the reservations policy, they suffered discrimination and domination. This led to a further sharpening of the tribals' desire for a greater share of power and control in determining their own life and destiny.

The emergence of regional political parties like the All People Hill Leaders Conference in erstwhile Assam, the Jharkhand Party in the adjoining districts of Bengal, Bihar, Orissa and the Gondwana Raj Party in Andhra Pradesh and Madhya Pradesh must be viewed in this context. With the formation of these political parties, there has been an increase in political consciousness and a demand for a greater share not only of political power (in the form of demands for statehood and autonomy) but also in employment, development benefits and even control over land, forests and other resources. Indeed the Panchayat Act, 1996 emerged out of this process—of this greater awakening and consciousness among tribes with respect to protection of their lands, forests, water and other resources.

Reservations in politics have been helpful to the tribes in another sense. It is an established fact that electoral politics require considerable material resources. Tribals in general lack such resources and would have been unable to compete with the non-tribals if there had been no provisions for reservations. This explains why electoral campaigns in tribal areas have generally been on a low key. Elections have been on the whole smooth, possibly also fair as stories of booth capturing are quite rare.

THE WORKING OF RESERVATIONS AT THE LOCAL LEVEL

Now the question is—how have reservations in the PRIs worked so far? They have been in force for too short a time to ascertain their exact working and consequences. One needs a great deal of field data before saying something concrete and definite on the matter. As of today, the data is either not forthcoming or extremely sketchy, as the process has only just begun and is in its infancy still.

Access of people from the weaker sections of society, including the tribals, to the rural power structure, has enlarged the social base of the PRIs. The experience prior to the 73rd Amendment has shown that the members of the dominant communities had control over the local power structure. Reservations have made the PRIs representative of the village community. Examples from a couple of states may not be altogether out of place here. In MP, following the election under the new act, 269 STs became members of the district panchayat, 2,737 of the janpad and 1,32,503 of the gram panchayat (Prasad et al., 1995: 158). In Rajasthan, the share of tribes stood at 154 at zilla panchayat, 804 at panchayat samiti, and 15,616 at the gram panchayat levels. Their share in the office of the chairperson stood at 6, 36 and 985 respectively in the zilla panchayat, panchayat samiti and gram panchayat (Srivastava and Sikligar, 1995: 245–6).

However, to understand how this system has been working, one could perhaps start with the reports that have been coming in. A number of problems have been encountered during implementation. These are structural and psychological. The lack of formal education and unfamiliarity with the structure, rules and regulations of panchayat institutions worked against people benefitting from reservations. Then there were men belonging to dominant social groups who refused to give any proper credence to the opinion of men and women from the SC/ST category. In the case of women, the handicaps were thus twofold. The non-cooperation of officials was another of the system's built-in depressants. In short, two factors have prevented SCs/STs from assuming their new responsibilities: (1) vested interests that do not allow them to discharge their duties; (2) their own ignorance of the system and powers assigned to them as most of them are first-generation entrants to politics (Rao, 1999: 580; Nayak 2001; Meher 2001).

A few cases are illuminating in the context. In Pilkod Panchayat of Jalgaon district in Maharashtra, a Koli woman from the ST category held the post of sarpanch. She was poor and illiterate and so was her husband. The two dominant groups in the village, viz., Malis and Marathas each tried to take advantage of the situation. In the process, the rivalry between the two so intensified that there was hardly any social intercourse between them. The gram sevak (secretary of the village assembly) also took advantage of the situation and misappropriated a few lakhs from the funds reserved under some of the project heads. Being illiterate and ignorant, the sarpanch was pressurized on some ground or the other to put her thumb impression on cheques and other documents (Baviskar, 2001).

Reservations have led to an increase in atrocities against SCs and STs. Some information is available on this aspect, especially with respect to women from these categories. Mishri Devi, an ST sarpanch was stripped while unfurling the national flag on 15 August 1998 at Thikari Gram Panchayat in Dausa district of Rajasthan (Nayak, 2001). Draupadi Bai, a ST woman panchayat member of Salheona village in Raigarh district (today in the new state of Chhattisgarh) was reportedly stripped in front of the Sariya block development officer in November 1995 (Mathew and Nayak 1996: 1766–7).

Where disputes exist between tribals and non-tribals over land and other resources, the provision of reservations has further intensified the conflict. An incident in Andhra Pradesh is a pointer in this direction. The extension of the act has led to a dispute over the number of mandal parishads to be reserved for the Scheduled Tribes, leading to the filing of a case by the tribes in the High Court. The government had provided for the reservation of 33 mandal parishad seats for the tribals. The tribals, on the other hand, made claims for 44 mandal parishad seats. The plea of the tribals is that under the 73rd Amendment, the state has no power to pass any law with respect to the panchayats in scheduled areas. They have also pleaded that there has been a large influx of non-tribals in the scheduled areas, leading to large-scale alienation of lands from tribals, despite protective legislation to the contrary. The result is a reduction in the size of the tribal population and hence the number of mandal parishads under their control (Sarumathy, 1999: 49–50).

Reservations have been significant for tribes in another respect. Although women in tribal society enjoy considerable freedom over a range of matters, they traditionally had a negligible place in the decision-making process pertaining to the public domain. The extension of reservations for women has dramatically changed this scenario. In fact, their participation has been much more than that stipulated in the enactment. The data from two states are a pointer to this. In Karnataka, out of 47 ST elected members at the zilla parishad level, 46.8 per cent were women, as against 38 per cent for SCs and

35.4 per cent for the general population. At the panchayat samiti level, their share was as high as 61.5 per cent as against 43.41 for SCs and 36.95 for the general population. In the gram panchayat, their share was as high as 78 per cent as against 41 per cent for SCs (Jayalakshmi, 1999: 321–24). The scenario in Himachal Pradesh was similar. All 120 gram pradhan posts reserved for tribes were held by women as against 152 out of 503 for the SCs. And so was the case with panchayat samiti chairpersons. That is, all 3 posts earmarked for tribes were held by women, as against 6 out of 14 among SCs (Reddi, 1999: 265–7).

CONCLUSION

Reservations were extended to tribals with a view to integrating them in the so-called mainstream of Indian life. In this, the Indian State has been greatly successful. The tribes have also made some gains, not so much in the direction of protecting their rights over land, forests and other resources, or in making a substantive contribution to the decision-making process, but in the direction of raising the political aspirations of the tribal people. Political empowerment has been the major gain of reservations in politics. This was not an intended outcome, but arose as an unintended consequence. Indeed provisions laid down through the 73rd Amendment and the Panchayat Act, 1996, especially the latter, have been the outcome of this process of political empowerment at work among the tribes. It is not at all surprising that the implementation of the provisions in those Acts has led to intense conflict and tension between tribals and non-tribals at the grass-roots level of politics. In short, unlike in the pre-Independence era when tribals were thought to be incapable of representing themselves, today they have reached a stage where they are not only able to represent their interests, but are probably able to do so even without the provision of reservations.

NOTES

1. There has been no such time frame in the case of reservations in employment and educational institutions, though this misconception prevails.

2. The designation of local units of administration, especially at the intermediate level, that is, between village and district, varies from state to state. The village, the basic unit of local self-government is called *gram* in most of the states and so is the case with the district, which is called *zilla*. The intermediary level, viz., the block is called *janpad* (in Madhya Pradesh), *anchal* (in Assam and West Bengal), *mandal* (in Andhra Pradesh), *taluka* (in Gujarat and Maharashtra), *samiti* (in Rajasthan). To add to the confusion, elected assemblies at all three levels may be called panchayat, samiti or parishad. Lastly the chairperson of a locally elected assembly may be called *pradhan* or *sarpanch*.
3. The 73rd Constitution Amendment Act came into effect from 24 April 1993.
4. It is a different matter that the ST status has not been accorded to the tea garden labour in Assam.

REFERENCES

Baviskar, B.S., 'Outline of a Study in Maharashtra', paper presented at a workshop on 'Inclusion of Excluded Communities Through Panchayati Raj', ISS, June 2001.

Choudhury, R.C. and S.P. Jain (eds), *Patterns of Decentralized Governance in Rural India*, 2 vols., Hyderabad: NIRD, 1999.

Durgaprasad, P. et al., 'Panchayati Raj Institutions in Gujarat', *Panchayati Raj Institutions in India. An Appraisal*, Hyderabad: NIRD, 1995.

Dutta, S.K., 'Tripura', in R.C. Choudhury and S.P. Jain (eds), op. cit., vol. 2, Hyderabad: NIRD, 1999.

Jain, S.P., 'Uttar Pradesh', in R.C. Choudhury and S.P. Jain (eds), ibid., vol. 2.

Jayalaksmi, 'Karnataka', in R.C. Choudhuri and S.P. Jain (eds), ibid., vol. 1, Hyderabad: NIRD, 1999.

Mathew, G. and R.C. Nayak, 'Panchayats at Work', *Economic and Political Weekly*, vol. XXXI, no. 27, 1996.

Meher, R., 'Panchayati Raj in Orissa', paper presented at the workshop on 'Inclusion of Excluded Communities through Panchayati Raj', ISS, June 2001.

Nayak, R.C., 'Panchayati Raj in Rajasthan', paper presented at the workshop on 'Inclusion of Excluded Communities through Panchayati Raj', ISS, June 2001.

NIRD, *Panchayati Raj Institutions in India: An Appraisal*, Hyderabad, 1995.

Planning Commission, *Tribes in India* (A Data Sheet), 2000.

Prasad, et al., 'Panchayati Raj Institutions in Madhya Pradesh', in NIRD, op. cit., 1995.

Rajiv Gandhi Foundation (RGF), *Panchayati Raj in India—Status Report 1999*, 2000.

Rao, Y. Bhaskar, 'Orissa', in R.C. Choudhury and S.P. Jain (eds), op. cit. vol. 2.

Reddi, R.G., 'Himachal Pradesh', in R.C. Choudhury and S.P. Jain (eds), op. cit., vol. 1.

Sarumathy, M., 'Tamil Nadu', in R.C. Choudhury and S.P. Jain (eds), op. cit., vol. 2.

Srivastava, K.B., 'Rajasthan', in R.C. Choudhury and S.P. Jain (eds), op. cit., vol. 2.

Srivastava, K.B. and P.C. Sikligar, 'Panchayati Raj Institutions in Rajasthan', in NIRD, op. cit., 1995.

Subrahmanyam, K.S. and R. Murugesan, 'An Appraisal of Panchayat Raj in Andhra Pradesh', in NIRD, op. cit., 1995.

Thapiliyal, B.K., 'Assam' in R.C. Choudhury and S.P. Jain (eds), op. cit., vol. 1.

The Constitution (Seventy-Third Amendment) Act, 1992.

Vithal, C.P., 'Madhya Pradesh', in R.C. Choudhury and S.P. Jain (eds), op. cit., vol. 1.

Xaxa, Virginius, 'Protective Discrimination: Why Scheduled Tribes Lag behind Scheduled Castes', *Economic and Political Weekly*, vol. XXXVI, no. 21, 2001.

CHAPTER 6

Empowered without Reservations: OBCs in Uttar Pradesh and Bihar

MEENAKSHI JAIN

Caste has been accepted by the modern Indian State as the principal criterion for identifying communities entitled to preferential treatment, despite the lack of consensus regarding the nature of caste itself. The 1950 constitutional directive prescribing measures for the upliftment of the socially and educationally backward classes did not use the word caste. However, two centrally constituted commissions relied mainly on caste as the indice for measuring backwardness. Indeed, the Constitution itself also implied caste when it referred to class, as subsequently clarified by Dr Ambedkar: 'what are called backward classes are . . . nothing else but a collection of certain castes' (Dirks, 2002: 281).

Even before Independence, Mysore, Bombay and Madras had defined backwardness exclusively on grounds of caste. Mysore, in 1921, classified as backward all castes other than Brahmins; and Bombay, in 1925, all except 'Brahmins, Prabhus, Marwaris, Parsis, Banias and Christians'. The Justice Party, founded in the Madras Presidency in 1916, too, focussed on caste as the principal factor determining status (Dirks, 2002: 282). In 1918, Brahmins in the Madras Presidency comprised about 20 per cent of the wealthiest urban inhabitants and 15 per cent of the rural rich (Washbrook, 1989: 211–12), yet the prosperous and numerically preponderant non-Brahmin castes demanded compensatory privileges on grounds of alleged historic disabilities.

Backwardness was thus almost wholly defined in terms of caste origins since colonial times, often ignoring the actual political, social and economic clout of the communities so designated. Nonetheless, unanimity about which groups constituted the all-India backward castes category remained elusive. While 'ritual exclusion' was accepted as the yardstick for identifying Scheduled Castes (Dirks, 2002: 277–8), there was no agreed criterion to locate backward castes. Scholars have attributed this partly to the amorphous nature of the Shudra Varna to which the backward castes are appended. As Prof. M.N. Srinivas noted, the term Shudra 'spans such a wide cultural and structural arch as to be almost meaningless. There are at one extreme the dominant, landowning, peasant castes which wield power and authority over local Vaishyas and Brahmins, whereas at the other extreme are the poor, near-Untouchable groups living just above the pollution line. The category also includes the many artisan and servicing castes . . .' (Srinivas, 1966: 10).

The absence of a clearly visible and cohesive backward caste category in the post-Independence period was compounded by the paucity of authentic all-India statistics on the social and economic standing of various caste groupings. The 1931 Census was the last to enumerate caste data, which meant that all available figures were outdated by at least half a century. Further, despite the unmistakable trend towards homogenization (as existed in the merger of smaller associated castes with the larger categories), there were wide variations 'in the size, extent and autonomy of classificatory rubrics around caste, and (it) . . . was still not a uniform system of reference' (Dirks, 2002: 283).

Undeterred by these pitfalls, the first Backward Classes Commission, constituted in 1953 under the chairmanship of Kaka Kalelkar, compiled a list of 2,399 backward castes (32 per cent of the total population, Bayly, 2000: 289) along with recommendations for their advancement. Amidst a welter of protests from groups that were excluded, the Commission failed to present a convincing defence of the methodology employed in preparing the list. The chairman himself virtually repudiated the report stating that 'it would have been better if we could determine the criteria of backwardness on principles other than caste' (Dirks, 2002: 283).

Academics also questioned the use of caste as the sole marker of backwardness. Arguing for the evolution of alternative norms, M.N. Srinivas stated that 'The criteria of literacy, land ownership and income in cash or grains should be able to subsume all cases of backwardness' (Dirks, 2002: 284).

The then prevalent atmosphere regarding the use of caste categories scuttled the Kalelkar report. But the issue of reservations for the indefinable category of backward classes was resurrected in 1977 when the Janata Party in its election manifesto pledged to 'reserve between 25 and 33 per cent of all appointments to government service for the backward classes. . .'. The Mandal Commission it constituted in 1978 also relied on caste and identified 3,248 communities (that is, 350 million people or 54.4 per cent of the population, Bayly, 2000: 295) for preferential treatment. It recommended 27 per cent reservation in government jobs and educational institutions for this group. Though the Janata Party was not in office when the Commission submitted its recommendations, the report was accepted a decade later by the Janata Dal government headed by V.P. Singh.

The frenzy that the decision evoked among upper caste students, who feared it would restrict their educational and career options, was but one facet of the problem. Far more serious and questionable was the complete resort to colonial analyses of caste by both Commissions, and their failure to acknowledge the changing nature of caste in modern times. The hierarchical underpinnings of the varna system had been so eroded by notions of equality (Fuller, 1996: 1–30), that scholars observed a 'deconstruction of the ideology underlying caste' (Weiner, 2001: 199). Alongside this modern makeover, caste after Independence became the most effective mechanism for the political empowerment of disadvantaged groups. Indeed, by serving as the natural foci of group consolidation, it enabled spatially dispersed non-elite and marginal sections to catapult to the very top of the polity. Indeed, the cornerstone of the criticism of the Mandal recommendations was that the groups it sought to privilege did not fall into the category of the deprived by any empirical yardstick, and in fact were the principal beneficiaries of government-sponsored economic reforms in the post-Independence period.

THE ABOLITION OF ZAMINDARI

In the early 1950s, the Central Government initiated 'a whole complex of changes' that simultaneously undermined 'the ideological legitimacy, social prestige, economic strength and monopoly over political power of upper castes' (Hasan, 1998: 138). The most significant of these was the abolition of zamindari,[1] which substantially dispossessed the big landholders and conferred ownership rights on erstwhile tenants, most of them belonging to the agricultural castes. It has been estimated that zamindari abolition turned roughly 20 million tenants into owners. The incidence of tenancy fell from 60 to 25 per cent and the percentage of owner-cultivators rose from 40 to 75 (Rudolph and Rudolph, 1987: 315). A bigger transfer of assets in peacetime is difficult to recall. In caste terms, the main victims in north India were Rajput-Thakurs and to a lesser degree Bania, Kayastha and Muslim landlords, while the principal beneficiaries were the erstwhile tenants among Jats, Yadavs, Kurmis and Koiris.

Virtually overnight, a substantial class of medium-sized owner cultivators came into being and began to dominate the countryside (Rudolph and Rudolph, 1987: 354). Variously called middle peasant castes, intermediate castes, backward castes, independent agricultural producers, bullock capitalists, these agricultural castes operated between 2.5 and 15 acres of land, used a pair of bullocks and 'the new inputs associated with the green revolution'. Lately also known as the Other Backward Castes (OBC) and Upper Shudras, they are to be distinguished from the less fortunate Lower Shudras (Hajjams, Kumbhars, Lohars, Telis, Tatwas, Dhanuks, Mallahs, etc.) who, though falling in the same varna category, are either poor marginal farmers or engage in ill-paid artisanal and servicing occupations.

By the early 1970s, the middle peasants were more numerous and controlled more land than any other agrarian class. Constituting 34 per cent of the population, they held 51 per cent of the land, as against the 33 per cent small-holders who owned 10 per cent land, and the 6 per cent large holders who retained 39 per cent land. The 27 per cent landless, of course, held no access to land (Rudolph and Rudolph, 1987: 52). In Uttar Pradesh, Yadavs, Kurmis, Lodhas and Gujars, who enjoyed merely 6 per cent of the zamindari rights in the pre-Independence period, now came to own 20 per cent of the land. Taking all the backward castes of UP together, their share increased from 8 per cent zamindari rights prior to Independence to control over 38 per cent of the land after enactment of the legislation (Hasan, 1989: 197).

THE GREEN REVOLUTION

The economic fortunes of the middle peasants were further boosted by parallel developments in agriculture, which ushered in the 'Green Revolution' and ended dependence on imported foodgrains. The need to sustain the Green Revolution promoted enhanced State investment in agriculture, especially under the heads of power and irrigation, that rose from 36 per cent in the first Plan to 58 per cent in the Fifth (Hasan, 1989: 194). In the Sixth and Seventh Plans as well, the outlays under this head were over 50 per cent. On the other hand, allocations to industrial development touched 6 per cent in the second Plan and thereafter fluctuated between 3 and 4 per cent of public expenditure. In the community development and social services sectors (whose principal beneficiaries were the landless), the outlays declined sharply from 27.5 per cent in the second Plan to 13.7 per cent in the Fifth and Sixth Plans (Frankel, 1989: 98). Moreover, from 1964–5 to 1978–9, the agricultural index (i.e. the relative value that farmers get for their produce over a period of time) rose from 147 to 198, largely due to the tremendous surge in wheat cultivation in Punjab, Haryana and western UP in the wake of the Green Revolution. By 1977, 70 per cent of the wheat-growing areas and 35 per cent of the rice-producing regions were under high-yielding varieties, illustrative of the magnitude of economic change wrought in the countryside (Rudolph and Rudolph, 1987: 323).

In UP, income from the agricultural and animal husbandry sectors tripled from Rs 1,072 crores in 1960–61 to Rs 3,563 crores in 1972–3. Western UP witnessed an annual growth rate of 3.5 per cent during the years 1970–83. Wheat productivity increased from 15.50 quintals per hectare in 1978–9 to 18.60 quintals per hectare in 1984–5, and maize from 6.85 quintals per hectare to 15.17 quintals during the same period. In western UP, the yield per hectare rose by a whopping 102 per cent from 1960–1 to 1982–3, as against 61 per cent in eastern UP, partly due to less improvement in rice cultivation in the state. Sugarcane production also made notable gains. Meanwhile, direct agricultural taxation declined sharply from over 2 per cent in 1960-61 to 0.83 per cent in 1972–3. As the UP Taxation Inquiry Committee Report noted, 'as a group, farmers did not have a bad bargain' (Hasan, 1998: 84–8).

Though technically belonging to the fourth varna and designated 'Other Backward Classes' (OBCs), the Upper Shudras can by no yardstick be regarded as deprived. Few groups in independent India have progressed as much as them, and it may be legitimate to question their continued inclusion in the Shudra category along with the Lower Shudra groups who are truly disadvantaged. At least since the 1960s, the Upper Shudras have also been in the political forefront with more voters than any other agrarian class (about 25 per cent of the total population, Rudolph and Rudolph, 1987: 550).

Politically, the ascent of the middle farmers was the single most important cause of the decline of the Congress Party. In 1967, in what is widely perceived as a turning point in Indian politics, they combined to dislodge the hitherto dominant upper castes (Jain, 1988: 254). Though this initial endeavour to alter power equations faltered, caste as an organizing principle of political mobility came into its own.

Despite some tentative efforts to accommodate these castes, they remained basically outside the Congress after 1967, prompting the party in the 1970s to devise a 'pro-poor agricultural strategy' in a bid to stem their influence (Rudolph and Rudolph, 1987: 325–8). Several programmes for employment and asset-creation for the weaker sections were launched, like the Small Farmer Development Agency (SFDA), the Marginal Farmers and Agricultural Labourers Scheme (MFAL), the Drought Prone Areas Programmes (DPAP), the Crash Rural Employment Scheme (CRES), among others (Brass, 1990: 226–68). The land legislation of 1972, which reduced the land ceiling to 18 acres, the state takeover of the wheat trade, and the efforts to redistribute surplus land, were all politics by other means, though to no avail. Economic power in the countryside remained firmly ensconced with the middle peasants.

As partners of the Janata coalition in 1977, the middle peasants even succeeded in installing a government committed to their welfare at the Centre. The Janata Government abolished all existing taxes on agricultural inputs, while the Agricultural Prices Commission for the first time accepted the principle of parity (between prices of inputs and procurement prices) demanded by the middle farmer lobby (Hasan, 1989: 166). Investment in the agricultural sector was raised above that in industry.

While cornering the benefits of agrarian legislation, the middle peasant castes were careful not to allow the gains to percolate to their weaker brethren, the Lower Shudras. In UP, after zamindari abolition and enactment of the first ceiling laws in 1960, virtually no reforms were permitted in the matter of land ceilings or tenures. In fact, remunerative agricultural prices rather than land reforms became the keynote of their demands. Issues affecting the Lower Shudras and other rural poor, such as minimum wages, housing and provision of fair price shops in villages figured nowhere on their horizon (Hasan 1998: 96–7). The OBCs obviously saw no contradiction between their demand for remunerative agricultural prices and the rejection of the plea for minimum wages in the countryside.

THE POLITICAL ASCENSION OF OBCs

In the political realm as well, there was a stark imbalance within the Shudra varna. In the two premier states of the Hindu heartland, the Lower Shudras saw their more privileged caste men push ahead. By 1967 itself, the Ahirs and Kurmis together constituted the third largest group in the UP Vidhan Sabha, whereas the Lower Shudras, who comprised 25 per cent of the total state population, were merely 2 per cent of the legislators in 1969 (Hasan 1998: 137). The Yadav, Kurmi, Lodha and Gujar presence in the UP Assembly was commensurate with their numerical strength by 1967, and reached a high of 23 per cent in 1974 (Hasan, 1989: 176).

With the formation of the Bharatiya Kranti Dal (BKD) in 1969, the OBCs acquired a political party devoted exclusively to their advancement. Scholars have estimated that the BKD in its various incarnations received the bulk of its support from Jats, Yadavs, Kurmis and Koiris (Frankel, 1977; Brass, 1981). However, other political parties were also solicitous of their well-being. Even in the upper caste-dominated Congress Legislature Party (CLP), the strength of the Yadavs, Kurmis, Lodhas and Gujars was a respectable 15 per cent in 1974 (Hasan, 1989: 186), and their representation in the UP Congress Governments increased from 9 per cent in 1980 to 20 per cent in 1989 (Chandra, 1999: 89).

Meanwhile, a succession of OBC-centred parties, such as the BKD, Bharatiya Lok Dal (BLD), and Lok Dal, held the middle peasant banner afloat. In 1992, a fresh phase in OBC mobilization commenced with the formation of the Samajwadi Party out of a series of splits in the Janata Dal. The OBCs remained well represented in other parties as well, and constituted the largest group in the UP Legislative Assembly in 1993, with 118 members in a house of 422 (Hasan, 1998: 162). Overall, the number of OBC MLAs rose from 13.7 per cent in

1980 to 29.9 per cent in 1993 and 24 per cent in 1996 (Jaffrelot, 2003: 362).

The 1990s also witnessed impressive OBC inroads into government. In the 1993 Samajwadi Party–Bahujan Samaj Party coalition, they comprised 60.7 per cent of the ministers. In contrast, there was only one upper-caste minister of cabinet rank. Though OBC representation went down to 48.5 per cent in the 1995 UP ministry and 40.4 per cent in the 1997 one, it was still way above that of every other caste grouping (Chandra, 1999: 91–2). What is more, the OBCs continued to be the most courted group in UP, actively wooed by all parties. Their strength in the Bharatiya Janata Party (BJP) remained constant at 16 per cent between 1989 and 1993, but swelled to 21 per cent in 1996. In fact, of the 420 seats the BJP contested in the 1996 Assembly elections, it fielded OBC candidates in as many as 190 constituencies (Jaffrelot, 2003: 486).

The OBC representation in the BJP ministry rose from 21 per cent in 1991 to 27 per cent in 1997 (Chandra, 1999: 67). Both the BJP governments of 1991 and 1997 were headed by an OBC chief minister. In the 2001 UP government, the BJP allotted 21 per cent of the ministerial portfolios to its OBC legislators (Jaffrelot, 2003: 490).

Time has not dimmed the value of the OBC vote. Even a self-consciously Dalit party like the BSP fielded nearly 30 per cent OBC candidates in the 1996 assembly elections, and 41 per cent in the 1998 parliamentary polls. However, the BSP allotted 66 per cent of the OBC tickets to the Lower Shudras in the latter election (Chandra 1999: 71). In the 1999 Lok Sabha elections, the party distributed the largest number of tickets (45 per cent) to the OBCs, with the next highest (23.5 per cent) to the Dalits (Jaffrelot, 2003: 402).

INTERNAL RIVALRIES

The all-too visible success of the OBCs, however, failed to mitigate the contradictions inherent in mobilization along castes lines. The original leadership and ideological articulation was provided by the Jats, who were technically excluded from the backward caste category to which the Yadavs, Kurmis, Gujars and Koiris belonged. But the Jats comprise a minuscule 1.6 per cent of the state's population and are concentrated in a few districts of western UP. They are outflanked, both numerically and in terms of geographical spread, by the Yadavs as also the Kurmis and Lodhas. Yet even so disadvantaged, the Jats under Choudhury Charan Singh had succeeded in welding the OBCs into a relatively coherent entity.

After Charan Singh's death in 1987, however, the competitiveness among the OBCs openly manifested itself. Though varna solidarity had been forged, it had not diluted the search for status within the group. Indeed, hierarchical considerations continued to pre-occupy middle peasant castes and actual ranking within the Shudra category remained fiercely contested. Jats regarded the Ahir and Gujar leadership as unacceptable, while the Yadavs were reluctant to acknowledge Jat claims to superior status. The Kurmis in turn were loathe to concede Yadav pretensions over them. The Upper Shudras were only united in their opposition to social parity with the Lower Shudras. These contradictory but simultaneous trends towards fission and fusion determined the direction of the movement following Charan Singh's demise.

An immediate fallout was the Yadav revolt against Jat leadership, resulting in a split in the Lok Dal (1987). An examination of the division in the legislative party shows that only 5 of the 18 Yadav Lok Dal MLAs supported Charan Singh's son and successor Ajit Singh, while not a single Jat legislator deserted him (Jain, 1996: 146–7). As Mulayam Singh Yadav sought to lead an OBC bloc under Yadav hegemony, there was a perceptible reversal in the fortunes of the Jats, who were now practically bereft of a political role. Instinctively recognizing this reality, they formed an overtly non-political organization to press the economic agenda of the middle peasants and assumed indifference to politics. The Bharatiya Kisan Union's (BKU) charter included higher prices for sugarcane, lower water and electricity tariffs, waiver of loans and greater public investments in agriculture. A formidable presence in the 1980s, its leaders took particular pride in the disdain with which they treated representatives of the Central and state governments.

But as the BKU grew in stature, it too fell prey to the intense status concerns of the OBCs. After initial unity, it was rent by the rivalry between the Jats and Gujars who inhabit the same region of western UP and are also numerically matched. Matters escalated to a point where a prominent Gujar politician, Hukum Singh, set up a parallel organization, the Kisan Mazdoor Panchayat, in 1990, because of the 'takeover' of the BKU by the Jats (Gupta, 1997).

The OBC movement was also undermined by the near-complete neglect of the Lower Shudras (now increasingly referred to as the Most Backward Castes or MBCs), who comprise the majority of the OBC population. The MBCs were grossly under-represented in the various OBC-led parties and governments, and this disparity held out the prospect of derailing the backward caste movement. Upper castes could checkmate the Upper Shudras by co-opting the Lower Shudras, or alternatively, the latter could align with upwardly mobile sections of the Scheduled Castes to create a coalition of the downtrodden. Both scenarios unfolded in UP. While the Samajwadi Party under Mulayam Singh remained the bastion of the Yadavs, a section of the Kurmis and Lodhas sought upward mobility through the BJP, as did some Lower OBCs. A number of the latter also responded to the BSP's call for unity among the weaker sections.

Sandwiched between the BJP and the BSP, the Yadavs turned to the Muslims for numerical strength, while simultaneously initiating moves to regroup the Upper OBCs. Following the 2002 Assembly elections, Mulayam Singh called for a new united front of backward castes with overtures to Kalyan Singh's Lodha-dominated Rashtriya Kranti Dal and Sonelal Patel's Kurmi-dominated Apna Dal.

THE DEMAND FOR RESERVATIONS

Economic empowerment, growing ascendancy in the electoral arena, and the strident demand for reservations in administration, culminated in the V.P. Singh Government's acceptance of the Mandal Commission report in 1990. Some points are in order on the reservation issue. That the OBCs were poorly represented in the bureaucracy was undeniable, but the reasons for their lagging behind deserve scrutiny.

Deriving their livelihood principally from agriculture-related occupations, the middle peasants were initially slow to take to modern education or to feel the need for administrative or professional employment. But this did not per se make them a disadvantaged group deserving preferential treatment. They had moved into the electoral arena without the aid of reservations and could equally have worked their way into the administration. There were no barriers to inhibit their progress. That is why their claims of social backwardness to buttress their demand for reservations were difficult to substantiate.

Indeed, the Upper Shudras, like the Jats and Yadavs, had never considered themselves socially inferior to the twice-born castes, and it was only the prospect of wresting power that 'facilitated the politicization of social cleavages' (Hasan, 1998: 149). As perceptive observers have pointed out, the demand for reservation was 'quintessentially political' (Hasan 1998: 149). OBC leaders were dissatisfied with the under-representation of their 'creamy layer' in Government, and sought to redress the imbalance. They were not motivated by 'a commitment to social equality or greater education' (Hasan, 1998: 135).

A major factor that fuelled the reservation demand was the political mobilization of the Scheduled Castes. Over the decades, compensatory discrimination had helped to create a middle class within the Scheduled Castes, estimated at roughly 6 per cent of the their population (Galanter, 1997). In sheer numerical terms, Scheduled Caste representation in the bureaucracy was impressive. In Class I jobs in the Central Government, it rose from less than 0.5 per cent in 1953 to 8 per cent in 1987, and in Class II jobs from 1 per cent to 10 per cent during the same period (Mendelsohn and Vicziany, 1998: 135–8). Available reports suggest that the number of Scheduled Castes in Class I positions now stands at 13 per cent, while their representation in Class III posts is a commendable 21.84 per cent (Chandra Bhan Prasad, *The Pioneer*, 25 August 2002). The BSP leader Kanshi Ram observed in 1994 that out of about 500 IAS officers in Uttar Pradesh, as many as 137 were from the Scheduled Castes. As against this, there were only seven IAS officers from the backward castes, of whom six were Yadavs. In 1997 (at the end of Ms Mayawati's second stint as chief minister), a quarter of the district magistrates and superintendents of police and more than a quarter of the principal secretaries were from the Scheduled Castes (Hasan, 2000: 160). It is significant that UP had no OBC Chief Secretary until the mid-1980s (Hasan, 1998: 153). The hierarchy-conscious OBCs would have found this unpalatable, but rather than augment their numbers through the normal avenues, they sought to muscle their way in.

The reservation demand has also been partly explained by the changing balance against the agricultural sector from the 1980s, when the increase in prices of agricultural produce failed to proportionately match those of non-agricultural goods. Moreover, between 1970–1 and 1980–1 in UP, there was a negative annual growth rate of 14 per cent of the price margin over cost in the case of wheat. The leveling of profits from agriculture is believed to have further spurred the demand for government jobs. In this context, it is interesting to note that eastern UP, where the bulk of the OBC population is concentrated, along with central UP, houses the majority of the state's 19 universities, most of whose arts graduates covet government jobs. But the economic argument cannot be pushed beyond a point, for the deteriorating terms of trade varied from crop to crop and did not automatically translate into a decline in income. What is more, investment in agriculture continued to show an upward trend (Hasan, 1998: 90–1, 152–3).

But as with representation in the legislature, the main beneficiaries of reservations in government jobs are the Upper OBCs. The Social Justice Committee constituted by the BJP Chief Minister Rajnath Singh found that the state's 9 per cent Yadavs had cornered approximately 34 per cent of the reservations. The Committee discovered that the disadvantaged MBCs were much worse off than the Scheduled Castes with respect to government jobs, and, therefore, recommended an MBC quota within the larger OBC quota (Kumar, 2001). It may be noted that even previously, the socialist leader Karpoori Thakur in Bihar and a dissenting Scheduled Caste member of the Mandal Commission, had both suggested a separate quota for the MBCs.

In UP itself, as far back as in 1975, the Cheddi Lal Sathi Commission had similarly concluded that the condition of the MBCs was pitiable: '. . . since the Scheduled Castes and Scheduled Tribes have reservations in jobs there has been some improvement in their condition, while MBCs have been denied any facilities. Hence their education, social, economic, commercial and employment conditions have worsened. This is most strikingly reflected in the virtual absence of representation of OBCs – in government services. In the 45 districts of UP there was only one person from MBC in Class I and approximately the same situation existed for Class II officers.' The Commission recommended 29.5 per cent reservations for the MBCs. In 1977, the state Janata Government introduced 15 per cent reservations, but abolished the distinction between the Upper Shudras and the Lower Shudras, thereby favouring the Ahirs, Kurmis, and Gujars (Hasan 1998: 145–6).

The current national debate on 33 per cent reservations for women in Parliament has also been vehemently opposed by the Upper OBCS, who are unwilling to countenance any dilution in their representation. A leader of the Samajwadi Party explained his party's resistance to the proposal on the grounds that '. . . if a proposal of this type is implemented, then our position will slip further. . . . In our state, hardly 15 per cent of the women are literate. And from among the backward castes, only 1–2 per cent women are literate. So when these 33 per cent reservations are implemented, which women are going to go to Parliament? Not the women from among the 54 per cent of the population. . . . We say, first give reservations to backwards, and then from this reservation, give 33 per cent to women in Parliament, we have no problem' (Chandra, 1999: 79).

THE CASE OF BIHAR

The political mobilization of the OBCs has proceeded apace in adjoining Bihar as well, where in fact it has displayed greater resilience in warding off challenge from other contenders for power. Though the OBC movement has splintered here as well, the Yadavs have not ceded ground and a government headed by them has been continuously in office since 1990.

As early as 1957 and 1962, 22 per cent members of the Congress Legislature Party came from the Upper Shudras. They received their due even in ministerial posts in state Congress governments. In 1963, the share of the Yadavs, Kurmis and Koiris in the ministry increased to 20 per cent from the previous less than 10 per cent (Frankel, 1989: 87). Thenceforth, till the formation of the Jagannath Mishra Government in 1980, the representation of the Upper Shudras in Congress governments never fell below 20 per cent (Frankel, 1989: 106–8, 118).

In the legislature as a whole, the Upper Shudras have constituted a sizeable group with the Yadavs being consistently over-represented. By 1967 itself, they had emerged as the second largest caste group in the Bihar Assembly, after the Rajputs. In 1977 they comprised 21 per cent of the legislature, which was almost twice their strength in the population (Blair, 1980). The following years witnessed a further augmentation in the political might of the Yadavs. They constituted the largest group in the Bihar Assembly in 1980, a position they have since retained. In March 1985, a record 41 Yadavs were elected to the Bihar Vidhan Sabha (Frankel, 1989: 119). Following the 1990 assembly elections, Laloo Prasad Yadav took over as Chief Minister, the third Yadav to rise to the office (the other two being B.P. Mandal and D.R. Rai). In the May 1991 parliamentary elections, the three principal parties, the Janata Dal, the Bharatiya Janata Party and the Congress, allotted the highest number of tickets to candidates belonging to the backward castes (*Sunday Mail*, 5 May 1991).

In Bihar as in UP, the Upper Shudras have demonstrated extreme reluctance to share power with the Lower Shudras, who comprise 40 per cent of the state's backward caste population. Representation of the Lower Shudras did not cross 4–5 per cent till 1977. Until 1983, their representation in ministries never exceeded 7 per cent even in OBC-led governments. It was only in the 1985 Congress ministry of Bindeshwari Dubey, that they achieved 12 per cent representation in government (Frankel, 1989: 118; Blair, 1980). In 1994 the representation of the OBCs in the state government was 46.5 per cent, which was almost twice that of the Upper Castes. Of this the share of the MBCs was 11.3 per cent, while that of the upper OBCs was 35.2 per cent (Jaffrelot, 2003: 353–4). In the Rabri Devi Government of 1995–2000, the share of the upper OBCs was 51.3 per cent and that of the lower OBCs 6.58 per cent, down from 11.3 per cent in the 1990–5 government of Laloo Yadav (Jaffrelot, 2003: 383).

The Upper OBCs maintained their dominance in Bihar throughout the 1990s, fortifying their position by wooing the minorities, Scheduled Castes and Scheduled Tribes. The Yadavs, in fact, emerged as major contenders for minority votes. In the 1995 assembly election, the Janata Dal, the party par excellence of the backward castes in Bihar, allotted 33 of the 260 seats it contested to Muslims (*Times of India*, 1 February 1995).

But as in UP, the backward caste movement in Bihar too has been plagued by dissensions. The Kurmi protest against the Yadavs in the 1990s is reminiscent of the Yadav challenge to Jat leadership in UP in the 1980s. An examination of the caste affiliations of the candidates fielded by the Janata Dal in the 1995 state elections lends credence to Kurmi charges of Yadav hegemony. The largest number of tickets was allotted to Yadavs. Of a total 260 seats contested, as many as 72 went to candidates belonging to this caste while the Kurmis had to be content with just 12 tickets (*The Times of India*, 1 February 1995).

The formation of the Samata Party on the eve of the assembly elections formalized the Kurmi rupture with the Yadavs. The Samata Party had only 11 Yadavs in its list of candidates, the lowest perhaps for any party in Bihar (*Hindustan Times*, 5 February 1995). Even the Congress accommodated 28 Yadavs and a total of 77 OBCs in the 324 seats it contested (*Times of India*, 24 January 1995). In the 1998 Lok Sabha election, Laloo Yadav's Rashtriya Janata Dal (RJD) contested 38 seats, leaving the rest to allies like the Congress and the Jan Morcha. Of these, the share of the Yadavs was 14, while Muslims and Koiris got 5 each, Rajputs 4, and Kurmis, Vaishyas and Nishads 1 each (Prasad, 1999: 132). The 12th assembly elections (2000), which resulted in a hung assembly, reiterated Yadav ascendancy in the RJD. As many as 102 of the 298 seats (34 per cent) it contested went to the Yadavs, of whom 38 Yadavs were eventually elected and constituted the largest single caste category in the party (Parkash, 2000).

CONCLUSION

The OBCs provide an instructive study of a group of related agricultural communities rallying under the banner of caste to emerge as an economically and politically influential cartel. Though the Mandal Commission recommendations were upheld by the Supreme Court and became part of the Indian landscape, the subsequent public discourse on this issue has increasingly centred round the issue of economic need (poverty), rather than caste per se. There is growing concern over the cornering of reservation benefits by the 'creamy layer' within the OBC category. The conscience of modern India appears to be exercised over the short shrift given to the disadvantaged MBCs. Although the MBC quota proposed by the then UP Chief Minister Rajnath Singh has been shelved for the present, it seems likely to emerge as the agenda of an insistently egalitarian Indian State.

NOTE

1. Zamindars were powerful landowners who functioned as intermediaries between the peasants and the State. Zamindari abolition sought to do away with their role as tax collecting intermediaries and promote the development of peasant proprietors.

REFERENCES

Baxter, Craig, 'The Rise and Fall of the Bharatiya Kranti Dal in U.P.', in John Osgood Field and Myron Weiner (eds), *Studies in Electoral Politics in the Indian States*, vol. 4, Delhi: Manohar, 1977.

Bayly, Susan, *Caste, Society and Politics in India*, in The New Cambridge History of India, IV. 3: Cambridge, Cambridge University Press, 2000.

Beteille, Andre, *Society and Politics in India: Essays in a Comparative Perspective*, London: Athlone Press, 1991.

Blair, Harry W., 'Rising Kulaks and Backward Classes in Bihar', *Economic and Political Weekly*, vol. XV, no. 2, 12 January 1980, pp. 64–74.

———, 'Structural Change, the Agricultural Sector and Politics in Bihar', in John R. Wood (ed.), *State Polities in Indira Gandhi's India: Continuity or Change?* Boulder: Westview Press, 1984.

Brass, Paul R., 'The Politicization of the Peasantry in a North Indian State', parts I and II, *The Journal of Peasant Studies*: vol. 7, no. 4, July 1980, pp. 395–426, and vol. 8, no. 1, September 1980, pp. 3–35.

———, 'Congress, the Lok Dal, and the Middle-Peasant Castes : An Analysis of the 1977 and 1980 Parliamentary Elections in Uttar Pradesh', *Pacific Affairs*, 54, Spring, 1981, pp. 5–41.

——— *The Politics of India Since Independence*, The New Cambridge History of India, IV. I, Cambridge, 1990.

Chandra, Kanchan, 'Post-Congress Politics in Uttar Pradesh: The Ethnification of the Party System and its Consequences', in Ramashray Roy and Paul Wallace (eds.), *Indian Politics and the 1998 Election*, Delhi: Sage, 1999.

Dirks, Nicholas B., *Castes Of Mind,* Delhi: Permanent Black, 2002.

Frankel, Francine R., 'Problems of Correlating Electoral and Economic Variables: An Analysis of Voting Behaviour and Agrarian Modernization in UP', in John Osgood Field and Myron Weiner (eds), *Electoral politics in the Indian States: The Impact of Modernization*, Delhi: Manohar, 1977.

———, 'Caste, Land and Dominance in Bihar: Breakdown of the Brahminical Social Order', in Francine Frankel and M.S.A. Rao (eds), *Dominance and State Power in Modern India*, vol. I, Delhi: Oxford University Press, 1989.

Fuller, C.J. (ed.), *Caste Today*, Delhi: Oxford University Press, 1996.

Galanter, Marc, 'Pursuing Equality: An Assessment of India's Policy of Compensatory Discrimination for Disadvantaged Groups', in Sudipta Kaviraj (ed.), *Politics in India*, Delhi: Oxford University Press, 1997.

Gupta, Dipankar, *Rivalry and Brotherhood: Politics in the Life of Farmers in Northern India*, Delhi: Oxford University Press, 1997.

Hasan, Zoya, 'Power and Mobilization: Patterns of Resilience and Change in Uttar Pradesh Politics', in Francine Frankel and M.S.A. Rao (eds), *Dominance and State Power in Modern India*, vol. 1, Delhi: Oxford University Press, 1989.

———, *Quest for Power Oppositional Movements and Post-Congress Politics in Uttar Pradesh*, Delhi: Oxford University Press, 1998.

———, 'Representation and Redistribution: The New Lower Caste Politics of North India', in Francine R. Frankel, Zoya Hasan, Rajeev Bhargava, Balveer Arora (eds), *Transforming India: Social and Political Dynamics of Democracy*, Delhi: Oxford University Press, 2000.

Jaffrelot, Christophe, *India's Silent Revolution*, Delhi: Permanent Black, 2003.

Jain, Meenakshi, 'Congress after 1967: Strategies of Mobilization', in D.A. Low (ed.), *The Indian National Congress: Centenary Hindsights*, Delhi: Oxford University Press, 1988.

———, 'Backward Castes and Social Change in UP and Bihar', in M.N. Srinivas (ed.), *Caste: It's Twentieth Century Avatar*, Delhi: Viking, 1996.

Kumar, Pradeep, 'Reservations within Reservations', *Economic and Political Weekly*, 15 September 2001, pp. 3505–7.

Mendelsohn, Oliver and Marika Vicziany, *The Untouchables: Subordination, Poverty and the State in Modern India*, Cambridge: Cambridge University Press, 1998.

Prasad, Binoy Shanker, 'Split the Votes and Win the Election: An Analysis of the 12th Lok Sabha Election in Bihar', in Ramashray Roy and Paul Wallace (eds), *Indian Politics and the 1998 Election*, Delhi: Sage, 1999.

Rudolph, L.I. and S.H. Rudolph, *In Pursuit of Lakshmi: The Political Economy of the India State*, Delhi: Orient Longman, 1987.

Srinivas, M.N., *Social Change in Modern India*, Delhi: Allied, 1966.

Washbrook, D.A., 'Caste, Class and Dominance in Modern Tamil Nadu: Non-Brahminism, Dravidianism, and Tamil Nationalism', in Francine Frankel and M.S.A. Rao (eds), *Dominance and State Power in Modern India*, vol. I, Delhi: Oxford University Press, 1989

Weiner, Myron, 'The Struggle for Equality: Caste in Indian Politics', in Atul Kohli (ed.), *The Success of India's Democracy*, Cambridge: Cambridge University Press, 2001.

CHAPTER 7

Reservations for Backward Classes in Karnataka's Panchayati Raj Institutions

K.S. Narayana

Karnataka is a pioneer state in terms of affirmative action policies. Preferential job opportunity on domicile consideration was originally sought by the Brahmins of the princely state of Mysore in an effort to end the Tamil Brahmins' monopoly of posts in the Palace administration. The slogan 'Mysore's jobs for Mysoreans', or the concept of 'sons of the soil' was thus born in 1831 (Thimmaiah, 1993; Galanter, 1984).

The local Brahmins' conscious effort against the Tamil Brahmins also marked the beginning of local non-Brahmins' awareness and revolt against the Brahmins' monopoly in posts and seats. Consequently, the non-Brahmins of Mysore started exerting pressure on the Palace administration in this regard. In response to these demands, the state of Mysore was the earliest in India, in 1874, to reserve 20 per cent of the middle and lower level jobs in the Police department for Brahmins and 80 per cent for other Hindus, Muslims and Indian Christians (Thimmaiah, 1993; Galanter, 1984).

To examine the merits of the reservation policy, the first Backward Classes Committee was formed in August 1918, under the Chairmanship of Sir Leslie Miller (the then Chief Judge of the Chief Court of Mysore). In its report (1919), the Committee recommended that with the exception of Brahmins, Europeans and Anglo-Indians, all others be treated as Backward Castes or Communities on the criteria of literacy in English and their share in government jobs. Castes with a literacy of over 5 per cent were eliminated from reservation benefits.

* I am deeply grateful to B.S. Bhargava, Vinod Vyasulu, G.K. Karanth, Anand Inbanathan, K.G. Gayathri Devi, V. Vijayalakshmi and Ms Mini G. for their useful comments and suggestions during the writing of this paper.

However, some castes and communities (Mudaliars, Pillais and Indian Christians) were classified as backward despite their English literacy of over 5 per cent. The report recommended an age relaxation for non-Brahmins, besides exemption from taking the civil service examination. The Committee was conscious of the possibilities of misuse of reservation benefits by dominant elements and in an effort to prevent such a misuse, it recommended 'reservation in reverse order': The reservation was to start first with the Depressed Classes (later called Scheduled Castes), followed by caste Hindus, Muslims, Europeans and Indian Christians, in that order; lastly unreserved posts were offered to Brahmins, to ensure the greatest benefit to the most needy.

A reservation policy was introduced on these lines for the Depressed and Backward Classes in the state. The Miller Committee Report held the position that the objective of reservation is to secure greater representation for BCs in public services, on the premise that increased opportunities may encourage them to strive for the betterment of their brethren as well. These measures were to be supplemented by offering BCs special facilities for higher and professional education.

From the 1930s onwards, several non-Brahmin associations came into being, demanding reservations in a larger number of jobs and seats. The BC movement received support from the Anti-Brahmin Movement in Tamil Nadu and the local Muslims. The local press also played a proactive role in raising its voice against the Brahmin monopoly of jobs and seats.[1]

THE CONSTITUTIONAL PREMISE

Having inherited a stratified society, the Constitution Drafting Committee set up under the chairmanship of Dr B.R. Ambedkar on 29 August 1947 realized that equality would not result from treating the unequal equally. This realization led to affirmative action policies and programmes considered necessary for the advancement of the depressed, the deprived, the oppressed and disadvantaged citizens (SCs, STs, OBCs and women). Indeed the quintessence of the Indian Constitution, as enunciated in the Preamble and Articles 14, 15(1–2), 16(1–2), 17, 29 (see Annexure for details) is to promote a greater degree of equality with social justice, so as to carve out a better social order. The Directive Principles of State Policy are a broad indicator for the legislature and executive to orient policies and programmes to realize these objectives. The judiciary has the onerous role of ensuring translation of the constitutional intent into reality on the social canvas.

The discriminatory provisions (under Articles 15(3, 4); 16(4); 17; 46; 330; 332, 243D) were created to 'level the playing field' with the hope that equality of opportunities for all segments of society might become a reality. On examination of the studies (Galanter, 1984; Maheshwari, 1995; Palkhivala, 1974; Prasad, 1997) on the subject, judicial interpretations and the constitutional intent, it is discernible that the main objective of reservation is to act as a social elevator and provide the disadvantaged with a much-needed boost towards social parity.

More specifically, the Indian Constitution provides for reservations for SCs/STs in jobs, educational institutions and electoral seats under Articles 15(4), 16(4), 330, 332 and 334. Reservation for OBCs was confined to public jobs and educational institutions only, under Articles 15(4) and 16(4). The 73rd and 74th Constitutional Amendments passed in 1992 provisioned for electoral reservation for women and for SC/STs in rural and urban local governments (Art. 243D). The states were given the option of reserving electoral seats for BCs at that level [Art. 243(6)].

HOW TO DEFINE BACKWARDNESS? THE ROLE OF COMMITTEES/COMMISSIONS AND COURTS

The terms Other Backward Classes (OBC) and Backward Classes (BC) are used both synonymously and interchangeably. Under the Constitution, OBCs are those who are socially and educationally backward. Thus, any caste/community (besides the SCs/STs) can be listed as OBCs. Before being categorized as backward, the castes/ communities should however be subjected to a socio-educational and economic means scrutiny. The Constitution has clearly pronounced that caste should not be the sole criterion of backwardness. Economic backwardness alone also does not qualify a class of citizens to be categorized as backward. Generally, a caste that is educationally backward, of low social status and living below the poverty line would qualify as OBC. Many Backward Classes Commissions also considered land holdings and housing conditions as elements of the composite indicators of backwardness.[2]

In 1958, the state of Karnataka issued an order deeming all non-Brahmins (excluding Muslims and Christians) as BCs, and offered them 57 per cent reservation in employment and education, while the quota for SCs/STs was set at 18 per cent. This was struck down by the Karnataka High Court in 1959, as the total quota exceeded the 50 per cent limit imposed by the apex court.[3]

Indeed, reservation policies (for jobs and education) often failed to pass legal scrutiny. Thus Commissions/Committees were regularly created by the state to identify backward classes entitled to benefits under Article 15(4) and 16(4), and to prevent the 'creamy layers' from cornering these benefits. These were as follows:

- Backward Classes Committee (Chairman: Nagana Gowda). Report: 1961.
- First Backward Classes Commission (Chairman: L.G. Havanoor). Report: 1975.
- Second Backward Classes Commission (Chairman: T. Venkata Swamy). Report: 1986.
- Third Backward Classes Commission (Chairman: Chinnappa Reddy). Report: 1990.
- Fourth Backward Classes Commission (Chairman: Ravivarma Kumar). Report: 2002.

The impact of these commissions however has been limited by a series of factors. One, the courts' directives to various commissions and governments regarding reservation policies can be summarized as: (a) not to use caste as the sole criterion to assign the OBC tag; (b) to subject castes to social, economic and educational scrutiny before assigning the BC tag; (c) to limit the overall quota to 50 per cent; (d) to evolve a proper mechanism to prevent the creamy layer from cornering the benefits; and (e) to evolve an effective system to ensure that benefits reach the most needy. BC commissions failed to comply with most of these directives. Despite clear terms of reference, none of these Commissions was able to conform to the prime objective of the Indian Constitution—of promoting equality—as they failed to evolve a mechanism by which benefits could accrue to the most needy. Both the High Court and the Supreme Court have treated the recommendations of the Commissions as unconstitutional and stalled them from being made operational.

Two, when these Commissions submitted their reports, the State either tried to tinker with their recommendations or chose to shelve it, guided by political compulsions or to avoid caste convulsions, and then appointed another commission. Since Independence, five commissions have been constituted, but at no time has the State demonstrated the will to accept their reports in totality. The Karnataka state government actually delegitimized the quota system by adding some castes to the BC list on purely political compulsions. For instance, the Nagana Gowda Committee (1961) recommended a BC tag for the Vokkaligas and excluded the Lingayats from the list. But the then Chief Minister who was a Lingayat had his community added to the BC list in the Committee's final report. The Havanoor Commission recommended keeping Brahmins, Lingayats, Rajputs, Muslims, Christians, Vaishyas and a few others outside the purview of reservations. However, the state government decided to accord BC status to all these groups, with the exception of Brahmins and Vaishyas. The Venkata Swamy Commission had suggested treating Vokkaligas and Lingayats as forward castes, but the sporadic, though widespread violence led by these caste groups compelled the state Government to confine the report to cold storage. Later, in 1986, it issued an order according the BC tag to these dominant castes. The Chinnappa Reddy Commission again recommended the exclusion of Vokkaligas and Lingayats from BC lists, as well as the prevention of the creamy layers (within the BCs) from cornering the benefits of reservations. This report again evoked widespread violence, obliging the State to shelve the report. Thus, the two dominant castes—the Lingayats and Vokkaligas—by virtue of their political clout in the state legislature, coercive tactics and numerical and economic strength, were able to retain the BC tag and hijack reservation benefits at the cost of the neediest (Narayana, 1998).

Three, in some cases the methodology used has been faulty. Out of these five Commissions/Committees, only the Venkata Swamy Commission could conduct detailed educational and economic household surveys, so essential for the purpose (Table 7.1).

TABLE 7.1: CASTE/COMMUNITY COMPOSITION OF THE POPULATION OF KARNATAKA

Total population	4,40,88,597	
Brahmins	15,23,598	3.45 %
Scheduled Castes	73,70,814	16.72 %
Scheduled Tribes	29,65,115	6.72 %
Muslims	51,47,071	11.67 %
Christians	9,15,252	2.07 %
Lingayats	67,62,703	15.33 %
Vokkaligas	47,65,348	10.80 %
Vaishyas	3,06,922	00.69 %

NOTE: This table shows that Backward Classes form about 70 per cent of the population, since they include all categories except Brahmins, Vaishyas, SCs, and STs.

SOURCE: Venkata Swamy Commission's detailed socio-economic and educational survey (1986)

Lastly, a scrutiny of various court cases and judgements makes it clear that the Commissions/Committees have failed to evolve an effective mechanism to deliver reservation benefits to the most needy. Also, no sincere attempt has been made to evaluate the socio-economic impact of reservation on the weaker sections, or to determine how far the policy has succeeded in weakening caste consciousness.[4] About 92 per cent of the state's population have been brought under the BC list, including the dominant Lingayat and Vokkaliga castes, who together account for over 22 per cent of the total population of Karnataka. They possess a significant portion of cultivable land and a large share in government jobs. They also wield considerable political power in the state legislature and use this power for personal gain by remaining in the BC category. Thus, both the legislature and executive have failed to create effective mechanisms to translate into reality the constitutional directive of carving out an equitable social order.

THE POLITICAL REPRESENTATION OF BCs BEFORE THE 73RD AMENDMENT

At the state level, the Congress Chief Minister Devaraj Urs played a critical role in limiting the preponderance of the Vokkaligas, and Lingayats, two caste groups that controlled the state's legislative power since the 1930s. Urs, who belonged to the Kshatriya community, succeeded in reducing the Vokkaliga and Lingayat monopoly by mobilizing Muslims, Backward Classes (minus Vokkaligas and Lingayats) and SCs. He was able to neutralize the dominant castes' political monopoly and in the process, the BCs emerged stronger in the state (Manor, 1989).

Urs was a freedom fighter who won elections as MLA right from the first Assembly, held important ministries and party positions and became Chief Minister from 1972 to 1979. He lost ground in the late 1970s, mainly due to the factional politics engineered by Indira Gandhi and Sanjay Gandhi, as they were determined to dissuade him from eyeing the prime minister's seat. Urs triggered the power-shift in favour of the BCs when he was Chief Minister of the state. During the pre-Urs era (1956–72) in the three elections to the state legislature, the Lingayats and Vokkaligas together shared more than 50 per cent of the seats. During the Urs era (1972–80) the share of the two dominant castes decreased, while the BCs improved their share. During the post-Urs era (1983 onwards), the dominant castes reconsolidated their positions. Even after his death, the BC power base appears to have stabilized, though their share has marginally diminished. Table 7.2 portrays the power matrix among the dominant castes during the three periods cited above.

The apex positions (of Chief Minister and important cabinet positions), except for a brief period, also have been held by Lingayat

TABLE 7.2: CASTE-WISE COMPOSITION OF MEMBERS OF KARNATAKA LEGISLATIVE ASSEMBLY, 1957–89

Caste	Election year							
	1957	1962	1967	1972	1978	1983	1985	1989
	Pre-Devaraj Urs era			Devaraj Urs Era		Post-Devaraj Urs Era		
Lingayat	69	61	81	56	52	66	65	57
Vokkaliga	42	50	45	44	43	45	48	43
Others	95	97	90	117	131	112	112	119
Total	204	208	216	217	226	223	225	219

SOURCE: L.R. Raghavendra Rao, 'Changing Pattern of Political Leadership in Karnataka', unpublished Ph.D. Thesis, ISEC, Bangalore, 1995.

or Vokkaliga MLAs. Two Brahmin MLAs (R. Gundu Rao and Ramakrishna Hegde) and two MLAs from the Backward Classes (S. Bangarappa and Veerappa Moily) managed to become Chief Minister for brief periods; none of them held office for a full term (for detailed analysis, see Rao, 1995). In spite of this, the BCs have improved their political base in the state legislature since the Devaraj Urs days.

At the national level, Narayana (2000) shows that in the 13th Lok Sabha elections (1999) more than 50 per cent of the MPs from Karnataka belonged to SC, ST and minority communities (Muslims and Christians), who together held 15 of the 28 seats. The dominant Lingayats and Vokkaligas combined had 9 seats while 4 seats were held by the 'general' category. In the absence of reservation of seats for OBCs, more than 50 per cent of the seats have been wrested by this category, which reflects its degree of political mobilization.

At the local level, in the 1987 elections to Panchayati Raj Institutions (PRIs) in Karnataka, there was no electoral reservation for BCs, so the dominant castes wrested most of the positions (including chair positions). The Reddy Commission (1990) notes that the Lingayats and Vokkaligas captured 25.4 and 18.7 per cent of the zilla panchayat seats, respectively (Aziz et al., 1994; Ray and Jayalakshmi; 1987, Reddy Commission, 1990). Lingayats and Vokkaligas were also able to wrest 10 out of 18 zilla panchayat president's posts in Karnataka. Though Lingayats formed 16.9 per cent and Vokkaligas 11.68 per cent of the state population, they could wrest 33 per cent and 22 per cent, respectively, of the chair positions (Ray and Jayalakshmi, 1987).

Since 1993, one-third of the constituencies and one-third of the chair positions in all the three tiers of Panchayati Raj Institutions (i.e. gram panchayat, taluk panchayat and zilla parishad/panchayat) have been earmarked for BCs in Karnataka, under the Panchayati Raj Act. Also, not less than one-third of these seats/positions should be earmarked for women.

DECENTRALIZATION AND ELECTORAL RESERVATIONS IN KARNATAKA

The draft constitution made no mention of panchayats, as Ambedkar famously considered these village councils as 'a sink of localism, den of ignorance, narrow-mindedness and communalism' (cited in

Mishra and Mishra, 1995: 27). Gandhi's persistent support to the institution of the panchayats, however, propelled Madhava Rao of Mysore not only to counter Ambedkar's views in the Constituent Assembly, but also to get the consent of the house to include Article 40 under Part IV of the Constitution, which reads: 'The state should take steps to organise village panchayats and endow them with such power and authority as may be necessary to enable them to function as units of self-government' (cited in Mathew, 2000: 5).

A few states initiated efforts in the 1950s in this direction but gradually the panchayat system became insignificant. When the Janata Government came to power at the Centre in 1977, steps were taken to revitalize panchayats by constituting the Asoka Mehta Committee: The Committee in its report of 1978 made far-reaching recommendations for reviving PRIs as rural local self-governments. The Sarkaria Commission (1987) also reiterated the need for evolving an effective decentralized political system for more effective implementation of community development programmes. It favoured the strengthening of panchayats with power, autonomy, finance and proactive State support. In 1992, the Union Government amended the Constitution, providing for the mandatory creation of panchayats in every state. However, in most states, PRIs are still not strengthened with adequate fiscal and administrative support. Also, all the 28 responsibilities listed under the 11th Schedule of the Constitution are yet to be transferred to the panchayats.

In Karnataka, a series of efforts to develop local bodies started with the Mysore Local Boards Act, 1902, under which a three-tier structure of union panchayats, taluk and district boards was created with a limited number of members, either elected, nominated or appointed *ex-officio.* The Act was revised in 1918 and 1926. The Venktakappa Committee and the Chandrasekharaiah Committee were constituted, respectively, in 1950 and 1954 to improve the structure and function of local government bodies. Both suggested substantive changes in the Act. The Balwantrai Mehta Committee Report mandated at the Centre (1957) also provided fresh impetus at the state level. As a result, the Mysore Village Panchayats and Local Boards Act, 1959 was passed, providing for a three-tier system of local self-government with elected members. Limited provisions for reservations for SCs, STs and women were included in the Act. Some of the positive elements of the Act were the transfer of some developmental functions, the power to levy taxes/surcharge on stamp duty and the allocation of funds to panchayats. The Kondajji Basappa Committee (1963) made some recommendations to further strengthen local bodies. Despite all this, successive state governments reduced the panchayats to the status of inconsequential institutions due to neglect. Some of the causes that undermined the growth of the PRIs included non-conduct of elections, supersession, dissolution and appointment of administrators for local tasks.

However, the panchayat movement took a positive direction in 1983, when the Janata Party came to power in the state. Ramakrishna Hegde as Chief Minister and Abdul Nazeer Sab as Minister for Rural Development and Panchayati Raj, were instrumental in reviving the PRIs. A model Karnataka Zilla Parishad, Taluk Panchayat Samiti, Mandal Panchayat and the Nyaya Panchayat Act, 1983 was enacted, which provided again for a three-tier local government structure. It envisaged the creation of the nyaya panchayat[5] as a dispute settlement forum at the local level. The Act provided for 25 per cent electoral reservation for women, and for SC/STs in proportion to their population. Section 5(3) of the Act included provisions for nominating two members from BCs. It stated: 'whenever no person belonging to Backward Classes is elected to Mandal Panchayat, the Zilla Parishad shall nominate two persons belonging to said classes to the Mandal Panchayat'. This Act demonstrated the state's willingness to divest itself of substantial powers and functions in favour of PRIs. Funds, planning and administrative support, powers and autonomy for PRIs were willingly made available. Elections, held in 1987, renewed hope among the rural people and encouraged them to participate in the decentralized political bodies.

There were some hiccups after the Congress-I won the state elections in 1988. It replaced the model 1983 Act with the Act of 1993, which altered certain positive elements of the earlier Act, in acquiescence to lobbying by MLAs/MPs and the bureaucracy. To clarify the point: in the 1983 Act, officials were subordinated to panchayat members elected at the local level, and as a result the MLAs and MPs felt that the panchayats negated their importance. Using their overriding power, they pruned the panchayats' autonomy and power, promised in the 1983 Act. Again, under the 1983 Act, the zilla panchayat (ZP) president was regarded as the 'Chief Minister' of the district, and the deputy commissioner, as its 'chief secretary' working under his directives. These proposals were modified in the 1993 Act by the Congress-I state government, to subordinate the PRIs to the state government (Sivanna, 1993). In a retrograde step, the MLAs/MPs were made ex-officio members of panchayat bodies, enjoying voting rights at meetings. Elections to the PRIs were postponed and local administration was brought under the bureaucrats.

However, the 1993 Act was made compatible with the 73rd Amendment regarding the women's quota. Based on the Nayak Committee recommendations, the 1993 PR Act was further improved by restoring some of the positive features of the 1983 Act. It provides for the constitution of district committees to prepare district plans, aligned with village level plans and priorities. The gram sabhas by order have to be convened not less than four times a year to pass the annual budget, define local plan priorities, identify programme beneficiaries and act as a forum for direct people's participation in the democratic process, as watchdogs and partners. Credit should go to Ghorpade (the then Rural Development and Panchayati Raj Minister) for some of these recently initiated positive developments. He is trying to re-popularize *jamabandhi* (social auditing)[6] under which panchayat activities are brought under people's scrutiny, in an effort to improve transparency and accountability in local governance. It may usher in responsible and responsive governance (for details see, Chandran, 2000; Mathew, 1994, 1986; Inbanathan, 1992; Sivanna, 1997).

Under the Karnataka Panchayati Raj Act, 1993, not less than one-third of the seats and offices in gram panchayats, taluk panchayats and zilla panchayats is reserved for BC-A (most backward classes) and BC-B (more backward classes) categories in the ratio of 80:20. Under BC-A, 190 castes and under BC-B 9 castes (with their numerous sub-castes) have been listed for the purpose of electoral reservation as per a government order, dated 13 January 1995. The latter category includes Christians and Jains, while Muslims are listed in the former group. The BC-B caste groups also include the Lingayats, Vokkaligas, Bunts, Mogaveeras, Kurubas, Idigas and others, although a large segment of these groups are dominant, own land/property and possess a fair degree of education. The Act also earmarks not less than one-third of the seats (including chair positions) for women in all the four categories, i.e. SCs, STs, BCs and general.

This provision is in compliance with the constitutional mandate. There is no upper limit on the quotas and, therefore, people entitled to reserved seats can contest from the general category as well.

Two elections have been held since the Act was passed. Narayana's (1997) analysis of the composition of Karnataka PRI members of 1993–4 elections shows that over 33 per cent of the chair positions were taken by Lingayats and Vokkaligas who were by then listed among BC-Bs.

A sample study covering the 1995 Karnataka Panchayat Elections in Bangalore, Mysore, Belgaum and Gulbarga reveals that Lingayats and Vokkaligas held 27.5 and 17.2 per cent of the seats. Thus, the dominant castes together obtained about 45 per cent of the seats, implying that unless dominant groups are kept outside the purview of reservations, electoral reservation would not result in power spread among the non-dominant sections. The dominant groups have wrested the lion's share of political positions in the PRIs in Karnataka as they have double advantage. Besides contesting the reserved seats, they stand from the general category as well, as their numerical and economic strength increases their likelihood of winning.

Yet, as shown by Narayana (1997), in 1995, the dominance of the numerically and economically stronger castes (Lingayats and Vokkaligas) in the PRIs was somewhat eroded. Thus, as compared to the 1987 situation, the power base has tilted slightly in favour of the BC-As. A similar situation is also noticed in the 2000 elections, as can be seen in Table 7.3, where about 27 per cent of seats and about 30 per cent of the chair positions in the PRIs are taken by BC-A members. SC/ST members together hold about 30 per cent and thus, over 60 per cent of the decision-making positions are with the disadvantaged sections. After the 2000 elections, 45 per cent of gram panchayat, 42 per cent of taluk panchayat and 38 per cent of zilla panchayat members were women, which is a significant and positive change. Women hold 38 per cent, 34 per cent and 33 per cent of the chair-positions, respectively, in the three tiers. These women members are distributed between SC, ST, BC and general categories: as per the constitutional mandate, not less than one-third of the seats in all the four categories must be earmarked for women. ST women have occupied much larger political space than the mandatory seats reservation. This is the reason why the women's total share in the local political space is so high.

TABLE 7.3: DISTRIBUTION OF ELECTED MEMBERS IN GRAM, TALUK AND ZILLA PANCHAYATS IN KARNATAKA IN THE LAST TWO ELECTIONS

(A) Gram Panchayats

Particulars	No. of GPs	Election Year	Total Seats	SCs	STs	BCs	Others
Total	5,640	1993-4	80,627	17,918	7,575	26,828	28,306
% to total				22	9.4	33	35
Women			35,305	7,373	5,933	10,721	11,278
% to total (in each category)			43.8	41	78	40	40
Chair positions			**5,640**	**1,025**	**296**	**1,880**	**2,439**
Women			1,880	342	99	626	813
% to total (in each category)			33	33	33	33	33
Total no.	5,659	2000	80,073	14,871	7,499	26,652	31,051
% to total				19	9	33	39
Women			35,922	7,218	5,873	10,716	12,115
% to total (in each category)			45	49	78	40	39
Chair positions			**5,659**	**1,033**	**296**	**1,886**	**2,444**
Women			2,144	407	173	690	874
% to total (in each category)			38	39	58	37	36

(B) Taluk Panchayats

Particulars	No. of TPs	Election Year	Total Seats	SCs	STs	BC-A	BC-B	Others
Total	175	1995	3,340	604	169	894	223	1,450
% to total				18	5	26.7	6.7	43.5
Women			1,341	261	104	395	46	535
% to total (in each category)			40	43	61	44	21	37
Chair positions			**175**	**32**	**9**	**46**	**12**	**76**
Women			59	11	3	15	4	26
% to total (in each category)			34	34	33	33	33	34

(contd.)

TABLE 7.3 (contd.)

Total no.	175	2000	3,255	583	244	876	217	1,335
% to total				18	7.5	27	6.7	41
Women			1,375	252	182	361	71	509
% to total (in each category)			42	43	75	41	33	38
Chair positions			**175**	**32**	**9**	**47**	**11**	**76**
Women			59	21	3	15	4	26
% to total (in each category)			34	66	33	32	36	34

(C) Zilla Panchayats

Particulars	No. of ZPs	Election Year	Total Seats	SCs	STs	BC-A	BC-B	Others
Total	20	1995	919	165	47	243	63	401
% to total				18	5	26	6.8	43.6
Women			335	63	22	87	21	142
% to total (in each category)			36.5	38	46.8	36	33	35
Chair positions			**20**	**4**	**1**	**6**	**1**	**8**
Women			7	2	-	2	-	3
% to total (in each category)			35	50	-	33	-	38
Total no.	27	2000	890	158	54	239	60	379
% to total				18	6	27	7	43
Women			339	63	31	84	25	136
% to total (in each category)			38	40	57	35	42	36
Chair positions			**27**	**5**	**1**	**7**	**2**	**12**
Women			9	2	-	2	1	4
% to total (in each category)			33	40	-	29	50	33

SOURCE: Computed from election figures provided by the Department of Rural Development and Panchayati Raj, Government of Karnataka.

Thus, the profile of the political personnel at the local level has changed significantly due to the reservation policy. The disadvantaged sections now occupy over 60 per cent of the political space in all the three tiers of local government, and the share of the general category has shrunk to 40 per cent. As borne out in many studies, in the absence of electoral reservation, access to power positions by the weaker sections may not have reached such an extent.

A CRITICAL ASSESSMENT OF DECENTRALIZATION

The impact of the power-shift resulting from reservations at the local level on the political leaders' socio-educational and economic status remains to be probed. Whether the situation has led to a positive dent on community welfare and development also needs to be examined.

As of today, no study is available that focusses on the role, degree of participation, and level of performance of BC members in the PRIs in Karnataka; that demonstrates how far the status of Backward Class members of the PRIs has improved after gaining access to political positions; or that examines the overall impact of electoral reservations on society. However, a few studies with an indirect implication in this context are reviewed here. The general impression one gets is that the PRIs need to strengthen their foundations if they are to play their expected role as local self-government institutions, as they are beset with structural, fiscal, and functional drawbacks.

Chandran (2000) summarizes concisely the status of PRIs in Karnataka and portrays the panchayat movement as forward looking, providing for the devolution of its functions with funds and personnel. These efforts have improved the delivery of services and opened opportunities for participation to a large number of people's representatives (including SCs, STs, BCs and women). He is critical of the fact that dominant castes play a major role in decision-making while the participation level of SC, ST and women representatives is low. The gram sabhas are non-functional, their degree of transparency and accountability is poor, corruption continues unabated, the panchayats have fallen short of making the mandatory allocation of 20 per cent on programmes benefitting SCs/STs, resource mobilization is inadequate, political commitment to decentralization is poor and a significant number of elected representatives are being used as proxies by dominant members. These concerns are accentuated by problems of illiteracy, the gender divide and social exclusion. The state government and the people at large should play a proactive role in making the PRIs more purposeful.

A comparative study of decentralized governance and planning in Andhra Pradesh, Karnataka and Tamil Nadu (Aziz et al., 1998) also observes that PRIs suffer from several maladies. It highlights the all-pervasive corruption (at official and non-official levels), poor planning, inefficient programme monitoring, improper programme prioritization, missing linkages between PRIs and civil society, paucity of funds, non-cooperation between officials and non-officials, members' disinterest, inexperience, illiteracy, the gender divide and inefficiency that have stifled the effectiveness of the PRIs.

More specifically, the gram sabhas (i.e. the gathering of all the panchayat's voters) are being used to settle political scores or as a battleground for caste/communal disputes, rather than to focus on the official agenda. Thus, Narayana (2001) narrates how a gram sabha meeting in Kattepura village (in Hassan district) turned violent. In the ensuing clash between rival groups, two village youth, who sustained severe head injuries, had to be shifted to Bangalore for treatment, leading to the abrupt shutting down of the gram sabha. Auctioning of sand (on the riverbed), community grazing land and the alleged misuse of village funds in the past had triggered the conflict. It is also pertinent to recall here the gruesome axing of one and burning alive of two gram panchayat members in Kamasamudra village (in Hassan district, Arasikere taluk) over the issue of wresting the gram panchayat president's position (*Deccan Herald*, 9 March 2002). Gram sabhas often are not held on schedule, but are shown on record to have been convened, by obtaining voters' signatures from their houses. Neither the officials nor the elected representatives take meetings seriously; the people lack enthusiasm, as they mistrust the institution.

Thimmaiah's study (1993), of the power politics behind OBC reservations in Karnataka points out that reservations have failed to prevent dominant castes from cornering opportunities. He says that the reservation policy has had many negative consequences, such as inefficiency, a dulling of the competitive spirit, indiscipline, indifference, intensifying of caste politics, poor performance, widespread caste prejudice, an extraordinary degree of corruption and intolerable level of arrogance. He favours socio-economic surveys to identify true BCs, and the introduction of severe penalties to prevent undeserving elements from monopolizing opportunities.

Every study acknowledges that electoral reservation has provided the disadvantaged with at least physical access to political space. Some studies are optimistic that in due course local governments may play a more effective role if these institutions receive the required support from the people and the State. Many studies are critical that physical access to political space has not led to an improvement in the status of elected members or the community they represent.

EMERGING SUGGESTIONS

As already mentioned, without electoral reservation, political power would have remained with the dominant and forward castes to a much larger extent. Circulation of power is an essential element of a progressive democracy. Electoral reservation has triggered the circulation of political power in favour of women, SCs, STs and BCs. Thus, the political representation of the weaker sections has been growing stronger from election to election, at national, state and local levels. While electoral reservation has triggered a power shift at the local level, the following issues have emerged:

- Is the power-shift hastening or slowing down the pace of societal development?
- Has access to political space led to the socio-educational and economic improvement of the disadvantaged sections?
- Is reservation creating a dependency syndrome?
- Has this created proxy leaders? If so, who are the beneficiaries? What is the impact of 'backseat driving' on society?
- Can the mechanism of electoral reservation in its present form provide opportunities to the most needy and prevent the creamy layers from cornering the opportunities?
- Is electoral reservation capable of effectively breaking the stronghold of the dominant castes over political positions? Karnataka's experience clearly shows that the Lingayats and Vokkaligas are numerically preponderant in government jobs, education and cultivable land. Using these advantages, the dominant castes would continue their hold over apex political power. Is there justification for electoral reservation for dominant castes? At national and state levels, the BCs have been able to corner a large share of political space without electoral reservation. At sub-state levels also, the BCs may find easy

access to political space, even if there is no electoral reservation. Is there no justification for limiting electoral reservation only in favour of SCs, STs and women?

The literature review already presented suggests that the electoral reservation has both positive and negative elements. It is time to free the reservation policy from its negative aspects so as to make it more purposeful. In this direction the following suggestions are offered.

Reservation should be time bound

The Constitution is clear that all preferential policies and programmes should aim at helping the disadvantaged and depressed sections to advance socially, educationally, economically and politically in order to level the playing field. As pronounced time and again by all court judgements, such measures should be temporary. The nation should be prepared to end all discriminatory policies in its march towards equality. Initially the stipulated period for electoral reservations was for 10 years. However, Parliament has already extended it to 50 years, without formulating a mechanism to prevent the creamy layers from cornering the reservation benefits. It is proposed that such reservations be reduced in a phased manner. As a complete withdrawal would stir up violence across the nation, reservations have to be tapered off gradually. Therefore, a cut by 1.5 per cent for all categories every five years, to be fully phased out by the turn of the century would perhaps be in order.

The creamy layer must be kept outside the reservation net

Electoral reservation would be more purposeful if its benefits reach the most backward, while the dominant or better-off were prevented from cornering its rewards. In Palkhivala's (1974) opinion, caste may carry class characteristics, but caste should not be used synonymously with class. Caste hierarchy, but also educational level, housing, means of livelihood, traditional occupation, property position, etc., should be considered in order to construct a socio-educational and economic (means) index for castes. This would enable not only to assign a BC tag to the most deserving, but also to eliminate the creamy layer so that the intended group derives the greatest benefit from the reservations policy. Courts have often directed the State to develop effective, scientific mechanisms to prevent the creamy layers within BC/SC/ST categories from monopolizing benefits.

Successive BC Commissions have proposed mechanisms in this regard, by defining a ceiling in terms of income. The Havanoor Commission (1975) suggested an annual household income not exceeding Rs 10,000; The Venkata Swamy Commission (1986) had suggested Rs 15,000 as the income ceiling for availing the quota benefit. The Karnataka Government fixed the ceiling at Rs 10,000 in 1986. However, under-reporting of income makes it difficult to use this indicator and remove the creamy layers from beneficiaries.

Based on the recommendation of the Fourth BC Commission (2002) the Karnataka Government recently modified its definition of the creamy layer. Accordingly, no quota for job or education is permissible to BCs with an annual income of over Rs 2,00,000. Candidates of high-income parents in top government/public sector / private sector jobs with a basic scale of Rs 6,000 to Rs 11,200 are also ineligible for the quota. Families owning over 10 acres of farmland or over 20 acres of plantation crops are eliminated. Children of legislators and parliamentarians who have completed a full term are also ineligible. Though the concept is laudable, the income and land ceiling limits are unreasonably high, defeating the purpose of these modifications.

This essay proposes that those possessing 5 acres of irrigated land or 10 acres of rain-fed land or with an annual family income exceeding Rs 50,000 should be ineligible for electoral reservation. Moreover, children of Class I officers, professionals, legislators and parliamentarians should be ineligible for quota benefits. The proposed property and income limit presupposes that these people do not need reservation for advancement. Last but not least, electoral reservation should not be available to castes that make up more than 25 per cent of the population in a constituency. Castes with a high concentration are well positioned to wrest political posts by sheer numerical strength.

Rectification of faulty BC lists

A reading of the Backward Classes Commission reports and the judicial pronouncements help us understand how caste lobbying, political expediency and bias influenced the inclusion of undeserving castes in the BC list. The number of castes recommended as BCs by various Commissions varies widely. A number of dominant castes have gained entry into these lists. Thus, the number of castes in the BC list goes on extending, like Hanuman's tail in the *Ramayana*.

Several caste-based associations and the truly backward and disadvantaged groups are raising their voice against the inaccurate listing of castes for reservation benefits. They are against this flawed system, which benefits the more assertive and privileged groups.

In Karnataka more particularly the fight between Holeyas and Madigas (both SCs) has reached a feverish pitch. The Holeyas have cornered most of the advantages while the Madigas, Chamar, Adhi Jambhava and others have received very few benefits.[7] The state is also witnessing a simmering discontent against the listing of the landed Lambanis as SCs.

Among the BCs, several caste groups are voicing their protests against the dominant Lingayats, Vokkaligas, Mogaviras (fishing community), Kurubas (shepherds), Edigas (toddy tapers), Kshatriyas and several other caste/community groups monopolizing the opportunities offered by reservation.

The demand for 'reservation within reservation' or for a mechanism to prevent the creamy layer from misusing benefits is being increasingly heard. This paper suggests that all castes/communities could be ranked according to socio-educational and economic indicators in reverse order (placing the lowest scoring caste at the top). The quota should also be offered in reverse order, starting with the most backward classes. In 1919, the Miller Committee was the earliest to suggest such a mechanism. This may help in reaching quota benefits to the more deserving. Besides, there should be a mechanism for a gradual reduction of quotas for groups of people within each caste/community as and when their socio-educational and economic position improves. Periodic socio-educational and economic status surveys of all castes/communities must be undertaken at least once in five years.

Minimum education for electoral candidates

Greater investment in education is important to create human capital, which has a positive correlation with both economic and social development. And proper education has the greatest potential for generating the transformation of individuals, society, nations and the world at large. Proper education not only improves productivity but can also break caste, class and gender barriers to promote greater socialization.

Literacy, democracy and development go hand in hand, as they are very closely linked. Therefore, it is time to make education a mandatory requirement for electoral candidates, from grass roots to national-level politics. We should note that these are the politicians who are involved in the preparation of local plans at sub-state levels, while at other levels they would participate in the process of policy making. These tasks require a good deal of education.

A seventh standard pass for gram panchayat, tenth standard (Secondary School Leaving Certificate), for taluk panchayat and twelfth (pre-university course) for zilla panchayat candidates should be made compulsory. Graduation should be compulsory for candidates contesting MLA/MP elections. Even though educational requirement prevents illiterates from contesting elections, we cannot afford to ignore the need for education on the part of elected representatives. Without ensuring quality input in the polity, the output cannot be positive. There should be no misunderstanding regarding the number of people that would be affected by an educational stipulation. As of now, not more than 10 per cent of those elected (and that too at the gram panchayat level) are illiterate, while at taluk and district levels illiterate members are even fewer. This does not imply that illiterates are uneducated, or that literacy ensures competence and commitment. However, it cannot be denied that a good formal education empowers members, enables them to reduce their dependence on officials and makes it more difficult to exploit such members as proxies. The educational requirement suggested is not confined to the reserved category alone; it should cover all categories.

Partyless democracy at the local level

Mahatma Gandhi did not favour party-based elections at the local level, as he felt they would encompass several undesirable evils. In Karnataka, as in most states, even at the local level elections are fought on party lines. Most of the mainstream political parties (including national parties) participate in local politics. This situation has over-politicized, criminalized and increased the cost of local politics. The party bosses allot tickets to the rich and dominant elements, as the criterion of 'winability' far outweighs all other considerations. This situation prevents distribution of power among the most backward groups. The fact is borne out in the study conducted by Rao (1995) at the state level. Party politics has badly divided the rural people. The acrimony witnessed in gram sabhas bears eloquent testimony to the political divide that rural India is subject to. The feasibility of introducing non-party based elections at panchayat levels is worthy of serious examination, even if the political pundits do not see merit in this proposition.

State funding of elections

As already emphasized, the reservation policy should have a built-in mechanism to provide benefits to the most deserving. However, electoral reservation is not well positioned to benefit the most backward. First of all, fighting an election even at the local level is not an easy proposition for the poor, who are battling for subsistence. Mere opportunity is not sufficient to enable the poor to avail of its benefits. At the gram panchayat level, a contestant would have to spend at least Rs 10,000 even to lose an election. There is justification in considering State funding of elections so as to make electoral reservation meaningful. To begin with, the State should finance the election expenditure of candidates contesting from reserved categories (including all women). In the absence of State funding, the dominant or better-off classes would continue to usurp political space.

Remuneration for elected members

The rendering of free service is unsustainable in the long run and it breeds corruption. Several studies have found that with the establishment of the PRIs, corruption is becoming truly decentralized (Prudhomme, 1995; Tanzi, 1995; Aziz et al., 1998; Narayanasamy et al., 2001). These authors are of the view that decentralized governance promotes inefficiency and provides scope for corruption owing to the influence of interest groups and discretion of local officials.

In Karnataka, the zilla panchayat and taluk panchayat members and chairpersons are paid monthly honorarium, guest allowance and sitting fee for attending meetings as shown in Table 7.4A. However,

TABLE 7.4A: CURRENT HONORARIUM/ALLOWANCES TO ZILLA PANCHAYAT AND TALUK PANCHAYAT MEMBERS IN KARNATAKA

No. of elected members in ZPs and TPs in 2000	Monthly Honorarium	Allowance for Attending Meeting	Guest Allowance	Estimated Annual Funds Required for Monthly Honorarium and Guest Allowance
Zilla Panchayat:				
a. President (27)	Rs 2,250	Rs 60	Rs 1,000	Rs 10,53,000
b. Vice-President (27)	Rs 1,750	Rs 60	Rs 8,000	Rs 8,26,200
c. Member (890)	Rs 1,000	Rs 60	NA	Rs 1,06,80,000
				Rs 1,25,59,200
Taluk Panchayat:				
a. President (175)	Rs 1,500	Rs 50	NA	Rs 31,50,000
b. Vice-President (175)	Rs 1,000	Rs 50	NA	Rs 21,00,000
c. Member (3255)	Rs 500	Rs 50	NA	Rs 1,95,30,000
				Rs 2,47,80,000
Gram Panchayat for all categories	NA	Rs 40	NA	

SOURCE: Worked out on the basis of present rate of honorarium in Govt. of Karnataka.

the gram panchayat members and chairpersons are not paid either the monthly honorarium or guest allowance; they are paid only the sitting fee for attending the monthly meeting. Paying the zilla and taluk panchayat representatives but not the gram panchayat members amounts to discrimination. Currently, the state Government is incurring about Rs 5 crore towards meeting these contingencies.

It is proposed that the gram panchayat members also be paid a monthly allowance. It is proposed to pay a monthly honorarium of Rs 750 to the members, Rs 1,000 to the vice-president and Rs 1,500 to the president of gram panchayats. It is also proposed that remuneration to the taluk and zilla panchayat members should be enhanced substantially, as shown in Table 7.4B. This would require an additional annual fund of about Rs 190 crore. In the light of these proposals, the existing guest allowance may be dispensed with.

TABLE 7.4B: ANNUAL FINANCIAL IMPLICATION OF PANCHAYAT REPRESENTATIVES' REMUNERATION ON KARNATAKA STATE

(*Rs in crores*)

Remuneration proposed per month	Gram Panchayat	Taluk Panchayat	Zilla Panchayat	Total
Rs 750 for 80,073 Members	72.06			
Rs 1,000 for 5,659 Vice-Presidents	06.79			
Rs 1,500 for 5,659 Presidents	10.18			
Rs 1,500 for 3,255 Members		5.85		
Rs 2,000 for 175 Vice-Presidents		0.42		
Rs 2,500 for 175 Presidents		0.52		
Rs 2,500 for 890 Members			2.67	
Rs 3,000 for 27 Vice-Presidents			0.09	
Rs 5,000 for 27 Presidents			0.16	
Total (as proposed)	89.03	6.79	2.92	98.74
Additional funds needed per annum				95.00

These measures may motivate elected members to become more enthusiastic about rendering better public service. The economically weak members in particular would benefit immensely from such a measure, which may enable their socio-educational improvement. It may encourage a more effective participation of members.

Training and capacity-building activities

Mere physical access by the disadvantaged sections to local political institutions is meaningless if increasing the competence of these members is not given due importance. Therefore, sufficient attention needs to be directed towards proper training and capacity-building activities. The training should enable members to internalize their responsibilities and prepare them for playing an effective role in translating the people's will into reality.

In Karnataka, the government has provisions for providing basic training to elected representatives. However, these training programmes are not properly designed. Currently the training is conducted over three days, largely as a token activity. Most people do not attend these training programmes, as they are not organized in nearby towns. In the 1990s, training courses for zilla panchayat members were held in Bangalore. Taluk panchayat members' training was organized in Mysore. These cities are far away and not easily accessible to a large number of people: women members—particularly those with families and small children—are burdened with domestic tasks, and many illiterate and less outgoing members need someone to escort them to the training centres.

Training needs to be imparted in various areas, such as the relationships and the cooperation that elected members need to maintain with officials, the rules of conduct in gram sabhas, the convening of meetings, the identification of local needs, the ways and means of local resource mobilization, etc. The resource persons involved in the training should be well versed in all aspects of the PRIs and be able to share their expertise with the trainees in their regional language.

Training and capacity-building activities should not be a one-time affair. The initial training should be provided within six months of the elections, while subsequent training should be compulsorily provided once a year thereafter. The training should be arranged in small groups in the most accessible towns within the taluk (for gram panchayat and taluk panchayat members) and at the district headquarters for the zilla panchayat members. Training centres should be equipped with all the facilities for a comfortable stay. While the initial training could focus on imparting basic information, the subsequent training courses should be participatory in nature, to allow members to discuss the difficulties they have encountered. Civil society can play a larger role than it does at present, in augmenting the capacity-building activities of elected representatives.

Data bank at village level

Caste-based information collection has been dispensed with by the decennial census with a view to weakening caste prejudice. In the absence of such information it has become difficult to evaluate the extent of socio-educational and economic improvements experienced by various classes.

It is suggested that there is need for evolving data banks at the gram panchayat level. Household information should be collected at the village level with the help of the gram panchayat secretary, who should ensure reliability and accuracy of information of the data. The information schedule should be prepared, covering all socio-economic aspects. The information thus generated should facilitate proper assessment of the socio-educational and economic status of the households. It should be open to the scrutiny of the households. Controversies if any, with regard to people's assets, livestock details, educational status, demographic details, employment particulars, sources of income, and so on should also be open to scrutiny by gram sabhas. To meet the diverse requirements of researchers, policy makers and other developmental agencies, it is recommended that these data be computerized and made easily accessible. The decennial census could draw all the required information from this data bank. The census authorities could be actively involved right from the initial stages to compile a comprehensive, multi-purpose village data bank. Population Census, Agricultural Census, Livestock Census, Census of Children, Child Labour Census, Unemployment Census, Census of the Aged, and several other types of surveys could avail the required information from village data banks. This would save time and resources currently being expended in the process of information retrieval.

Such an effective data bank would greatly help the administrative machinery and the policy makers to assess the impact of various community development programmes and undertake the changes needed to better reach programme benefits to their target groups. The Eleventh National Finance Commission has offered financial assistance for the creation of village data banks. This suggestion needs to be urgently taken to its logical end.

CONCLUSION

Many studies suggest that preferential policies pursued hitherto are contrary to the professed goals of the Constitution and have perpetuated inequalities instead of creating an egalitarian order.

Compensatory discrimination policies have strengthened caste consciousness instead of neutralizing it. Reservation for the BCs is a political expedient that has pit caste against caste (Galanter, 1984; Lieten, 1996; Malik and Kapur, 1998; Singh and Saxena, 1998; Thimmaiah, 1993, to cite a few).

This paper emphasizes the need for evolving effective mechanisms for translating the constitutional intent about reservation into a reality. Electoral reservation cannot benefit the most needy unless the State funds elections. For proper identification and elimination of creamy layers, effective socio-educational and economic composite index must be formulated and surveys conducted. Minimum education should be made compulsory for contestants. There is a need to focus on training and capacity-building activities to instil in both officials and elected members the necessary skills and motivation to discharge their responsibility. In order to enhance the commitment and motivational levels of members, this paper proposes remuneration to gram panchayat members. It is also of utmost importance to develop a multipurpose village data bank to identify the most backward classes among the population and to limit the benefits of reservations to include only the most deserving. Lastly, electoral reservation should be offered to castes that comprise not more than 25 per cent of the population in the constituencies.

Conscious efforts must be made towards ending all types of reservations in a phased manner, with a view to ensuring that Indian society conforms to the basic tenets of the Constitution of promoting equity, equality, liberty and justice. All policies and programmes should play the role of social equalizer. It is hoped that the suggestions flowing from this paper may help in freeing the electoral reservation from drawbacks and inadequacies and thereby enhance its effectiveness.

NOTES

1. For more details on Backward Classes movements in princely Mysore and post-Independence Mysore/Karnataka state, refer to Galanter, 1984; Manor, 1989; Rao, 1984; and Thimmaiah, 1993.
2. In Karnataka, the state government has deemed 190 castes/communities as Most Backward and 9 castes (with numerous sub-castes) as Backward, thus entitled to electoral reservation.

3. The reservation issue for employment and education has a long and convoluted history (see Galanter, 1984; Manor, 1989; Rao, 1984; Thimmaiah, 1993), which is not the main focus of this chapter.
4. The aforementioned efforts focussed on reservations in employment and education, but none examined the issue of electoral reservation for OBCs.
5. This 'people's court' was meant to administer justice at the grass-roots level without a government appointed judge. The chairman of the gram panchayat would act as the nyaya panchayat chairman. This mechanism would avoid delays in dispute settlement and prevent expenditure.
6. This is an administrative mechanism introduced in Karnataka in 2000 to assess the performance of gram panchayats against their objectives and expectations of the stakeholders. This mechanism is assumed to enhance transparency, accountability and good governance. Though the practice of *jamabandhi* was in vogue long ago, its rejuvenation in the context of PRIs is due to Ghorpade's relentless efforts (Sivanna and Babu, 2004).
7. The Holeyas identify themselves as the 'Right-hand caste group' while the Madigas, Chamars, Adhi Jambhavas, etc., are considered as 'Left-hand caste groups'. This distinction or identification with left or right hand is difficult to explain for both the groups. Certainly there are certain social taboos between these castes. They do not co-dine or entertain marriage alliances. The right-hand groups consider themselves superior to the left-hand groups. The fight between the right-hand and left-hand SCs in Andhra Pradesh has, quite often, unleashed feverish social conflicts. Each group wants separate per centage of quota as otherwise, the right-hand SCs will corner most of these reservation benefits and hardly leave anything for the left-hand SCs.

REFERENCES

Aziz, Abdul, *Decentralisation: Mandal Panchayat System in Karnataka*, Hyderabad: NIRD, 1994.

Aziz, Abdul et al., 'Decentralised Governance and Planning: A Comparative Study in Three South Indian States', Bangalore: ISEC, 1998 (Mimeo).

Chandran, Satish, 'Karnataka', in G. Mathew (ed.), *Status of Panchayati Raj in the States and Union Territories of India 2000*, Delhi: Concept, 2000.

Galanter, Marc, *Competing Equalities – Law and the Backward Classes in India*, Delhi: Oxford University Press, 1984.

Inbanathan, Anand, *The New Panchayati Raj in Karnataka: An Evaluation*, Delhi: ISS, 1992.

———, 'Karnataka Panchayats Under Administrators', ISS Occasional Paper Series 14, Delhi, 1994.

India, Govt. of, *Report of the Team for Study of Community Projects and National Extension Service* (Chairman: Balwantrai Mehta), New Delhi, 1957.

———, *Report of the Committee on Panchayati Raj Institutions* (Chairman: Ashok Mehta), Delhi, 1978.

———, *Report of the Commission on Centre-State Relations* (Chairman: Justice R.S. Sarkaria), Delhi, 1987.

Karnataka, Govt. of, *Report of First Backward Classes Commission* (Chairman: L.G. Havanoor), Bangalore, 1975.

———, *Report of Second Backward Classes Commission* (Chairman: T. Venkata Swamy), Bangalore, 1986.

———, *Report of Third Karnataka Backward Classes Commission* (Chairman: O. Chinnappa Reddy), Bangalore, 1990.

———, *Report of Fourth Backward Classes Commission* (Chairman: Ravivarma Kumar), Bangalore, 2002.

Lieten, G.K., *Development, Devolution and Democracy—Village Discourse in West Bengal*, Delhi, Sage, 1996.

Maheshwari, Shriram, *Mandal Commission Revisited—Reservation Bureaucracy in India*, Delhi: Jawahar Publishers and Distributors, 1995.

Malik, Y.K. and S. Padmanabh Pillai, 'Fifty years of State, Society and Political Culture in India—Continuity and Change', in Y.K. Malik and A. Kapur (eds), *Fifty Years of Democracy and Development*, Delhi: APH Publishing Corporation, 1998.

Manor, James, 'Karnataka: Caste, Class, Dominance and Politics in a Cohesive Society', in Francine R. Frankel and M.S.A. Rao (eds), *Dominance and State Power in Modern India – Decline of a Social Order*, vol. 1, Delhi: Oxford University Press, 1989.

Mathew, George (ed.), *Status of Panchayati Raj in the States and Union Territories of India 2000*, Delhi: Concept, 2000.

———, *Karnataka Rajakiya Duranta*, H.M. Kemparaju (trans.), Bangalore: ISS, 1994.

———, *Panchayati Raj in Karnataka Today*, Delhi: Concept, 1986.

Mishra, S.N. and S. Mishra 'Future of Panchayati Raj After 73rd Constitutional Amendment Act', *Kurukshetra*, April 1995, pp. 26–30.

Mysore, Govt. of, *Miller Committee* (Chair: Leslie C. Miller), Govt. Press, Mysore, 1919.

———, *Report of Mysore Backward Classes Committee* (Chair: Nagana Gowda), Bangalore, 1961.

Narayana, K.S., 'Policy Intervention and Emerging Patterns of Leadership: Study of ZP Chairpersons in Karnataka', in Vinod Vyasulu (ed.), *Facets of Development—Studies in Karnataka*, Jaipur: Rawat, 1997.

Narayana, K.S., 'Drawbacks Impeding Success of Positive Discrimination', *Journal of Indian Institute of Public Administration*, vol. 44, no. 3, July–Sept. 1998, pp. 520–33.

———, 'Annotated Bibliography of Literature on PRIs in India', FAIR and GPC, Bangalore (Mimeo), 1998.

———, 'Policy Efforts and Status of Empowerment, Participation and Development Achieved through PRIs', *Vision*, vol. 19, nos 3-4, Jan.–June 2000, pp. 1–14.

———, 'Review of Social Movements in India: A Critique', *Vision*, vol. 20, nos 1-2, July–Dec. 2001, pp. 51–64.

———, 'Thirteenth Lok Sabha Elections: State Review (Karnataka)', *Madhya Pradesh Jr. of Social Sciences*, vol. 5, no. 1, Jan.–June 2001, pp. 95–125.

Narayanasami, N. et al., *Corruption at the Grassroots: The Shades and Shadows*, Delhi: Concept, 2001.

Palkhivala, N.A., *Our Constitution Defaced and Defiled,* Delhi: Macmillan, 1974.

Prasad, Anirudh, *Reservational Justice to Other Backward Classes – Theoretical and Practical Issues*, Delhi: Deep and Deep, 1997.

Prudhomme, Remy, 'The Dangers of Decentralisation', *The World Bank Research Observer*, vol. 10, no. 2, 1995, pp. 201–20.

Rao, L.R. Ragavendra, 'Changing Pattern of Political Leadership in Karnataka', unpublished Ph.D. thesis, Bangalore, 1995.

Ray, Amal S. and K. Jayalakshmi, 'Zilla Parishad Presidents in Karnataka: Their Social Background and Implications for Development', *Economic and Political Weekly*, vol. 22, nos 42-43, 17–24 Oct. 1987, pp. 1825–30.

Singh, M.P. and Rekha Saxena (eds), *Ideologies and Institutions in Indian Politics*, Delhi: Deep and Deep, 1998.

Sivanna, N., 'Less Power to the People', *Deccan Herald*, Bangalore, 25 December 1993.

———, 'Amendments to Panchayati Raj Act', *Deccan Herald*, Bangalore, 28 September 1997.

Sivanna, N. and M. Devendra Babu, 'Panchayat Jamabandhi in Karnataka: A Case of Transparency, and Accountability in Good Governance', Working Paper No. 142, Institute for Social and Economic Change, Bangalore, 2004.

Tanzi, Vito, 'Fiscal Federalism and Decentralisation: A Review of Some Efficiency and Macroeconomic Aspects', in Michael Bruno and Boris Pleskovic (eds), *Annual World Bank Conference on Development Economics*, Washington D.C.: The World Bank, 1995.

Thimmaiah, G., *Power Politics and Social Justice: Backward Castes in Karnataka*, Delhi: Sage, 1993.

ANNEXURE

Relevant Provisions of the Indian Constitution

PREAMBLE

We, the people of India, having solemnly resolved to constitute India into a sovereign democratic republic and to secure to all its citizens JUSTICE (social, economic and political), LIBERTY (of thought, belief, faith and worship), EQUALITY (of status and of opportunity; and to promote among them all) FRATERNITY (assuring the dignity of the individual and the unity of the nation) . . . hereby adopt, enact and give to ourselves this Constitution.

PART III: FUNDAMENTAL RIGHTS

Article 14

The State shall not deny to any person equality before the law or the equal protection of the laws within the territory of India.

Article 15

(1) The State shall not discriminate against any citizen on grounds only of religion, race, caste, sex, place or birth or any of them;

(2) No citizen shall, on grounds only of religion, race, caste, sex, place of birth or any of them, be subject to any disability, liability, restriction or condition with regard to (a) access to shops, public restaurants, hotels and places of public entertainment, or (b) the use of wells, tanks, bathing ghats, roads and places of public resort maintained wholly or partly out of State funds or dedicated to the use of the general public;

(3) Nothing in this article shall prevent the State from making any special provision for women and children.

(4) Nothing in this Article or in clause (2) of Article 29 shall prevent the State from making any special provision for the advancement of any socially and educationally backward classes of citizens or for the Scheduled Castes and the Scheduled Tribes.

Article 16(4)

Nothing in this article shall prevent the State from making any provision for the reservation of appointments or posts in favour of any backward class of citizens which, in the opinion of the State, is not adequately represented in the services under the State.

Article 17

'Untouchability' is abolished and its practice in any form is forbidden. The enforcement of any disability arising out of 'untouchability' shall be an offence punishable in accordance with law.

Article 29

No citizen shall be denied admission into any educational institution maintained by the State or receiving aid out of State funds on grounds only of religion, race, caste, language or any of them.

PART IV: ARTICLE 46

The State shall promote with special care the educational and economic interests of the weaker sections of the people, and, in particular, of the Scheduled Castes and Scheduled Tribes, and shall protect them from social injustice and all forms of exploitation.

PART XVI: ARTICLE 330

(1) Seats shall be reserved in the Houses of the People for (i) Scheduled Castes, (ii) Scheduled Tribes. . . .

Article 332

(i) Seats shall be reserved for the SCs and the STs, except the STs in the tribal areas . . . in the Legislative Assembly of every State.

PART IX: ARTICLE 343(D)

1. Seats shall be reserved for (a) the Scheduled Castes; and (b) the Scheduled Tribes in every Panchayat and the number of seats so reserved shall bear, as nearly as may be, the same proportion to the total number of seats to

be filled by direct election in that Panchayat as the population of SCs and STs in the Panchayat area. . . .

2. Not less than one-third of the total number of seats reserved under clause (1) shall be reserved for women belonging to the SCs or, as the case may be, the STs.
3. Not less than one-third (including the number of seats reserved for women belonging to SCs and STs) of the total number of seats to be filled by direct election in every Panchayat shall be reserved for women. . . .
4. The offices of the Chairpersons in the Panchayats at the village or any other level shall be reserved for the SCs, the STs and women in such manner as the Legislature of a State may, by law, provide. . . .

CHAPTER 8

Reservations for Women in Urban Local Bodies: A Tentative Assessment

STÉPHANIE TAWA LAMA-REWAL

The decentralization policy often referred to as 'Panchayati Raj' actually comprises two distinct, if very similar, dimensions: a rural dimension, defined by the 73rd Constitutional Amendment Act (CAA), and an urban dimension, defined by the 74th CAA. Both Acts were passed in 1992, and subsequently conformity legislations were passed and progressively implemented by different states from 1994 onwards. One of the major provisions of the 73rd and 74th CAAs concerns the mandatory reservation of a number of seats (including that of chairperson) for women (33 per cent) and for the Scheduled Castes (SC) and Scheduled Tribes (ST) in proportion to their respective demographic weight,[1] at all levels of local self-government. This paper is specifically concerned with the provisions of the 74th CAA according to which 33 per cent of seats in the elected assemblies of municipal corporations, municipal councils and nagar panchayats[2] shall be reserved for women.

Women (as well as Other Backward Classes/Castes, or OBCs) are the latest social category to benefit from compensatory discrimination in the form of electoral reservations or quotas, in the Indian polity. In the first instance, reservations (in favour of the SCs and STs) were provided in the founding text of Indian democracy, the Constitution, and have been implemented since 1952 at the parliamentary and state assembly levels.

As far as their rationale is concerned, reservations pertain to the logic of real, as opposed to formal, equality. They are part of a set of affirmative action measures intended to compensate for the multi-dimensional prejudice suffered over the centuries by some groups, resulting in their present backwardness. Social justice is, therefore, the core concern of reservations.

More specifically, electoral reservations are supposed to ensure political representation of those groups identified as backward. Concretely, a number of constituencies, whose population is characterized by a high percentage of people from the SCs and STs, have been reserved for SCs or STs (which means that all candidates to general and state elections in these constituencies must belong to either group), so as to ensure that the number of elected representatives belonging to these social categories would at least be proportionate to their demographic weight in the Union or in the state.

The women's category is obviously different in nature from that of the SCs, STs and OBCs: women constitute half the population, do not live in isolation from men, and are divided according to all possible social, cultural and economic criteria. In other words, women, unlike castes and tribes, are not a group. Yet women's quotas, both in their rationale and in their design, are closely modelled on the reservations for the SCs and STs, with two exceptions. First, women have been considered by legislators as too large a group to benefit from quotas in proportion to their demographic importance. Quotas for women are thus limited to 33 per cent of the total number of seats, a figure usually justified by the 'critical mass' theory, according to which 33 per cent is the threshold from which a minority is able to have an impact on the decisions of the whole group (Dahlerup, 1988). Second, women are too evenly dispersed over the national territory for any 'women's constituency' to be permanently defined. Thus, the principle of rotation of reserved constituencies (for women, but also for SCs, STs, and OBCs wherever applicable) has been adopted for local elections—even though the pace of rotation and the modalities of selecting reserved constituencies differ from state to state.

In order to assess the implementation of reservations for women in the Indian urban local bodies, I will first outline the expectations attached to these reservations, and then confront these expectations with what is known of the way in which quotas function today.

WHY DO WE NEED RESERVATIONS FOR WOMEN?

The first question that arises when one tries to assess reservations for women is: what are these reservations meant to achieve, what is their *raison d'être*, and what is their yardstick?

Even though the provisions concerning reservations for women in elected local bodies have largely contributed to the interest evoked by the decentralization policy, as they were deemed a bold step towards democratization in general and gender justice in particular, they were in fact hardly discussed in Parliament during the long debates preceding the enactment of the two constitutional amendment bills. One has therefore, to look beyond the parliamentary debates of the years 1989–92 to find an explicit discussion on electoral reservations for women.

The issue of women's political representation and of the means thereof is actually an old one; it was raised as early as 1917, when Indian women's organizations started lobbying the British government, demanding that women be included in the broader franchise base provided by the constitutional reforms of British India.

As far as independent India is concerned, the option of reservations for women appeared for the first time in the report written by Kaka Kalelkar, chairman of the first Backward Classes Commission, who stated that:

> The position of women in India is peculiar. We have always felt that they have lived under great social handicaps and must, therefore, as a class be regarded as backward. But since they do not form a separate community it has not been possible for us to list them among the backward classes. (GOI, 1955: 31)

The same question was later addressed by the Committee on the Status of Women in India (CSWI), formed in 1974 to prepare for the Women's Decade (1975–85) proclaimed by the United Nations. In its report, *Towards Equality*, it discussed the pros and cons of resorting to quotas in order to improve the abysmally low political representation of women. After listing the arguments in favour of reservations for women in elected assemblies, this option was finally rejected on the following grounds:

> Separate constituencies for women would narrow their outlook. (…) Women's interests as such cannot be isolated from economic, social and political interests of groups, strata and classes in society. (…) The minority argument cannot be applied to women. Women are not a community, they are a category. (GOI 1974: 304)

For the second time, then, the fact that 'women are not a community'—for they are not 'separate' from the rest of society but on the contrary, are scattered among all existing groups—was invoked as a major obstacle to the option of resorting to affirmative measures to improve their political representation.

The question resurfaced in the late 1980s, when it became clear that the alternative measures suggested by the CSWI—such as the creation of women's panchayats, or councils, at the local level or the adoption by political parties of internal quotas for women—were not being considered seriously. The women's movement then took up the issue, making women's political representation, for the first time, one of its priorities. It found an ally in Rajiv Gandhi who had reasons to publicly defend electoral reservations for women: such a posture fitted well with the image he wanted to project of his government as committed to social (and economic) modernization. The following declaration of the Prime Minister shows what expectations *he* attached to women's quotas at the local level:

> We believe the presence of women in large numbers in the panchayats will not only make the panchayats more representative but will also make them more efficient, honest, disciplined and more responsible. (Gandhi, 1989: 12–13)

This view of the rationale for women's quotas was not challenged at the time, indeed these quotas were hardly discussed. It is only after the 73rd and 74th CAAs were passed that a public debate over electoral reservations for women really took place. It was triggered in 1996 by the introduction in the Lok Sabha of a new constitutional amendment bill, seeking to extend women's quotas to state Assemblies and Parliament. The Women's Reservation Bill (WRB), as it has since been called, seems today to have been definitely shelved; it nevertheless generated an intense debate in the years following its introduction, a debate that took place in Parliament as well as in the media, and at a number of seminars and conferences throughout the country.

This debate clearly spelt out a series of positive and negative expectations attached to women's quotas, and more generally it gave a hearing to the many voices that wanted to discuss the objectives and means for greater political representation of women. I have elsewhere analysed the debate over the WRB (Tawa Lama-Rewal,

2001), but this paper will simply list the seven main arguments that emerged in the course of the debate.

First, a set of three arguments in favour of women's quotas on the *objectives* of such a policy:

1. By guaranteeing a minimal representativeness of elected assemblies in terms of gender, women's quotas will promote *gender justice*;
2. The increased presence of women in legislative bodies will ensure better *representation of women's interests*;
3. Women's quotas will enable elected assemblies, and, therefore society at large, to profitably tap *the resource base constituted by women's specific talents*.

Second, a set of negative arguments, highlighting the flaws in the quota system as a *means* towards a more equitable political representation of women:

4. Only *upper class women, or female relatives of politicians, will actually benefit* from reservations;
5. Not enough women are presently ready to work as legislators; therefore, a large number of *incompetent people are likely to be elected*;
6. A *male backlash* is to be expected, which will confine women to a political ghetto, in terms of the constituencies open to them and the positions they can occupy within the legislative Assemblies.[3]

WHAT IS UNIQUE ABOUT THE DEBATE OVER WOMEN'S QUOTAS?

If we take all the arguments expressed at various intervals in the past 50 years, for and against electoral reservations for women, it appears that the debate over women's quotas has, by and large, focussed on the same issues as the debate over reservations for the other social categories concerned (i.e. SCs, STs and OBCs).

The first major issue is *the potential of reservations as instruments of social change*. Will reservations benefit the group or only a few individuals? Can reservations per se promote the representation of the group's interests? What are the chances that the redistribution of political opportunities resulting from reservations will actually be registered through the non-integration of the beneficiaries of reservations?

This issue is clear in argument 2, about the representation of women's interests. It also permeates argument 4, i.e. whether elected women happen to be upper class women or female relatives of male politicians. What is at stake here is the representativeness of women representatives: in both cases gender consciousness is implicitly suspected to be no match for class- or family-based solidarity. Lastly, the danger of a male backlash (i.e. argument 6) also comes within the purview of this issue.

The second issue relates to *the criteria adopted to define backwardness* since, according to the Indian Constitution, the backwardness of a given group is the *raison d'être* of all reservation policies. Can women, *as women*, be considered backward? This question permeates the older argument that women are not a community (i.e. women's social status varies widely depending on their class, their caste/community, their age, their marital status, etc.). Moreover, the fear, expressed since 1996 by OBC representatives across political parties, that reservations for women would result in increasing the hold of the elite on politics (argument 4), clearly shows that gender is fiercely contested as a ground for backwardness.

The third issue relates to what André Béteille calls the '*well-being of institutions*' affected by reservations (Béteille, 1998). Even though Béteille excluded electoral reservations from his analysis, the fear that women's quotas would result in incompetent people being elected (argument 5) pertains to the same concern. But the argument 3, according to which women constitute a political resource is an interesting, indeed a unique position on this issue. It finally appears, then, that in the course of the debate over electoral reservations, the sub-theme of women's quotas is unique only as far as the 'resource' argument is concerned. Only women have been said to embody, as women, qualities such as peacefulness, honesty, devotion, etc. One has only to imagine similar qualities being attributed to SCs, STs or OBCs to realize the patronizing, essentialist (and therefore politically dangerous) nature of this argument.

Having spelt out the expectations attached to reservations for women, and the way these fit into the larger debate over electoral reservations, this paper will now turn to the implementation, since 1993, of these reservations in the urban local bodies.

SOURCES AND LIMITS OF THE ASSESSMENT OF RESERVATIONS FOR WOMEN

Any assessment of the decentralization policy defined by the 74th CAA is subject to three major difficulties. First, the current status of local self-government is extremely heterogeneous throughout the Indian Union. Some states have just organized local elections, while others are now well into their second term in the context of the new legislative framework. Moreover, while local democracy has been a reality in some states (such as West Bengal) for the past 25 years or so, in other states (such as Tamil Nadu) it had, until 1993, largely remained a dead letter.

Secondly, the decentralization policy is 13 years old. What is therefore being assessed is only the first phase of its implementation, and one must keep in mind that the time factor may strongly affect today's observations.

Lastly, information is comparatively limited: there has not been sufficient research on the implementation of women's quotas in urban local bodies as compared to the wealth of studies conducted on women in Panchayati Raj Institutions. The following analysis will be based on six studies dealing respectively with Punjab (Gill, 1999), Haryana (Arora and Prabhakar, 1997 and MARG, 2000), Delhi (MARG, 2000), Maharashtra (Nanivadekar, 1997), and West Bengal (Ghosh 1996, Tawa Lama-Rewal, 2001).

Despite the absence of a southern perspective, these studies together provide a fairly diversified sample of what has been observed in urban India. In order to get a consistent view across the different states surveyed, the author had to focus on concerns common to all or most of them, including the profile of elected women in terms of education levels and occupation, the number of representatives by proxy, or 'proxies', the difficulties they have experienced and their achievements.

What, then, do we know today of the implementation and impact of women's quotas in Indian cities?

WHO ARE THE BENEFICIARIES OF WOMEN'S QUOTAS?

All available studies provide data about the education level and previous occupation of women representatives, which gives us some clues about two questions: (i) Are upper class women over-represented among the beneficiaries of reservations? (ii) How many proxies are there among elected women?

Table 8.1 gives a picture of the education level of women elected to the local bodies reviewed in the above mentioned studies. On the one hand, it highlights the predictably higher level of education in the metropolises as compared to the small towns. On the other, it shows that women representatives are relatively more educated in West Bengal as a whole, which is consistent with the generally high level of education of the Bengali political class (Tawa Lama-Rewal, forthcoming). It also highlights the high number of illiterate representatives in Punjab and Haryana, which raises questions about the capacity of these women to fulfill their political functions.

Table 8.2 highlights the same contrasts as Table 8.1, and gives us some clues as to the number of proxies. Ex-housewives constitute the majority of women representatives everywhere but in West Bengal, where the large proportion of teachers among elected women is again consistent with the sociological profile of the Bengali political personnel as a whole. After West Bengal, the largest number of ex-working women is to be found in Maharashtra and in Delhi, i.e. in big cities. On the contrary, the proportion of ex-housewives is particularly high in Punjab and in Haryana.

The above findings suggest that two factors play an important role in the local impact of the 74th CAA. Firstly, contrasts between the different states are considerable, which testifies to the weight of the regional (political) culture. Thus, in West Bengal the high education levels of elected women, the large proportion of former teachers among them, but also the large proportion of upper caste members (67 per cent) among elected women is typical of the elite character of the local political personnel (Ghosh, 1996: 33).

Secondly, the contrasts between the different types of local bodies suggest that the size of cities also matters. But the large number of illiterates and the high proportion of former housewives among elected women in Punjab, where the cities surveyed are big enough to have a municipal corporation, suggest that this factor is less important than

TABLE 8.1: EDUCATION LEVEL OF WOMEN MEMBERS OF URBAN LOCAL BODIES

(% of the total number of women surveyed)

	Calcutta Municipal Corporation	West Bengal (2 Municipal Corporations, 2 Municipal Councils, 1 Nagar Panchayat)	Punjab (3 Municipal Corporations)	Delhi Municipal Corporation	Karnal Nagar Panchayat	Rohtak Municipal Council	Maharashtra (12 Municipal Corporations)
University degree	73	54	36	66	19	30	7
Middle level (Primary to Matric)	14	12.5	52	33	31	60	NA
Illiterate	0	0	25	0	5	10	NA

SOURCES: Gill, 1999; Arora and Prabhakar, 1997; MARG, 2000; Nanivadekar, 1997; Ghosh, 1996; Tawa Lama-Rewal, 2001.

TABLE 8.2: OCCUPATION OF WOMEN MEMBERS OF URBAN LOCAL BODIES

(% of the total number of women surveyed)

	Calcutta Municipal Corporation	West Bengal (2 Municipal Corporations, 2 Municipal Councils, 1 Nagar Panchayat)	Punjab (3 Municipal Corporations)	Delhi Municipal Corporation	Karnal Nagar Panchayat	Rohtak Municipal Council	Maharashtra (12 Municipal Corporations)
Housewife	24	33	84	54	81	70	59
Teacher	38	25	0	21	0	0	4
Self-employed	7	17	8	21	19		18
Professional	14	NA	8	0	0	10	
Employee	10	12.5	0	4	0		

SOURCES: Gill, 1999; Arora and Prabhakar, 1997; MARG, 2000; Nanivadekar, 1997; Ghosh, 1996; Tawa Lama-Rewal, 2001.

political culture.[4] Indeed, both Haryana and Punjab are characterized by societies in which male domination is particularly strong.

The lack of homogeneous information on the social status (in terms of caste/community identity) and income of elected women in the studies herein referred to is obviously a major limitation for our tentative assessment. Let us mention, however, that in Rohtak (Haryana) 'most candidates belonged to the middle economic category' (Arora and Prabhakar, 1997: 923); in Maharashtra 'financial resources at the disposal of the aspirants (is one of) the most crucial criteria for getting party nomination' (Nanivadekar, 1997: 20); in Calcutta financial resources were also found to be very important, not only for the campaign but also to meet the demands of the councillor's job (Tawa Lama-Rewal, 2001: 15). While these examples do not allow us to conclude as to the elite character, in terms of income, of the majority of elected women, they nevertheless strongly suggest that poor people are indeed excluded from municipal contests.

HOW MANY 'PROXIES' ARE THERE?

'Most of the women elected to local bodies in Haryana are the proxy of their husband' (MARG, 2000: 16). In Maharashtra, 32 per cent of the women surveyed said that 'the sole reason for contesting the election was the conversion of the constituency hitherto nursed by their close male relative . . . into a constituency reserved for women' (Nanivadekar: 16), which fits the definition of proxy representatives. In Calcutta, it was found that 11 per cent of the women elected in 1995 occupied a seat previously held by a male relative. All these women could therefore be qualified as inheritors. But further investigation revealed that all inheritors were not proxies, as was proved by the fact that some of them got elected a second time, and what is more, in a general ward. And all proxies were not inheritors: women representatives could be puppets in the hand of their party, for instance (Tawa Lama-Rewal, 2001: 16).

These facts suggest that an analysis in terms of political resources would actually tell us more about the potential of elected women than just their relationship with the sitting councillor of the ward from which they were elected. Thus, the proportion of illiterate women, and ex-housewives, benefitting from reservations in Punjab, is a strong indicator of the lack of political resources (such as education, contacts, money and political experience) of elected women in this state. As such they suggest that a large number of them are probably proxies and at the very least quite susceptible to being manipulated by male politicians.

Table 8.3 shows the distribution of two political resources among elected women in three states. The data provided earlier about the occupation and education levels of women give us some hints as to how to interpret these figures. Thus, the high proportion of women with a family tradition of political participation in Punjab confirms our hypothesis that a large majority of female representatives there are proxies. On the contrary, the most widely distributed political resource among women councillors in Calcutta is the former membership of a political party (or of a front organization of a political party), which fits in with the small number of proxy candidates observed in this city. The figures for Maharashtra highlight the non-exclusive character of these two resources. Indeed, while a prior political activism can guarantee political experience, contacts, and often party support, a family tradition of political participation ensures some familiarity with political activism, a legitimate (male) patronage, and family support, which are all important political resources.

WHAT ARE THE MAJOR DIFFICULTIES FACED BY ELECTED WOMEN?

The lack of time seems to be the most widely shared problem faced by women politicians. In Maharashtra, elected women 'continued to

TABLE 8.3: POLITICAL BACKGROUND OF ELECTED WOMEN

(% of the total number of women surveyed)

	Calcutta Municipal Corporation	Punjab (3 Municipal Corporations)	Maharashtra (12 Municipal Corporations)
Family tradition of political participation	37.5	72	58
Previous political activism	77	16	50

SOURCES: Gill, 1999; Nanivadekar, 1997; Tawa Lama-Rewal, 2001.

perform all those duties that are expected of a full time housewife' (Nanivadekar, 1997:17). In Punjab they lamented their 'over-indulgence in household affairs' (Gill, 1999: 55). In Calcutta, too, all respondents identified the perpetual shortage of time as a major problem (Tawa Lama-Rewal, 2001: 23). The difficult task of juggling domestic responsibilities with public obligations is familiar to all working women. But for women politicians the difficulty is even greater, because one feature common to domestic and political work is that both involve total commitment (Laufer, 1995: 378).

The second major handicap experienced by many elected women is the lack of training. This is, of course, related to the fact that many beneficiaries of reservations are newcomers to politics, a state of affairs aggravated by the substantial proportion of former housewives among them. Unfortunately, nowhere have urban local bodies thought of providing minimal training to the new councillors, at least not during the first electoral term under the 74th CAA.

Thus, none of the women representatives interviewed in Karnal had received formal training for their new job, while in Delhi 42 per cent of the women councillors had been provided some training by their respective political parties (MARG, 2000: 98–9). The authors suggest that this might be due to the unique political status of Delhi, and that the high level of involvement of parties in the local affairs of the capital is not necessarily representative of the situation in most metropolises (MARG, 2000: 105). Indeed in Calcutta all the women interviewed said they had had to learn their new functions hands on, and it is only after the second municipal election under the 74th CAA, in 2000, that the Calcutta Municipal Corporation as well as the political parties organized training sessions for the newly elected councillors.

The third problem commonly faced by female representatives is male prejudice on the part of fellow councillors or of officials, which can take various forms, from not taking their women colleagues seriously to active discrimination in the distribution of important positions. Thus, Nanivadekar reports the under-representation of female corporators in the more important committees of Maharashtra's municipal corporations, while in the 'Women and Child Development Committee, [which] has 75 per cent seats reserved for women, usually all 100 per cent members are women because men find it embarrassing to be a member of this committee' (Nanivadekar, 1997: 36).

In Calcutta however, even though women are under-represented in the decision-making positions within the Corporation, one must note that (i) already prior to the implementation of the 74th CAA a woman was in charge of the all important Water department; and that after the implementation of women's quotas (ii) a woman has become deputy mayor for the first time, and (iii) the number of women chairpersons of borough committees has increased (Tawa Lama-Rewal 2001: 43).

Here again being a proxy or an inheritor means benefitting from comparatively greater political support. In Maharashtra again, 'without reservations (in the various committees of the municipal corporations), the proxies find it relatively easier to get elected to the committees (since) their husbands do all the manoeuvring necessary in acquiring for them a position on important committees' (Nanivadekar, 1997: 36).

WHAT HAVE FEMALE REPRESENTATIVES ACHIEVED SO FAR?

Another major theme common to all studies is the performance of the beneficiaries of reservations, once elected. What have been the achievements of women councillors? More particularly, have they done anything to improve the lives of women in their cities? And finally, has the greater presence of so many women changed anything in the working of urban local bodies?

The major concern of elected women both in Delhi and Karnal was the construction, repair and maintenance of roads, bridges and streets (MARG, 2000: 84), while on problems likely to affect women more specifically, such as public toilets, only 7 per cent of the Karnal representatives and 21 per cent of the Delhi representatives had done anything. As far as health issues were concerned, 8 per cent of elected women in Delhi, but no one in Karnal, had done anything (ibid.: 84). However women representatives in both cities did mention their work on pensions for widows (ibid.: 91), but in the absence of analogous information on the work of men representatives, one cannot determine whether this is an affirmation of some gender based solidarity.

In Calcutta, the women councillors interviewed mentioned water, drainage and roads as their chief concerns; only 12 per cent of them mentioned the lack of toilets, and 6 per cent the need for maternity homes. Moreover, an analysis of the proceedings of the Corporation meetings over a five year period showed that among the issues discussed in the House, those which could be identified as women's issues—such as health, pensions for widows or public toilets—were in fact raised mostly by male councillors. Women councillors generally intervened less often than the male councillors and mostly on water-related problems (Tawa Lama-Rewal, 2001: 35)

The 'critical mass' theory therefore is not substantiated through the implementation of women's quotas in Indian cities, at least not during the first five years. Numbers, obviously, are not enough. Several observations point to the fact that gender consciousness is, if not absent, at least not thought to be legitimate by women representatives.

Indeed, a gender-based agenda is conspicuously absent at every stage of municipal politics, starting with the selection of candidates. Thus, in Maharashtra 'the women's wings of all the parties . . . have not played any decisive role in the selection of women candidates for the municipal elections' (Nanivadekar, 1997: 28). Moreover, even in that state, which has for long been the headquarters of the Indian women's movement, 'most women corporators have had no involvement in the feminist movement . . . they do not display any primary commitment to the women's cause' (ibid.: 29).

My own survey showed that most women councillors in Calcutta actually differentiate between their concerns as private individuals and as public persons. None of them were women's rights activists, yet they did express concern for the problems faced by women in their ward, and underlined the fact that being a woman enabled them to better understand them. But at the same time, they considered that dealing with these problems was not their main function, but rather an additional burden to their existing workload as councillors. Moreover, they dismissed any idea of a common front of women councillors, cutting across party lines, on important women's issues; the party, clearly, was their unique reference (Tawa Lama-Rewal, 2001: 44). Similarly, in Maharashtra, 'there was some evidence of local attempts at forming a women's alliance on the basis of some common agenda, but the affiliations and loyalties to political parties were the obstacle to the formation of such an alliance' (Nanivadekar, 1997: 29).

Lastly, the question of the achievement of women representatives' encompasses that of the impact of their presence on the working of urban local bodies. On this respect, the data is scarce and heterogeneous. But the studies on Maharashtra and Calcutta mention incidents of physical violence displayed by women representatives (Nanivadekar, 1997: 20; Tawa Lama-Rewal, 2001: 47). Moreover, 'in Mumbai, out of 511 women candidates, 6 were reported to have links with the underworld' (Nanivadekar, 1997: 21). This proves that men do not have the monopoly of violence.

CONCLUSION

The six studies used for the present assessment present many contrasting observations, and a few common findings. The contrasts, obviously, are striking both between different states, and between metropolitan cities and small towns. While Calcutta looks like a success story, Karnal raises many doubts as to the efficacy of reservations for women.

In Punjab and in Haryana indeed all negative expectations attached to women's quotas seem to be validated. A majority of elected women appear to be proxy representatives; moreover the relatively large number of illiterate people among the representatives, and the fact that most of them used to be housewives mean that many of them are deprived of most of the resources necessary for political participation. As a consequence, their performance as councillors is likely to be poor, and they are obviously not armed to resist male attempts to sideline them. Women's quotas are thus, as expected, largely ineffective in social situations characterized by strong male domination.

But the findings on Delhi, Maharashtra and West Bengal suggest that the general picture presents more nuances. In these three states, the educational, professional and political background of elected women is quite varied and so is, most probably, their performance. However, one commonly expressed need in this respect is training, which is all the more necessary as most women representatives are newcomers to municipal politics. Both political parties and the officials in urban local bodies could make an important contribution in this regard, to the success of women's quotas.

The other problem commonly faced by elected women is the lack of time. This highlights the importance of family support as a political resource, since only the family can provide the necessary assistance on the domestic front. It can also, as said earlier, be a source of training and patronage. Because family is such a rich political resource, it is important to refrain from equating inheritors with puppets, or proxies, as has often been done in media reports.

As far as the male backlash, and more generally the danger of 'ghettoization' of elected women is concerned, a follow-up study is essential. Only a detailed analysis of the *second* election, after the implementation of reservations, can enlighten us as to the real extent of male resentment, by showing whether elected women were given a ticket by their party even if their constituency is de-reserved. Such an analysis would also help differentiate proxies from inheritors, since one can assume that a woman who is given a ticket for the second time, although her male relative might have been eligible, has definitely become a politician in her own right.

Moreover, a follow-up study is necessary to assess the impact of the time factor. Time indeed is likely to have a positive effect on at least two problems faced by elected women today: their lack of training, and male prejudice.

The major finding common to all studies is that elected women have not set out to work for the representation of women's interests. If there is any gender consciousness among elected women, then it expresses itself at the margins of their field of activity. Clearly, they do not consider themselves as representatives of women first, and they do not consider women's issues as major issues. In other words, quotas have not transformed a category into a community so far. This situation calls for the intervention of women's organizations, whether party based or autonomous, in the municipal electoral process. Women's organizations could provide the much-needed support and training to candidates and elected women. Most importantly, by openly lobbying urban local bodies, they could work to assert the legitimacy of women's issues as urban development issues.

The one undisputable achievement of women's reservations, which was inscribed in the very implementation of the decentralization policy, is the greater representativeness of elected urban local bodies in terms of gender. This achievement is obviously of a symbolic nature, but as such its psychological impact might not be negligible. The sheer presence of a number of women among local representatives might help popularize the notion that politics is not necessarily a male-dominated field of activity.

NOTES

1. In addition to these three categories, the 73rd and 74th CAAs also leave open the option of similar reservations for the Backward Castes.
2. These three types of urban local bodies are principally defined on the basis of the size of their population: cities with a population of 10,000 to 1,00,000 have a nagar palika or municipal committee; cities with a population of 1,00,000 to 5,00,000 have a municipal council, and cities with a population over 5,00,000 have a municipal corporation.
3. A seventh argument, focussing on a technical point specific to quotas at the local level, concerned the rotation of constituencies reserved for women. It was argued that this rotation would prevent women from getting any political weightage, and from building any kind of female solidarity.
4. One must note, however, that the capital city of Punjab, Chandigarh, is not included in the three cities surveyed by Gill (which are Ludhiana, Amritsar and Jalandhar), whereas in the studies on Maharashtra and West Bengal the state capital is included.

REFERENCES

Arora, Subhash and R.K. Prabhakar, 'A Study of Municipal Council Elections in India: Socio-Economic Background of Women Candidates in Rohtak, Haryana', *Asian Survey*, vol. 37, no. 10, October 1997, pp. 918–26.

Beteille, André, 'Distributive Justice and Institutional Well-Being', in G. Mahajan (ed.), *Democracy, Difference and Social Justice*, Delhi, Oxford University Press, 1998, pp. 463–88.

Dahlerup, Drude, 'From a Small to a Large Minority: Women in Scandinavian Politics', *Scandinavian Political Studies*, vol. 11, no. 4, 1988, pp. 275–98.

Gandhi, Rajiv, *Prime Minister Rajiv Gandhi on Panchayati Raj*, Delhi: Ministry of Information and Broadcasting, Government of India, 1989.

Ghosh, Archana, 'Municipal Governance in West Bengal: People's Perception and Participation', ISS Manuscript, Report 9, Institute of Social Sciences, Delhi, 1996.

Gill, Rajesh, 'Seventy Fourth Constitutional Amendment and Political Empowerment of Women in Punjab: A Study in Urban Governance', *Urban India*, vol. XIX, no. 1, 1999, pp. 39–58.

Laufer, J., 'Introduction: l'égalité et la différence en débat', in EPHESIA, *La place des femmes. Les enjeux de l'identité et de l'égalité au regard des sciences sociales*, La Découverte, Paris, 1995.

MARG, *Daughters of the 74th Amendment: A Study of Women Elected to Municipal Bodies in Karnal and Delhi*, Delhi, 2000.

Nanivadekar, Medha, *Empowering Women: Assessing the Policy of Reservations in Local Bodies – A Report*, Mumbai: Rambhau Mhalgi Prabodhini, 1997.

Tawa Lama-Rewal, Stéphanie, 'Women in the Calcutta Municipal Corporation: A Study in the Context of the Debate on the Women's Reservation Bill', CSH Occasional Paper no. 2, 2001.

———, 'The Resilient Bhadralok: A Profile of the West Bengal MLAs', in Christophe Jaffrelot (ed.), *The Changing Profile of the Indian Political Class, Caste, Education and Occupation of the MLAs since 1952*, Delhi: Permanent Black, forthcoming.

Contributors

WALTER FERNANDES is currently Director of the North Eastern Social Research Centre, Guwahati. He has done much research on forests and tribals, tribal women and displacement. He has recently published (with Sanjay Barbora) *Modernisation and Women's Status in North Eastern India: A Comparative Study of Six Tribes* (Guwahati: North Eastern Social Research Centre, 2002).

MEENAKSHI JAIN is currently Fellow, Nehru Memorial Museum & Library, Delhi. She is working on inter-community relations in early modern India and has published a number of articles on this theme. She is also the author of *Medieval India* (NCERT, 2002).

PRAKASH LOUIS is currently Executive Director of the Indian Social Institute, New Delhi. A sociologist by discipline, he has edited and authored several books, including *People Power: The Naxalite Movement in Central Bihar* (Delhi: Wordsmith, 2002) and more recently *Political Sociology of Dalit Assertion* (Delhi: Gyan, 2003). He also contributes to various national and international journals

K.S. NARAYANA joined the Institute for Social and Economic Change, Bangalore, in 1976 and is currently in-charge of the Ph.D. Programme. His research interests include positive discrimination, decentralization and Karnataka politics.

SUDHA PAI teaches at the Centre for Political Studies, School of Social Sciences, Jawaharlal Nehru University, New Delhi. Apart from papers in reputed journals on the party system and electoral politics in India, her recent publications include *Democratic Governance in India: Challenges of Poverty, Development and Identity* (co-edited with Niraja Gopal Jayal, Delhi: Sage, 2001) and *Dalit Assertion and the Unfinished Democratic Revolution, The BSP in Uttar Pradesh* (Delhi: Sage, 2002). She is also interested in issues of governance and globalization in India.

BHUPINDER SINGH has devoted the best part of his career in the Indian Administrative Service (1956-89) to the cause and study of the weaker sections of the society. After retirement, he has been mainly responsible for drafting the reports of three important committees set up by the Government of India: as a member of the Committee on Jharkhand Matters (1990), as chairman of the Three-Members Expert Committee on Plains Tribes of Assam (1992) and as an expert member of the Committee of MPs and Experts for Law on Extension to Scheduled Areas of the Provisions of the 73rd Constitutional Amendment (1994). Currently, he is a member of the Second Commission on Scheduled Tribes and Scheduled Areas appointed in 2002 by the Government of India. He has recently published *Autonomy Movements and Federal India* (Jaipur: Rawat, 2002).

STÉPHANIE TAWA LAMA-REWAL is a research fellow in political science at the Centre d'Etudes de l'Inde et de l'Asie du Sud (CNRS-EHESS), Paris, and an affiliate researcher at the Centre de Sciences Humaines, New Delhi. Her research interests include political representation of groups in general and of women in particular, decentralization and urban governance. Her latest publication is (with Archana Ghosh) *Democratization in Progress: Women and Local Politics in Urban India* (Delhi: Tulika, forthcoming).

VIRGINIUS XAXA teaches in the Sociology Department of the Delhi School of Economics, University of Delhi. He is the co-author of *Tea Plantation Labour in India* (jointly with Sharit K. Bhowmik and M.A. Kalam, Delhi: Friedrich Ebert Stiftung, 1996) and the author of *Economic Dualism and Structure of Class: A Study of Plantation and Subsistence Settings in North Bengal* (Delhi: Cosmos, 1997). His research interests are tribal studies, agrarian relations and development studies.